MODERN ENGLISH WA

Tim Kendall's study offers the fullest account to date of a tradition of modern English war poetry. Stretching from the Boer War to the present day, it focuses on many of the twentieth-century's finest poets—combatants and non-combatants alike—and considers how they address the ethical challenges of making art out of violence. Poetry, we are often told, makes nothing happen. But war makes poetry happen: the war poet cannot regret, and must exalt at, even the most appalling experiences. *Modern English War Poetry* not only assesses the problematic relationship between war and its poets, it also encourages an urgent reconsideration of the modern poetry canon and the (too often marginalised) position of war poetry within it. The aesthetic and ethical values on which canonical judgements have been based are carefully scrutinized via a detailed analysis of individual poets, including Thomas Hardy, Rudyard Kipling, Wilfred Owen, Charlotte Mew, Edward Thomas, Ivor Gurney, W. H. Auden, Keith Douglas, Ted Hughes, and Geoffrey Hill.

Tim Kendall is Professor of English at the University of Exeter. He is the editor of *The Oxford Handbook of British and Irish War Poetry*.

Modern English War Poetry

TIM KENDALL

OXFORD
UNIVERSITY PRESS

p. cm.
Includes bibliographical references and index.
ISBN-13: 978-0-19-956202-2(Pbk.) (alk. paper)
ISBN-10: 978-0-19-927676-9(Hbk.) (alk. paper)
1. War poetry, English—History and criticism. 2. English poetry—20th century—
History and criticism. 3. English poetry—19th century—History and criticism. I.
Title.
PR605.W3K46 2006 821'.9109358—dc22 2006011796

Typeset by Laserwords Private Limited, Chennai, India
Printed in Great Britain
on acid-free paper by
the MPG Books Group

ISBN 978-0-19-927676-9(Hbk.) 978-0-19-956202-2(Pbk.)

1 3 5 7 9 10 8 6 4 2

Cover illustration : John Nash, 'Over the Top. 1st Artists' Rifles at Marcoing, 30th December 1917'.
Imperial War Museum, London (IWM ART 1656).

To the Memory of
Francis Charles Bennett (1919–1989)
and
Charles George Kendall (1908–1979)

Acknowledgements

I am grateful to the editors of the following publications, where earlier versions of several chapters first appeared: *Essays in Criticism, P. N. Review, The Yale Review*. Other chapters began life as public talks. Chapter 8, on Keith Douglas, was delivered at the British Academy as the Thomas Chatterton Lecture in English Poetry for 2001, and was subsequently published in *The Proceedings of the British Academy* (volume 117; 2002). Abbreviated versions of Chapter 4, on Edward Thomas and Charlotte Mew, and Chapter 12, on anti-war poetry, were given as lectures at (respectively) the Edward Thomas Fellowship in Gloucester and the Seamus Heaney Centre at Queen's University, Belfast.

I should like to thank the AHRC for awarding me matching research leave in 2004. It is also a pleasure to acknowledge the friends whose advice and encouragement have made this book considerably stronger: Dawn Bellamy, Fran Brearton, George Donaldson, John Lee, John Lyon, Peter McDonald, Andrew McNeillie, John Redmond, Ben Sonnenberg, Jon Stallworthy.

My largest debts of gratitude are to my wife Fiona, and our children Charlie, Milly, and (the latecomer in the vineyard) Rosie.

Corsham
October 2005

T. K.

Contents

Introduction

War poetry, Edward Thomas could still claim as late as December 1914, had always been unlikely to stand the test of time: 'No other class of poetry vanishes so rapidly, has so little chosen from it for posterity.'[1] Where, he wondered, were the poems and songs of Marlborough's wars, or Wolfe's battles in Quebec, or the Napoleonic campaigns? All the surviving poems that had been written 'under the direct pressure of public patriotic motives' would fit into 'one tiny volume'.

Thomas's essay appeared in the early months of a conflict destined to break for ever the equation of war poetry with 'public patriotic motives' and produce more significant poets than any war before or since. But even without the gift of foresight, Thomas understood the challenges facing war poets, who learn at times of national crisis that 'The demand is for the crude, for what everybody is saying or thinking, or is ready to begin saying or thinking'.[2] Only the strongest poets can resist the siren song of public opinion, the harmonies of which changed through the twentieth century. Denouncing Rupert Brooke's 'begloried sonnets' in 1916, Isaac Rosenberg maintained that war should be approached in 'a colder way, more abstract, with less of the million feelings everybody feels'.[3]

[1] Edward Thomas, 'War Poetry', in *A Language not to be Betrayed: Selected Prose*, ed. Edna Longley (Ashington and Manchester: MidNag/Carcanet, 1981), 131.

[2] Ibid. 132.

[3] Isaac Rosenberg to Mrs Herbert Cohen, ?1916, in *The Collected Works*, ed. Ian Parsons (London: Chatto & Windus, 1979), 237.

It is now less often Brooke's patriotism than a well-rehearsed pity and outrage which 'everybody feels'. Nevertheless, whatever orthodoxy happens to prevail at a given moment, the best war poets of the twentieth century reject the acceptable in favour of the true. Or, as W. H. Auden puts it in an essay on war poetry, 'the serious poetry of any given moment is always at odds with the conscious ideas of the majority'.[4] The truths told by war poets continue to disconcert, not least because they encompass what Wilfred Owen called the 'exultation'[5] of war as well as the futility, the imaginative opportunities as well as the senseless horrors. War poets cannot wholly regret even the most appalling experiences, as they transform violence, death, atrocity, into the pleasing formal aesthetics of art. Poetry, we never cease to be told, makes nothing happen; but war makes poetry happen.

The same duty towards truth falls, albeit less consequentially, to the scholar of war poetry. When in *Don Juan* Byron complains of a misprint in the *Waterloo Gazette*, more is at stake than bad copy-editing:

> Thrice happy he whose name has been well spelt
> In the despatch: I knew a man whose loss
> Was printed *Grove*, although his name was Grose.[6]

Byron detects a fundamental indifference underlying the nation's shows of sorrow and commemoration. What verdict, then, should be handed down to the well-known poet-anthologist who ventures that 'Brooke gets a lot of stick these days for his sonnets of 1914'—as if he were a football manager enduring a run of defeats—and that 'even

---

    [4] W. H. Auden, 'W. H. Auden Speaks of Poetry and Total War', in *Prose*, ii: *1939–1948*, ed. Edward Mendelson (Princeton: Princeton University Press, 2002), 153.

    [5] Wilfred Owen to Colin Owen, 14 May 1917, in *Collected Letters*, ed. Harold Owen and John Bell (Oxford: Oxford University Press, 1967), 458. Owen describes the experience of going over the top: 'There was an extraordinary exultation in the act of slowly walking forward'; 'When I looked back and saw the ground all crawling and wormy with wounded bodies, I felt no horror at all but only immense exultation at having got through the Barrage.'

    [6] Lord Byron, *Poetical Works*, ed. Frederick Page (London: Oxford University Press, 1970), canto 8, stanza xviii, p. 755.

Isaac Rosenberg greeted the outbreak of war with enthusiasm'?[7] (Far from enthusiastic, Rosenberg had stated from the start that he 'despise[d] war and hate[d] war',[8] that it was 'against all [his] principles of justice', and that although he finally enlisted to escape poverty, he 'would be doing the most criminal thing a man can do'.[9]) The treason of the clerks replaces intellectual accuracy with easy complaisance. As a result, the war poets' emphasis on truth-telling, against the grain of a dominant contemporary discourse which mistakes opinion for truth, always risks being smoothed into an acceptable narrative by the critic's dishonouring inattention.

'Obviously no poet would wish to be a war poet still less a "war poet".'[10] To readers of war poetry concerned with weighing textual minutiae, Jeffrey Wainwright's comment serves as a reminder of the horrific realities about which those texts speak. But Wainwright also makes a point about the reception of war poetry, which has often been marginalized by critics suspicious of its readership. A common travesty has been to allege that, circumscribed by events, war poetry distracts from, and cannot accommodate, more universal concerns: as John Lehmann advised in 1946, poets should now turn their attention to experiences of a 'wider and more generally valid scope'.[11] The history of the twentieth century has demonstrated how generally valid the war poet's experiences continue to be. The most urgent issue addressed by the poetry of the period is the relationship between art and violence: how, and with what difficulties and ethical questions, can one communicate with and about the other? War poetry, this study contends, is the arena in which those questions are most powerfully resolved. It is hard to think of a modern English poet of any significance—combatant or non-combatant—who has

---

[7] Andrew Motion, 'Introduction', in Andrew Motion (ed.), *First World War Poems* (London: Faber, 2003), p. xii.

[8] Rosenberg to Edward Marsh, 8 Aug. 1914, in *Collected Works*, 205.

[9] Rosenberg to Sydney Schiff, 8 June 1915, ibid. 216.

[10] Jeffrey Wainwright, 'Introduction', in Sidney Keyes, *Collected Poems*, ed. Michael Meyer (Manchester: Carcanet, 2002), p. ix.

[11] John Lehmann, quoted by Andy Croft, 'Introduction', in Randall Swingler, *Selected Poems*, ed. Andy Croft (Nottingham: Trent Editions, 2000), p. xiii.

not contributed substantially to the poetry of war. That the post-war work of writers as otherwise diverse as Ted Hughes and Geoffrey Hill should share a profound indebtedness to the soldier-poets points to the continuing force of the legacy.

No single study can do full justice to the variety of twentieth-century war poetry or to the quantity and quality of its poets. All books having to end somewhere, my range is temporal more than geographical. The concentration on English war poetry has the advantage of reducing the number of inexcusable omissions; and those which remain are the result either of a value judgement or of a belief that I can add little to existing scholarship. To the criticism that modern poets are limited by linguistic and not national boundaries, it should be countered that war, more than anything else, obliges individuals to address questions of nationhood. I have therefore chosen to analyse poets whose attitudes to England cannot be disentangled from their portrayals of war. Accordingly, my study charts the continuities and disjunctions of a living lyric tradition created out of a shared historical as well as aesthetic experience.

1

Thomas Hardy's Witness

On 20 October 1899, Thomas Hardy cycled to Southampton to watch the British fleet set sail for the Boer War in South Africa. The embarcation of the troopships, he later told Edmund Gosse, had presented 'a most impressive scene';[1] and to another correspondent he confirmed its special significance as 'a sight I wish you could have witnessed with me'.[2] Hardy used the same word—'witnessed'—twice within three lines in his autobiography, first in relation to his visit to Southampton, and then to describe how he had watched the departure of a battery of artillery stationed at Dorchester.[3] His credentials as witness were important to Hardy: under the heading 'War Poems' in *Poems of the Past and the Present* (1901), the first three poems are marked, in parentheses, 'Southampton Docks: October 1899'; and the fourth, 'The Going of the Battery', has a date of 2 November 1899. These war poems were, emphatically, eyewitness accounts, claiming an authority denied to absentees.

The witness does more than merely see: he testifies to the truth of contentious and possibly even criminal events. This emphasis on experience over hearsay and propaganda is affirmed many times by war poets throughout the following century. Closing Plato's gap between representation and truth, poet-witnesses are liable to be banished from the Republic not as liars but for the opposite reason:

---

[1] Thomas Hardy to Edmund Gosse, 26 Oct. 1899, in *The Collected Letters*, ii: *1893–1901*, ed. Richard Little Purdy and Michael Millgate (Oxford: Clarendon Press, 1980), 233.

[2] Thomas Hardy to Edward Clodd, 29 Oct. 1899, ibid. 235.

[3] Florence Emily Hardy, *The Life of Thomas Hardy* (London: Macmillan, 1962), 305.

in their ambition to educate the ignorant, provide an authentic testimony, and challenge tyranny, they speak with a prerogative which threatens the founding fictions of their societies. Seamus Heaney defines the 'poet as witness' as 'any figure in whom the truth-telling urge and the compulsion to identify with the oppressed becomes [*sic*] necessarily integral with the act of writing itself'.[4] Heaney's focus on the oppressed reveals his own preoccupation with the poetry of Eastern Europe, but his reference to the 'truth-telling urge' recognizes the inspiration of the testimonial poet, who will typically risk hardship and death to speak the truth to power. As a non-combatant living continents away from the battlefields of the Boer War, Hardy suffered wounds only to his reputation, the most severe being the *Daily Chronicle*'s denunciation of him as a pacifist on (of all days) Christmas Day, 1899. Nevertheless, together with Rudyard Kipling, who observed the fighting at first hand in South Africa, he ensured that the Boer War inaugurated a tradition of witness among English poets which would characterize the poetry of later and larger conflicts.

Hardy responded to events as they happened, and published quickly: 'Embarcation' appeared within five days, and 'The Going of the Battery' within nine days, of the scenes they describe, while 'The Souls of the Slain' was sent to the *Cornhill Magazine* with a request for a prompt reply, 'since, whatever interest [it] may possess for readers, would be probably of a temporary kind'.[5] This was more than a strategy to rouse unforthcoming editors: Hardy believed that the poems were news unlikely to stay news. Writing to Florence Henniker, whose husband commanded a battalion of the Coldstream Guards in South Africa, he grew increasingly deprecating about the occasional nature of his Boer War poems. They were, he assured her, mere 'scraps of verse',[6] and 'The Dead Drummer' (later retitled

[4] Seamus Heaney, 'The Interesting Case of Nero, Chekhov's Cognac and a Knocker', in *The Government of the Tongue* (London: Faber, 1988), p. xvi.

[5] Hardy to Reginald Smith, 2 Mar. 1900, in *Collected Letters*, ii. 249.

[6] Hardy to Florence Henniker, 9 Nov. 1899, ibid. 236.

'Drummer Hodge') embodied a passing thought 'of no profundity'.[7] He had not purposely looked for this new subject-matter:

The fact is, the incidents of departure have rather come in my way by accident. The latest was the going of our Battery of Artillery (stationed in this town) & as they left at 10 at night, & some at 4 in the morning, amid rain and wind, the scene was a pathetic one.[8]

Beginning with a redundant protestation—'The fact is'—Hardy lets slip a nervousness over the factuality of his account. The unsociable circumstances of departure contradict his claim that the scene came in his way 'by accident', as those favourite climatic effects of 'rain and wind', later employed in some of Hardy's greatest lyric poetry, help to create the desired pathos. The letter tactfully attempts to conceal an opportunism at transforming the sufferings of others into high tragedy. Florence Henniker, as Hardy knew, was obliged to endure the apprehension and the suffering which became his raw material.

Hardy's anxiety helps to explain his emphasis on the accuracy of his poetic accounts, which by offering themselves as first-hand reports of events encountered accidentally, sought to avoid accusations of exploiting others' griefs. 'The Going of the Battery', Hardy told Henniker, 'was almost an exact report of the scene & expressions [he] overheard.'[9] At other times, however, his war poetry succumbed to a temptation born of his limited exposure to events: witness could be faked. The fifth of his sequence of war poems, 'At the War Office, London', again gives the impression of a first-hand account, and following the Southampton and Dorchester poems of departure, it announces a similar precision in its parenthetical subtitle: '(Affixing the Lists of Killed and Wounded: December 1899)'. But Hardy had not visited London for many months, and the poem was purely an act of imagination: he admitted to Henniker that, although having pictured the scene 'with painful realism', he had 'not witnessed it'.[10]

[7] Hardy to Florence Henniker, 24 Nov. 1899, ibid. 238.
[8] Hardy to Florence Henniker, 9 Nov. 1899, ibid. 236.
[9] Hardy to Florence Henniker, 24 Nov. 1899, ibid. 238.
[10] Hardy to Florence Henniker, 19 Dec. 1899, ibid. 241.

'At the War Office, London' inadvertently discloses the gap between 'realism' and the real by substituting vague philosophical complaint for the actualities of life:

> Last year I called this world of gaingivings
> The darkest thinkable, and questioned sadly
> If my own land could heave its pulse less gladly,
> So charged it seemed with circumstance that brings
> The tragedy of things.[11]

'Circumstance' is a word that Hardy uses more potently later in his career. Here, its etymological meaning (*circumstare*—to stand around) suggests the awkwardness of a line which overstates its claims: Hardy neither acts nor even stands around, but stays at home imagining the scene. William Empson's critique of Peacock's 'War Song'—'He makes a cradle and rocks himself in it'[12]—would serve equally well as a description of Hardy's self-satisfied pessimism. The lumbering iambics, the banal oppositional rhyme of 'sadly/gladly', and the dead weight of 'things' suit a poem of mood rather than witness. Nor is it defensible to describe the world, even at the time of the Boer War, as 'The darkest thinkable' unless owning up to a profound failure of imagination. The second of the two stanzas does refer tongue-twistedly to 'hourly posted sheets of scheduled slaughter',[13] but that is the poem's only concession to its title. Hardy betrays the duty of the witness: in his eagerness to provoke a desired emotional response, he counteracts one kind of insidious war propaganda with another.

'At the War Office, London' impugns the integrity of the earlier of Hardy's 'War Poems', because it justifies a question which confronts any complacent faith in the witness's truth-telling urge: what is the truth? Like all poetry, testimonial poetry may remain dependent on linguistic techniques, but Hardy assumes that those techniques are all that matter, and that the reality of experience can be replaced

---

[11] Hardy, *The Complete Poems*, ed. James Gibson (Basingstoke: Palgrave, 2001), 89.
[12] William Empson, *Seven Types of Ambiguity* (London: Pimlico, 2004), 22.
[13] Hardy, *Complete Poems*, 90.

by a reality effect. In this confidence he follows Philip Sidney's Aristotelian belief that 'a fained example hath as much force to teach, as a true example'.[14] The poet, according to Sidney, 'nothing affirmeth, and therefore never lieth':[15] consequently, his ejection from Plato's Republic must constitute a miscarriage of justice. By this standard, 'At the War Office, London' would be deficient only because Hardy failed to imagine the scene convincingly enough. Yet the failure ought to be considered ethical as well as imaginative: claiming to report the truth, testimonial poetry can be guilty of lying. As Christopher Ricks insists,

By proffering factuality, a work is released from certain obligations—for example, our tests of plausibility rightly become different and may even lapse. But (nothing coming easier in art which is true both to itself and to all which is not art) by the same token, a work which proffers factuality will enter into other obligations.[16]

The best war poetry after Hardy gleans its authority from being determinedly and, at times, aggressively true to 'all which is not art'. Hardy, by contrast, manipulates the truth, or offers a plausible account of it, for the benefit of his art and politics, laying false claim to the authority of witness in order to exert an emotional coercion.

The inauthenticity of 'At the War Office, London' alerts the reader that even the witness poems of Southampton and Dorchester do not content themselves with merely reporting the circumstances of departure; they also deduce from those circumstances a tacit message of opposition to the war. Hardy finds 'None dubious of the cause' as he watches the fleet setting sail in 'Embarcation',[17] but his condemnation of the failures of politicians, expressed earlier in the poem and throughout the sequence, hints that he knows better. Even if war has become ineluctable as the soldiers sail towards the 'Tragical

[14] Philip Sidney, 'The Defence of Poesie', *The Prose Works*, iii, ed. Albert Feuillerat (Cambridge: Cambridge University Press, 1968), 17.
[15] Ibid. 29.
[16] Christopher Ricks, 'Literature and the Matter of Fact', in *Essays in Appreciation* (Oxford: Oxford University Press, 1996), 286–7.
[17] Hardy, *Complete Poems*, 86.

To-be', it does not follow that, for Hardy, its cost in human misery is justified. Writing to Florence Henniker late in 1900, he noted that none of his Boer War poems had been 'Jingo or Imperial—a fatal defect according to the judgment of the British majority at present, I dare say'.[18] At least one reviewer of *Poems of the Past and the Present* confirmed that judgement, regretting that the Boer War had inspired no 'enthusiasm' in Hardy,[19] who had advertised his allegiances by allowing his Boer War poem, 'A Christmas Ghost-Story', to be reprinted by W. T. Stead in a periodical titled *War Against War in South Africa*. This opposition to the war put Hardy at odds with the dominant mood of the nation. As Henry Newbolt approvingly recalled three decades later, 'the great majority of us saw no reason to disbelieve in the goodness of our cause'.[20] Nevertheless, Newbolt remembered having been acutely aware of a 'small but indignant minority, belonging mostly to the modern category of "highbrows": the loyalists labelled them pro-Boers, and were genuinely hurt by their passionate reproaches'.[21] The schism which Newbolt detected during that 'very unhappy time' plays itself out in his own poetry's political challenge to Hardy's sequence.

Newbolt took his prompt from Hardy's preoccupations not just during the Boer War but subsequently: the first book of Hardy's *The Dynasts*, which included a detailed account of the Battle of Trafalgar and events immediately before and after, was published in 1904; Newbolt's book-length history, *The Year of Trafalgar*, appeared in 1905 with an extract from Hardy's work included. A dedicated follower of Hardy's poetry, Newbolt seems to have sought out and read the Southampton poems as they appeared. Yet, although he describes the same events as Hardy in the title poem of *The Sailing of the Long-Ships* (1902), his poem's message of duty, patriotism, and martial glory comprehensively opposes Hardy's subdued pessimism.

[18] Hardy to Florence Henniker, 24 Dec. 1900, in *Collected Letters*, ii. 277.
[19] T. H. Warren, quoted in Martin Seymour-Smith, *Hardy* (London: Bloomsbury, 1994), 648.
[20] Henry Newbolt, *My World as in My Time* (London: Faber, 1932), 249.
[21] Ibid. 249–50.

Like Hardy, Newbolt writes a date under his title: 'October, 1899'. And, like Hardy, Newbolt observes the reactions of those left on the quayside. Hardy's 'Embarcation' concludes with an account of predominantly female grief: 'Wives, sisters, parents, wave white hands and smile, | As if they knew not that they weep the while.'[22] (Adopting his customary apologetic tone, he later wrote to Florence Henniker, 'I fancy you thought my sonnet on the departure too tragic?'[23]) The third of Hardy's Southampton poems, 'The Colonel's Soliloquy', does muster a passing excitement—' "The quay recedes. Hurrah! Ahead we go! . . ." ' —but the colonel soon turns his attention to the ache of his old wounds, his rheumy eyes, his wrinkled face, and his wife 'waving from the wharfside, palely grieving'.[24] Newbolt's 'The Sailing of the Long-Ships' is more ready to acknowledge the 'tumult' of diverse responses: 'They saw the cables loosened, they saw the gangways cleared, | They heard the women weeping, they heard the men that cheered.'[25] Whereas Hardy scarcely admits any cheering, Newbolt's is a more exhilarated poem, for which the weeping women are a brief passing reference, rather than a pitiful concluding image. Three times in his twenty-four lines Newbolt mentions 'fathers', as he focuses on a paternal tradition, in order to place the Boer War in the context of previous military victories. His soldiers are not decrepit colonels but 'tireless fighters, flushed with a youth renewed'.[26]

'The Sailing of the Long-Ships' also engages with Hardy in its broad historical perspectives. Hardy's 'Embarcation', the first of his 'War Poems', starts with lines which seem to augur a vindication of the war effort, before suddenly descending into outraged criticism of such continuing folly:

> Here, where Vespasian's legions struck the sands,
> And Cerdic with his Saxons entered in,

---

[22] Hardy, *Complete Poems*, 86.
[23] Hardy to Florence Henniker, 9 Nov. 1899, in *Collected Letters*, ii. 236.
[24] Hardy, *Complete Poems*, 87–8.
[25] Henry Newbolt, *The Sailing of the Long-Ships and Other Poems* (London: John Murray, 1902), 7.
[26] Ibid. 8.

> And Henry's army leapt afloat to win
> Convincing triumphs over neighbour lands,
> Vaster battalions press for further strands,
> To argue in the selfsame bloody mode
> Which this late age of thought, and pact, and code,
> Still fails to mend.[27]

Although Hardy educes two successful invasions of England, his progression to Henry V's campaign in France, and his apparent pride in vaster battalions and further strands, promise a poem in the heroic vein. Only in line 6 does he surprise and punish the reader tempted to glory in ancient battles, as the grandiose polysyndeton of the first stanza ('Here ... And ... And') is remembered but diminished in the second: 'thought, and pact, and code'. The 'white hands' of the poem's third, and shrunken, triplet—'Wives, sisters, parents'—indicate that those relatives, like the wife 'palely grieving' in 'The Colonel's Soliloquy', do not have blood on their hands. (In 'At the War Office, London' it is again the 'feature blanched of parent, wife, or daughter' which conveys Hardy's pathos;[28] and 'The Going of the Battery', subtitled '*Wives' Lament*', refers to the women's pale faces.) This contrasts with the warmongers in one of Hardy's Great War poems, 'England to Germany in 1914', perceived as a 'flushed few' with 'face aflame';[29] and that later poem may itself recall Newbolt's positive reference to soldiers 'flushed' with renewed youth. While Newbolt celebrates ruddy men, Hardy sympathizes with pale women, who are innocent victims of a history viewed as repetitive bloodshed. However, 'Embarcation' needs to conceal geographical diversity in order to introduce the defeats: Henry may have set sail from 'Here', in Southampton, but Vespasian's legions landed in Kent, and Cerdic at Portsmouth.

There is nothing inevitable about Hardy's selective version of history. Needing to make an opposing political case, Newbolt is drawn to different (but no less appropriate) historical events. A singing sea-wind recalls earlier fleets as the ships pull away from dock:

---

[27] Hardy, *Complete Poems*, 86.   [28] Ibid. 90.   [29] Ibid. 540.

'I came by Cape St. Vincent, I came by Trafalgar
I swept from Torres Vedras to golden Vigo Bar,
I saw the beacons blazing that fired the world with light,
When down their ancient highway your fathers passed to fight.'

'O race of tireless fighters, flushed with a youth renewed,
Right well the wars of Freedom befit the Sea-Kings' brood;
Yet as ye go forget not the fame of yonder shore,
The fame ye owe your fathers and the old time before.'[30]

'The Sailing of the Long-Ships' eulogizes what Hardy had condemned as the 'bloody mode' of war. Hardy alludes to historical events in order to grieve that the present day has learnt nothing and is bent on repeating the old mistakes; Newbolt welcomes his generation's opportunity to achieve a fame equal to that of its historical 'fathers', and to repay them by continuing to defend what they fought and died for. Like Hardy's, this interpretation of the Boer War requires its own emphases, omissions, and guiles, as Newbolt groups the conflict with previous 'wars of Freedom'.[31] (Disputes over the rights of British subjects in self-governing Boer territories had contributed, whether as cause or excuse, to the breaking out of hostilities.) Newbolt borrows the authority of pseudo-biblical rhetoric to award the campaign a godly sanction. His challenge to Hardy's poem is made in a battle between rival rhetorical devices, as his extravagant anaphora trumps the mildly cumulative effects of Hardy's polysyndeton: 'They strove and knew not hatred, they smote and toiled to save, | They tended whom they vanquished, they praised the fallen brave.'[32] Onward Christian soldiers: the British male, Newbolt implies, is never more Christian than on the battlefield. As Hardy would wryly observe in his autobiography, one feature of the 'warlike and patriotic poetry' inspired by the Boer War was 'the disguise under Christian terminology of principles not necessarily wrong from the point of view of international politics, but obviously anti-Christian, because inexorable and masterful'.[33]

---

[30] Newbolt, *Sailing of the Long-Ships and Other Poems*, 8.
[31] Ibid.   [32] Ibid. 8–9.
[33] Quoted in F. E. Hardy, *Life of Thomas Hardy*, 311.

The modern-day desire to reject such distorting glorifications has been partly responsible for a neglect of Newbolt's work which is almost entirely deserved. Yet an age which denounces any hint of pro-war propaganda may often be blind to, or even complicit in, the same strategies employed for an anti-war agenda. 'The Sailing of the Long-Ships' warrants sustained attention because of its power to disturb the acquiescent reader of Hardy's poetry: if Newbolt is guilty, Hardy should not escape whipping either. Both poets cunningly dress opinion as *réportage*, most obviously in their fashioning of other voices to deliver authorial beliefs. Those voices are heard as authoritative after the din of the multitudes wanes. 'Departure', the second of Hardy's 'War Poems', begins: 'While the far farewell music thins and fails';[34] Newbolt, similarly, recounts the moment when 'Far off, far off, the tumult faded and died away'.[35] In each poem, the brief calm which follows is broken by a message—sung, in Newbolt's case, by the sea-wind, and in Hardy's, created out of a 'sense of severance' which 'shapes the late long tramp of mounting men | To seeming words':

> 'How long, O striving Teutons, Slavs, and Gaels
>
> Must your wroth reasonings trade on lives like these,
> That are as puppets in a playing hand?—
> When shall the saner softer polities
> Whereof we dream, have sway in each proud land
> And patriotism, grown Godlike, scorn to stand
> Bondslave to realms, but circle earth and seas?'[36]

Hardy's vocative places the blame for war squarely on other races, but his complaint about a patriotism which is 'Bondslave to realms' also implicates the British jingoism about which he expresses such disgust in his letters. What Hardy anatomizes as the cause of war is exalted by Newbolt into a requirement for 'Freedom': patriotism, enslaved by national boundaries in Hardy's work, becomes the defender

---

[34] Hardy, *Complete Poems*, 86.
[35] Newbolt, *Sailing of the Long-Ships and Other Poems*, 7.
[36] Hardy, *Complete Poems*, 86–7.

and liberator of nations in Newbolt's. And whereas 'Embarcation' and 'Departure' deal in the severances of families and individual lives, Newbolt's frequent allusion to the 'fathers' stresses continuity by transforming war into a necessary paternal inheritance which strengthens family ties. The triumph of 'The Sailing of the Long-Ships' grows out of its redeployment of Hardy's images and its redirection of their energies for opposing political ends. Newbolt exposes and exploits the prejudices inherent in poetic witness, unmasking Hardy's 'seeming words' as the cajoling product of an all-too-palpable design: there is nothing either pro- or anti-war in Hardy's account, as in Newbolt's, but thinking has made it so.

Hardy's Boer War poems prefigure his celebrated elegies for his first wife, Emma, in their attempt to guide interpretation by inscribing a ventriloquized voice. Emma's ghost, overheard by the reader, remains tantalizingly out of her husband's earshot, and yet her words are the creation of the poet who supposedly cannot hear her: she becomes, like Hardy's soldiers, a puppet in a playing hand. Just as Emma's speech represents Hardy's own 'wish-fulfilling fantasy'[37]—the product not of her independent volition but of his prosopopoeia—so his Boer War poems are haunted by voices which say nothing more or less than he requires. The 'seeming words' in 'Departure', fashioned out of 'the long tramp of mounting men', expose a chasm so vast, between monotonous tramping and a complex question about the desirability of patriotism, that even Hardy's governing presence must strain to bridge it. Other voices are equally accommodating of the poet's philosophies and politics. The 'puzzled phantom' of a 'mouldering soldier' in 'A Christmas Ghost-Story' provides a conspicuous example, as it moans on the breeze some ironic questions about the failures of Christian nations:

'I would know
By whom and when the All-Earth-gladdening Law
Of Peace, brought in by that Man Crucified,

[37] Jahan Ramazani, *Poetry of Mourning: The Modern Elegy from Hardy to Heaney* (Chicago: University of Chicago Press, 1994), 56.

Was ruled to be inept, and set aside?
And what of logic or of truth appears
In tacking 'Anno Domini' to the years?
Near twenty-hundred liveried thus have hied,
But tarries yet the Cause for which He died.'[38]

The phantom sounds as if it might have read Hardy's report of his
meeting with a 'religious man': 'I said, We the civilized world have
given Christianity a fair trial for nearly 2000 years, & it has not yet
taught countries the rudimentary virtue of keeping peace.'[39] Hardy
grants such opinions a spurious authority by placing them in the
mouth of a war victim. John McCrae's 'In Flanders Fields' employs
the technique over a decade later for more bellicose purposes: 'We
are the Dead', the poem's unified voice declares, before insisting that
the 'quarrel with the foe' must be pursued lest the living 'break faith
with those who die'.[40] Like McCrae after him, Hardy exploits the
dead to force his political argument. He does not speak for the dead;
the dead are obliged to speak for him.

Dramatic monologues always involve an act of presumption,
as the poet puts words into the mouths of others. The peculiar
difficulty for Hardy's Boer War poems, however, is that the aged
colonel, the mouldering soldier, and the lamenting wives are drawn
so sketchily that the poems barely summon any kind of drama.
Hardy's greater presumption is that he should feel entitled to reduce
his characters to convenient ciphers, chosen for their proximity to
the effects of war. When he encounters, in Florence Henniker, a
woman condemned to endure the emotional complexities of what he
simplistically imagines, he must acknowledge that his poems sound
too tragic. 'I was not meaning to write like that, & you must forgive
me,' he disingenuously asserts, having just asked her whether she
thinks the 40,000 war-dead 'wish to wake up again'.[41] Whatever his

[38] Hardy, *Complete Poems*, 90.
[39] Hardy to Florence Henniker, 25 Feb. 1900, in *Collected Letters*, ii. 248.
[40] John McCrae, 'In Flanders Fields', in Jon Silkin (ed.), *The Penguin Book of First World War Poetry* (Harmondsworth: Penguin, 1981), 85.
[41] Hardy to Florence Henniker, 22 Oct. 1900, in *Collected Letters*, ii. 269.

audience, he finds his often mordant inclination towards the 'tragedy of things' hard to resist. In what may be a direct allusion, Geoffrey Hill's *Scenes from Comus* points out that 'The tragedy of things is not conclusive; | rather, one way by which the spirit moves.'[42] For Hardy it is the only way. Even when 'The Going of the Battery' offers him the power of witness, he prefers to efface himself and writes, instead, a poem from the wives' perspective. Wives, not wife—all the women are one woman, speaking in the first person plural, as Hardy disallows any discrepancy in their reactions to their husbands' departure. Only in the penultimate stanza does the tragedy of things reassert itself, as a stray voice rejects the wives' faith that their men will return safely:

Some one said: "Nevermore will they come: evermore
Are they now lost to us." O it was wrong!
Though may be hard their ways, some Hand will guard their ways,
Bear them through safely, in brief time or long.

—Yet, voices haunting us, daunting us, taunting us,
Hint in the night-time when life beats are low
Other and graver things . . . Hold we to braver things,
Wait we, in trust, what Time's fulness shall show.[43]

These stanzas cause problems for Hardy's claim that the poem constitutes almost an exact report, and raise questions about how the soldiers' wives who read 'The Going of the Battery', in *The Graphic* nine days later, would have reacted to his imputation of private fears. Those fears are not only described but created by Hardy himself (albeit with help from Poe's 'The Raven'). The suspiciously anonymous 'Some one' in dispute with the wives is another of his manipulative voices, like the words formed from tramping men or the phantom's moan. Its punning hint of 'graver things' implies an ominous destiny which the women's apparently naïve trust in 'Time's fulness', or the protective 'Hand' of a beneficent God, cannot

42 Geoffrey Hill, *Scenes from Comus* (Harmondsworth: Penguin, 2005), 3.
43 Hardy, *Complete Poems*, 89.

countermand. A later poem in the sequence, 'Song of the Soldiers' Wives and Sweethearts', rejoices in the imminent return of the men, again with a united voice, and explicitly rebuts such fears: 'Some told us we should meet no more'.[44] However, that is separated from 'The Going of the Battery' by five poems concerned with the war-dead. Not all the soldiers' wives, Hardy has already illustrated at length, have something to sing about.

A week before the fleet left Southampton, Hardy confided to Florence Henniker that, much as he loathed war, as soon as it became inevitable he could not help but feel a passion for it: 'few persons are more martial than I, or like better to write of war in prose & rhyme'.[45] He had not waited for contemporary events to bestow the pleasure: the first book of *The Dynasts*, his epic diorama of the Napoleonic campaigns, may not have appeared until 1904, but the idea had come as early as 1891, and research began in earnest during 1897. The differences between Hardy's Boer War poems and *The Dynasts* are not confined to matters of scale. His extensive reading allowed him to write detailed representations of political intrigues and of battle in *The Dynasts*. Yet, on the Boer War's causes, its key protagonists, its pivotal moments, its battle scenes, and even its outcome, his poetry stays silent: a reader of Hardy's sequence would learn nothing of the conflict, beyond guessing from references to the 'Karoo' and a 'kopje-crest' (in 'Drummer Hodge') that the battleground must be South Africa. Although Hardy reported that his thoughts were 'all Kahki colour' [*sic*],[46] his poetry concerns itself almost exclusively with departures, burials, returns, and the women left behind.

This last emphasis raises ethical difficulties for a poet who confessed himself appalled by war but enjoyed writing about it. When the speaker of the slightly later Boer War poem, 'The Man He Killed' (1902), imagines how he and his victim would in other circumstances have been drinking partners in 'some old ancient inn',[47] Hardy

44 Hardy, *Complete Poems*, 97.
45 Hardy to Florence Henniker, 11 Oct. 1899, in *Collected Letters*, ii. 232.
46 Hardy to Winifred Thomson, 6 Feb. 1900, ibid. 247.
47 Hardy, *Complete Poems*, 287.

foreshadows Great War poets in his portrayal of the enemy as a brother or mirror-image. But the Boer War sequence in *Poems of the Past and the Present* parades a more dubious sympathy which leaves itself vulnerable to a kind of condemnation similar to that voiced by Theodor Adorno against Holocaust art:

Victims are used to create something, works of art, that are thrown to the consumption of a world which destroyed them. The so-called artistic representation of the sheer physical pain of people beaten to the ground with rifle-butts contains, however remotely, the power to elicit enjoyment out of it.[48]

Hardy's authorial enjoyment, so often founded on female suffering, glibly translates pain into poetry. The desire to notice and commemorate victims always risks falling into a voyeuristic exploitation of their sufferings. It is not so much Hardy's fascination which repels, as his disguising of it as moral concern. His sympathy becomes not only manipulative but mawkish—literally so in 'A Wife in London', where news of the husband's death is inevitably followed by a letter from 'His hand, whom the worm now knows'.[49] The irony is pleased with its own neatness, as it remembers the wives in 'The Going of the Battery' who had placed their faith in another 'Hand'—the 'Hand [that] will guard their ways'.

Such failures are also partly the exaggerations of an aggressive disillusionment which Hardy attributed to a recent shift in human sensibility: 'Down to Waterloo war was romantic, was believed in', he told Arthur Quiller-Couch, but now 'we see ... too many details'.[50] The final poem in his sequence, 'The Sick Battle-God', makes a similar point, remembering the days when 'men found joy in war' and worshipped the 'crimson form' of the God of Battles.[51] ('Great is the battle-god, great,' Stephen Crane bitterly reported

[48] Theodor Adorno, 'Commitment', in Ernst Bloch *et al.*, *Aesthetics and Politics*, trans. Francis McDonagh (London: NLB, 1977), 189.
[49] Hardy, *Complete Poems*, 92.
[50] Hardy to Arthur Quiller-Couch, 9 Feb. 1903, *Collected Letters*, iii: *1902–1908*, ed. Richard Little Purdy and Michael Millgate (Oxford: Clarendon Press, 1982), 51.
[51] Hardy, *Complete Poems*, 97.

in 1899, 'and his kingdom—| A field where a thousand corpses lie'.[52]) Hardy claims that under the new dispensation of 'sympathy' and 'amity', modern-day 'champions' are as 'pale of brow' as their women, and—in a phrase that Wilfred Owen may have recalled when complaining of a civilian poet's 'high zest' for battle[53]—their 'zest grows cold':

> Let men rejoice, let men deplore,
> The lurid Deity of heretofore
> Succumbs to one of saner nod;
> The Battle-god is god no more.[54]

'The Sick Battle-God' credits this decline in the influence of the martial deity to three possible causes: 'modern meditation', 'penmen's pleadings', and 'crimes too dire'.[55] Hardy's own penman's pleadings set about encouraging the transformation of public consciousness, and enjoy implicit self-congratulation as the Boer War sequence unfolds. 'Departure' despairingly evokes the 'saner softer polities | Whereof we dream', but the dream of the sequence's second poem turns into the reality of the last as 'The Sick Battle-God' charts the fall of the 'lurid Deity'. The dethroning of the God of Battles takes place during the sequence, as if brought about by the act of writing the poems.

Hardy's Boer War poetry most effectively contributes to this succession when it avoids the comfortable pathos and the anti-war hectoring. *The Dynasts* holds the advantage of being sufficiently distanced from contemporary events to allow brutally attentive accounts of battlefield slaughter: depriving death in battle of even the scutcheon of honour, its ruthless candour refuses to be distracted by sentiment. In book III, for example, as the English guards at Waterloo surround some French battalions and methodically cut

---

[52] Stephen Crane, *War is Kind* (New York: Frederick A. Stokes, 1899), 9.
[53] Wilfred Owen, 'Dulce et Decorum Est', in *The Complete Poems and Fragments*, i: *The Poems*, ed. Jon Stallworthy (London: Chatto & Windus, Hogarth Press, and Oxford University Press, 1983), 140.
[54] Hardy, *Complete Poems*, 99.	[55] Ibid. 98.

them down with rifle fire, Hardy tallies up the squalor of war and
the cost of heroism:

> COLONEL HUGH HALKETT (shouting)
> Surrender! And preserve those heroes' lives!
>
> CAMBRONNE (with exasperation)
> Mer-r-r-de! . . . You've to deal with desperates, man, to-day:
> Life is a byword here!

Hollow laughter, as from people in hell, comes approvingly from the
remains of the Old Guard. The English proceed with their massacre, the
devoted band thins and thins, and a ball strikes CAMBRONNE, who falls, and
is trampled over.[56]

Jon Silkin calls this passage 'as horrific and affecting as anything in
the poetry of the First World War'.[57] But its power is dissipated by
cliché—the heroes and desperadoes, the infernal hollow laughter,
the defiant officer's dishonoured corpse. The one powerfully effective
moment comes in describing the business-like aspects of battle, where
victory has been secured but the job still entails a dutiful and thor-
ough killing: 'The English proceed with their massacre'. Although
Hardy never dares to attempt such battlefield reconstruction in his
Boer War poems, the best are distinguished by a similar dispassion.

'Drummer Hodge' and 'The Souls of the Slain', written during
November and December 1899, offer a new war lyric for the
twentieth century, undeceived but unflinching. The entire Boer
War sequence resists consolation, discovering neither earthly nor
heavenly reward for the men's sacrifice. However, those two poems
stand apart, because they also resist a cathartic purging of, and relief
from, the distressing emotions they arouse: there are no tears and
no politics to assuage the reader's response. Both poems awaken
a visceral fear greater even than fear of death in battle—a fear of
being lost for all eternity, far from home, without hope of restitution.

---

[56] Hardy, *The Dynasts* (London: Macmillan, 1978), 695.
[57] Jon Silkin, *Out of Battle: The Poetry of the Great War* (Oxford: Oxford University
Press, 1972), 36.

'A Christmas Ghost-Story' had briefly broached that prospect of exile as it located the mouldering soldier 'South of the Line, inland from far Durban';[58] his phantom moans 'to clear Canopus', the second brightest star in the night sky but invisible as far north as England. Although 'Drummer Hodge' is less astronomically specific, each of its three stanzas ends with the unfamiliarity of the stars above the drummer-boy's grave: they are 'foreign constellations', 'Strange stars' and 'strange-eyed constellations'.[59] (Compare Housman's indebted Boer War elegy 'Astronomy', which describes the final resting-place of a dead soldier: 'And now he does not even see | Signs of the nadir roll | At night over the ground where he | Is buried with the pole.'[60]) Hardy deals in stark binaries—Northern/Southern, home/foreign, homely/unknown—as the irruption of Afrikaans words such as 'kopje', 'Karoo', and 'veldt' stresses the incompatibility of the boy 'Fresh from his Wessex home' with the landscape in which he is compelled to 'rest' for all eternity. Over a decade later, Rupert Brooke in 'The Soldier' renders safe what Hardy had shown to be terrifying: Brooke's lines, 'there's some corner of a foreign field | That is for ever England',[61] convert into patriotic pride the horror of Hardy's 'Yet portion of that unknown plain | Will Hodge for ever be'; and Hardy's alien constellations are replaced in Brooke's final image by the comforts of 'an English heaven', as God and *patria* are united. Hardy, typically, had evoked Wessex as Hodge's home; home is local. For Brooke, home means a rural nation and the succours of patriotism. Brooke reinstates what Hardy had conspicuously denied: a beneficent God, a divinely sanctioned cause, a national unity, a consolation, and a victory even in death. In doing so, he exposes the negation of 'Drummer Hodge', itself founded on a rejection of the 'elegiac topos of stellification'[62] and of Wordsworthian solace. Hodge is rolled round in earth's diurnal course, but the natural world which was

    [58] Hardy, *Complete Poems*, 90.   [59] Ibid. 90–1.
    [60] A. E. Housman, *The Poems*, ed. Archie Burnett (Oxford: Clarendon Press, 1997), 86.
    [61] Rupert Brooke, *The Poetical Works*, ed. Geoffrey Keynes (London: Faber, 1960), 23.
    [62] Ramazani, *Poetry of Mourning*, 42.

sustaining for Wordsworth has become alien and manipulative: 'His homely Northern breast and brain' will 'Grow to some Southern tree'. 'The Souls of the Slain', like 'Drummer Hodge', passes over the circumstances of death to dwell on commemoration and its absence. Hodge's corpse is unceremoniously dumped by an anonymous 'They' who may be Boer or British: the unbridgeable division is between living and dead, rather than rival nations, and it behoves the poet to provide the monument which Hodge would otherwise have lacked. In 'The Souls of the Slain', the revenants look forward to feasting on fame, and reach the south coast of England before learning that their 'glory and war-mightiness' go unappreciated at home. Standing at Portland Bill, the poet witnesses this disappointment as the dead soldiers are told of their posthumous reputations by their general:

VIII
'Some mothers muse sadly, and murmur
Your doings as boys—
Recall the quaint ways
Of your babyhood's innocent days.
Some pray that, ere dying, your faith had grown firmer,
And higher your joys.

IX
'A father broods: "Would I had set him
To some humble trade,
And so slacked his high fire,
And his passionate martial desire;
And told him no stories to woo him and whet him
To this dire crusade!"'

X
'And, General, how hold out our sweethearts,
Sworn loyal as doves?'
'—Many mourn; many think
It is not unattractive to prink
Them in sables for heroes. Some fickle and fleet hearts
Have found them new loves.'

XI

'And our wives?' quoth another resignedly,
          'Dwell they on our deeds?'
          — 'Deeds of home; that live yet
     Fresh as new—deeds of fondness or fret;
Ancient words that were kindly expressed or unkindly,
          These, these have their heeds.'[63]

Hardy's willingness to acknowledge such complication carries into
a slightly later poem, 'A Wife and Another', which makes a love
triangle out of the soldier-husband's return as his wife discovers
that another woman is pregnant with his child. In 'The Souls
of the Slain', however, it is the men who are betrayed, by fickle
sweethearts and, more painfully, by a society prepared to sacrifice
its youth in a distant war but seemingly indifferent to the soldiers'
achievements.

Some of the souls are reconciled to this fate, immediately under-
standing that they should value those loved ones who recall their
'old kindness' more than they value martial fame. But while they
are restored to their homes, others among the 'trooped appar-
itions' choose to leave England again rather than endure such
a destiny:

XV

And, towering to seaward in legions,
          They paused at a spot
          Overbending the Race—
That engulphing, ghast, sinister place—
Whither headlong they plunged, to the fathomless regions
          Of myriads forgot.

XVI

And the spirits of those who were homing
          Passed on, rushingly,
          Like the Pentecost Wind;
And the whirr of their wayfaring thinned

---

63 Hardy, *Complete Poems*, 94–5.

And surceased on the sky, and but left in the gloaming
Sea-mutterings and me.[64]

These stanzas epitomize the confrontations and negotiations which
Hardy's Boer War sequence enacts. To the north of the poet is home
and solace; to the south, estrangement and the oceanic depths. 'The
Souls of the Slain' leaves Hardy stationary and undecided, witnessing
with a truth which this time seems to accommodate no bias. Yet a
hint of allegiance does linger in the last lines. The 'Pentecost Wind'
has rushed past the poet without filling him with the Holy Spirit or
inspiring him to teach others of Christian consolation. Instead, he
is left behind with those 'sea-mutterings' — 'mutterings' suggesting
that the complaints of the unreconciled souls who plunged into the
sea's 'fathomless regions' are audible and unceasing. The sea cannot
drown the voices of the dead, but nor this time do the tears which
flow all too freely earlier in the sequence.

[64] Ibid. 95–6.

2

Rudyard Kipling's Dress Parade

Hardy's Boer War poetry shows little interest in soldiers until they die. More concerned with the effects of their departure and return—or failure to return—it allows them only a posthumous voice, so that they may confront the cause for which they were sacrificed. Soldiers are tragic figures in Hardy's work, tramping gloomily to their inevitable fates. Of their experiences in battle, their daily routines, their sense of duty, their camaraderie, even their attitudes to military and civilian leaders, Hardy says nothing. It falls to Rudyard Kipling, a long-standing veteran of the barrack-room, to break that silence; in doing so, he (more than Hardy) fosters the earliest significant generation of soldier-poets, which will emerge during the Great War over a decade later.

Kipling had always been well placed to study the military, first as a schoolboy in the United Services College which trained sons of officers to follow their fathers, and then as a tyro journalist in the Punjab where the British army controlled the civil administration. By instinct a war poet (and prose writer) long before his nation was at war, Kipling in his early work returned frequently to tales heard around 'a Mess-table at midnight'[1]—tales of skirmishes at the frontiers of Empire, in Afghanistan, Sudan, Burma, Khartoum, and north-west India. The fascination was profound and enduring: army men, Kipling gratefully concluded, do not 'spout hashed

---

[1] Rudyard Kipling, 'The Drums of the Fore and Aft', in *Wee Willie Winkie*, ed. Hugh Haughton (Harmondsworth: Penguin, 1988), 300.

libraries | Or think the next man's thought'.[2] Whether they avoided thinking Kipling's thought is a different matter. As Sir George Younghusband, a retired subaltern, recalled in 1917,

> I myself had served for many years with soldiers, but had never heard the words or expressions that Rudyard Kipling's soldiers used ... But sure enough, a few years after, the soldiers thought, and talked, and expressed themselves exactly like Rudyard Kipling had taught them in his stories ... Kipling made the modern soldier.[3]

Kipling's poetry proved as influential as his prose. The *Barrack-Room Ballads* of 1892 offered a model for soldier-poets, who produced what Malvern Van Wyk Smith has described as a 'small library of Kiplingesque verse' during the Boer War.[4] That level of productivity reflected new educational circumstances. The conflict in South Africa was the first to involve a predominantly literate British army, and its poets' overwhelming indebtedness to Kipling signalled the extent to which literature had previously neglected the experiences of private soldiers. As Lionel Johnson had remarked when reviewing the *Barrack-Room Ballads*, 'of the British army, as a way of daily life, as composed of individual men, as full of marked personal characteristics and peculiarities, our poets great and small have had little conception'.[5] Kipling attempted to rectify that ignorance, but not every British soldier in South Africa was persuaded of the authenticity of his portrayals. 'Rudyardkiplingese', published in the Bloemfontein *Friend* (an information sheet for soldiers which Kipling helped to edit briefly), pointedly suggested that the famous poet need not bother researching his subject:

---

[2] Quoted by Michael Edwardes, '"Oh to meet an Army Man!"': Kipling and the Soldiers', in John Gross (ed.), *Rudyard Kipling: The Man, his Work and his World* (London: Weidenfeld & Nicolson, 1972), 38.

[3] Ibid. 44.

[4] M. Van Wyk Smith, *Drummer Hodge: The Poetry of the Anglo-Boer War 1899–1902* (Oxford: Clarendon Press, 1978), 111.

[5] Lionel Johnson, quoted in Peter Keating, *Kipling the Poet* (London: Secker & Warburg, 1994), 54.

> The man that writes a poem
> In praise of our Tommy A.'s
> Ain't got no call to study
> Their manners, nor talk, nor ways,
> 'E's only to fake up something
> What's Barracky—more or less—
> And civilians don't know as it's rubbish and so
> The Ballad's a big success.[6]

This barracking of the more or less 'Barracky' constitutes an ambivalent criticism, forged out of what it purportedly condemns: attacking Kipling's depiction of soldiers' 'manners', their 'talk' and 'ways', as fake, the poem depends on his Cockney dialect for its expression. The more serious charge against Kipling predicts the anger of Great War poets against long-range civilian commentators. However much he may know of the barrack-room compared with other civilians, Kipling will never be a 'Tommy A.'. Like Hardy, he wants to serve as advocate for the downtrodden and dispossessed, but the act of giving the voiceless a voice remains ethically fraught. He teaches them poetry, and (in poems like 'Rudyardkiplingese') their profit is that they know how to curse him. If such criticisms are to be trusted, Kipling also shares with Hardy a reluctance to draw distinctions between speaking *for* and speaking *through*. Hardy's soldiers think and sound like Hardy; the issue is whether, for all their disguise of Cockneyfication, Kipling's think and sound like Kipling.

Arguments in favour of an experiential war poetry did not begin with the Boer War. Tennyson's 'The Charge of the Light Brigade', inspired by an account of the incident in *The Times*, had become possible because the Crimean War was the first to be covered by reporters and photographers. Yet, within a decade, Walt Whitman in *Drum Taps* (1865) had created a war poetry based on first-hand experience. Spending the American Civil War as a voluntary hospital help and wound-dresser, Whitman concluded that only the witness

---

6 Quoted in Van Wyk Smith, *Drummer Hodge*, 110.

could understand the nature of the conflict: 'I now doubt whether one can get a fair idea of what this war practically is . . . without some such experience as this I am having.'[7] Kipling had once considered Whitman his favourite poet,[8] and the American's example may have influenced Kipling's own behaviour in the Boer War. Just as Whitman had travelled with a trainload of wounded soldiers, tending their injuries, so Kipling joined a Red Cross ambulance train to collect casualties from the Battle of Paardeburg; and Kipling, like Whitman before him, wrote letters on behalf of wounded soldiers to their families. (He would later recall in *Something of Myself* that, among the rank and file, he unofficially gained a status 'above that of most Generals'.[9]) Nevertheless, Kipling's three-month visit to South Africa during early 1900 does not sustain comparison with Whitman's years of altruism in the field hospitals. As war correspondent, politician, tourist, entertainer, celebrity, and charity-worker, he enjoyed feeding his intellectual curiosity, reporting after his return to England that 'there happened to be a bit of a war on, and I had the time of my life. Carrie and the children stayed at Cape Town and I sort of drifted up country looking at hospitals and wounded men and guns and generals.'[10] One glimpse of Kipling in early 1900 describes him with 'his nose to the ground for subject-matter' as he examines 'every mortal thing from the Maxims to the officers and privates'.[11] Whereas Whitman never saw fighting, Kipling seized the opportunity to spectate when the British advanced on some Boer positions just north of Bloemfontein. Even his having unexpectedly come under fire, as he watched from a nearby farmhouse, brought writerly compensations: 'I wasn't hit, which was the main thing; and

---

[7] Walt Whitman, 'Specimen Days', in *Complete Poetry and Collected Prose*, ed. Justin Kaplan (New York: Library of America, 1982), 735.

[8] See Andrew Lycett, *Rudyard Kipling* (London: Weidenfeld & Nicolson, 1999), 91.

[9] Kipling, *Something of Myself*, ed. Robert Hampson (Harmondsworth: Penguin, 1987), 121.

[10] Kipling to James M. Conland, 24 July 1900, in *The Letters*, iii: *1900–1910*, ed. Thomas Pinney (London: Macmillan, 1996), 26.

[11] Quoted by George Shepperson, 'Kipling and the Boer War', in Gross (ed.), *Rudyard Kipling*, 86.

I certainly managed to pick up a good deal of mixed and valuable information.'[12] Kipling's Boer War poetry exploits the authority of experience. Most of his output divides between the Cockney poems spoken by low-ranking soldiers, and the high pronouncements, *in propria persona*, on the justifications for war and (subsequently) the lessons to be learnt from it. These two types might be expected to enjoy a symbiotic relationship. As the soldiers' friend, witnessing war at first hand, Kipling accumulates the right to a political poetry. But his own politics rarely informs the attitudes of his soldiers, who convey a diversity of responses which resists dilution to a simple pro-war message. So often caricatured as a jingoist and apologist for empire, Kipling writes a poetry which can be tentative, self-doubting, and compassionate. Received wisdom requires that his Boer War writings do not live up to expectations: 'neither in his Boer War poetry nor in his prose, did Kipling produce the South African book which many of his admirers expected of him';[13] 'the Boer War stories are very disappointing';[14] 'the fifteen "Service Songs" in *The Five Nations*, in the style of *Barrack-Room Ballads*, are inferior to their predecessors';[15] '[during this period] he published verse that was too fluently and easily written';[16] 'The war inevitably prompted him to much writing both in prose and verse, but it cannot be said to have elicited any of his best work.'[17] Not all universally acknowledged truths warrant an instant dismissal, but these critical judgements neglect Kipling's success in achieving a polyvocal range in prose and poetry which at least gestures towards the variety of opinions about, and experiences of, the Boer War. Although he writes no individual poem as great

[12] Kipling to James M. Conland, 24 July 1900, in *Letters*, iii. 26.
[13] George Shepperson, 'Kipling and the Boer War', in Gross (ed.), *Rudyard Kipling*, 85.
[14] Angus Wilson, *The Strange Ride of Rudyard Kipling* (London: Secker & Warburg, 1977), 217.
[15] Van Wyk Smith, *Drummer Hodge*, 107.
[16] Philip Mason, *Kipling: The Glass, the Shadow and the Fire* (London: Cape, 1975), 145.
[17] J. I. M. Stewart, *Rudyard Kipling* (London: Gollancz, 1966), 146.

as Hardy's 'Drummer Hodge' or 'The Souls of the Slain', Kipling creates a body of Boer War poetry which is, *in toto*, the match of any contemporary.

The Five Nations appeared in 1903, the year after the end of the war. Collecting most of his Boer War poems from the previous four years, Kipling emphasizes through his title a broader theme: the mutually beneficial relationship (as he saw it) between Britain and her daughter nations of Canada, Australia, New Zealand, and South Africa. Their willingness to aid the British Empire during the Boer War is celebrated in the balladic fourteeners of 'The Parting of the Columns', as the British troops bid farewell to a mixed detachment of 'colonials' who, despite having ''ad no special call to come', had lent brave support to the imperial cause:

> We'll never read the papers now without inquirin' first
> For word from all those friendly dorps where you was born an' nursed.
> Why, Dawson, Galle, an' Montreal—Port Darwin—Timaru
> They're only just across the road! Good-bye—good luck to you![18]

The war, such poems argue, might yet strengthen a sense of identity and shared purpose amongst the scattered nations of the Empire: as Kipling reported in early 1901, the regular regiments and the colonials had become brothers who 'eat out of the same dish'.[19] His work does its best to honour that brotherhood, although hope for the future exists alongside a greater fear that British decadence will bring about defeat. The Boer War may have been, as Kipling's British general says in his story 'The Captive', ' "a first-class dress parade for Armageddon" ',[20] but the repeated insistence on the urgency of preparing for a still more catastrophic conflict—in poems like 'The Dykes' and 'The Lesson'—indicates the extent of their author's foreboding. Ignoring chronology, Kipling ends *The Five Nations* with 'Recessional', written two years before the outbreak of war in 1897. This arrangement frames the Boer War poems and invites

---

[18] Kipling, *The Five Nations* (London: Methuen, 1903), 178.
[19] Kipling to James M. Conland, 20 Feb. 1901, in *Letters*, iii. 42.
[20] Kipling, *Traffics and Discoveries* (London: House of Stratus, 2001), 20.

understanding of the conflict as another confirmation of the dangers of national complacency. Calling on the 'Judge of the Nations' to 'spare us yet',[21] 'Recessional' is a fitting conclusion to a volume which is at least as preoccupied with the war to come as with the Boer War.

If 'Recessional' indicates Kipling's belief that urgent lessons needed to be learnt even before the Boer War, the Boer War proves that most were not learnt. Kipling's campaign in poetry and prose to raise the status of the British soldier among civilians—'For it's Tommy this an' Tommy that, an' "Chuck him out, the brute!" | But it's "Saviour of 'is country" when the guns begin to shoot'[22]—blames a national hypocrisy which he fears will lead, if uncorrected, to destruction. His letters of the period harp on the potentially purifying effects of the war: in May 1901 he remembers how before its outbreak, 'We were bung-full of beastly unjustified spiritual pride as we were with material luxury and over much ease'; whereas now 'Every thing we have—church school and craft—has, so to speak, been challenged to show cause why it should continue on the old unthinking hide-bound lines.'[23] The Boer War may have been 'new and terrible', but out of it, Kipling hoped, would come the opportunity for 'immense gain both to the land and the Empire—not to mention the Army'.[24] His call for military reform and for a shift in public opinion, given added passion by his expectations of a larger and looming war against Germany, would end in angry disappointment. Yet, even if their prophecies go unheeded, the poems of *The Five Nations* do their duty for their country, attacking failures and shortcomings in the hierarchies of power in ways which Great War poets would have ample reason to repeat. Proleptic but not prophylactic, 'Stellenbosh' expresses an appalled disdain for the generals whose incompetence prolongs the war and wastes the courage of their young charges:

---

[21] Kipling, *Five Nations*, 214.
[22] Kipling, 'Tommy', in *The Complete Verse* (London: Kyle Cathie, 1996), 322.
[23] Kipling to Charles Eliot Norton, 19 May 1901, in *Letters*, iii. 53.
[24] Kipling to William Charles Scully, 14 Feb. 1900, ibid. 12.

The General saw the mountain-range ahead,
    With their 'elios showin' saucy on the 'eight,
So 'e 'eld us to the level ground instead,
    An' telegraphed the Boojers wouldn't fight.
For 'e might 'ave gone an' sprayed 'em with a pompom,
    Or 'e might have slung a squadron out to see—
But 'e wasn't takin' chances in them 'igh an' 'ostile kranzes—
    He was markin' time to earn a K.C.B.[25]

The poem's perspective is that of the low-ranking everyman soldier, whose criticisms of army strategy suggest that he would make a better leader than the leaders. Kipling's General, inevitably, 'got 'is decorations thick', leaving the rank and file with 'the work to do again'. His direct descendants are Sassoon's scarlet majors toddling safely home to die in bed, or the cheery old General who 'did for' his men 'by his plan of attack'.[26] But although the result is the same, 'Stellenbosh' encounters the opposite problem: there is no 'plan of attack', the General's reputation being more important to him than a military strategy which, striving for victory, would risk defeat by engaging directly with the enemy.

Kipling plays out the same battle between high-ranking idiocy and low-ranking wisdom in his Boer War short stories. 'The Way That He Took', for example, relates a captain's discovery of a Boer ambush. When he tells his colonel not to advance because of the trap, the colonel doubts the wisdom of the advice: ' "D'you expect any officer of my experience to believe that?" ' Against such arrogance, the only possibility is to acquiesce: ' "As you please, sir," said the Captain hopelessly.'[27] It is the colonel who, tactically 'hopeless', instils that lack of hope in the soldiers serving under him; and so the story ends, in the expectation that the colonel will sacrifice his men by marching blithely into an ambush about which he has been fully warned.

---

[25] Kipling, *Five Nations*, 195–6. The ' 'elios' are heliographs—mirrors which reflect sunlight to flash messages in Morse code.
[26] Siegfried Sassoon, 'The General', in *Collected Poems 1908–1956* (London: Faber, 1984), 69.
[27] Kipling, *War Stories and Poems*, ed. Andrew Rutherford (Oxford: Oxford University Press, 1990), 144.

Kipling's own experiences in South Africa exacerbated his dismay. 'I knew for sure we were fools,' he wrote in the summer of 1900, 'but I didn't know how thick and wide and consistent our folly was.'[28] The conflict in his poems and stories is not so urgently between Empire and Boer as it is between generations of Englishmen: the 'old men', in Kipling's poem of that title, 'shall abide till the battle is won ere [they] amble into the fray'.[29] They—the ruling classes in both the political and the military sphere—are the cowards, and Kipling denounces them angrily and often as the product of a society more interested in 'the flannelled fools at the wicket or the muddied oafs at the goals' ('The Islanders').[30] Poem after poem reports the betrayal: the nation has neglected the dykes left by its fathers, and the sea will sweep over its defences to drown it imminently. Kipling's letters continue the theme. England has been 'criminally weak', he tells one correspondent,[31] and to another he complains that if only 'the Show had been run *as a war* in this Colony, instead of as a cross between a lying-in-hospital and a Sunday school picnic it might have been over a good long time ago'.[32] That desire for a thorough, committed, and, consequently, brief and less costly war should not be mistaken for bloodlust. Kipling's grudging admiration for the Boer stands apart from the murderous hatred he directs at the Russians, who had provided a steady threat to British rule of India during the 1880s. His anti-Russian parable in *The Five Nations*, 'The Truce of the Bear', illustrates the dangers of sympathizing with your enemy when he is at your mercy. The speaker remembers how he hunted down the bear, but hesitated as he was 'Touched with pity and wonder'.[33] The next touch, as the bear totters towards him 'with paws like hands that pray', is altogether more decisive: 'From brow to jaw that steel-shod paw, it ripped my face away!' Hesitation born out of pity, this lesson concludes, is a self-mutilating weakness.

[28] Kipling to Walter Lawrence, 21 June 1900, in *Letters*, iii. 23.
[29] Kipling, *Five Nations*, 50.   [30] Ibid. 135.
[31] Kipling to Edward Lucas White, 11 Nov. 1902, in *Letters*, iii. 112.
[32] Kipling to an unidentified recipient, 14 Jan. 1902, ibid. 83.
[33] Kipling, *Five Nations*, 46.

If Kipling's portrayal of the Boers harbours no such animosity, it is not least because he preoccupies himself so completely with his own nation's shortcomings. While Swinburne could call on God's England to 'scourge these dogs agape with jaws afoam, | Down out of life',[34] and by so doing, come to embody what he attacked, Kipling's more measured tones dignify a worthy adversary. 'I'm offended with no one except the "simple and pastoral" Boer who seems to be having us on toast,'[35] he acknowledged, immediately before sailing to South Africa and observing British incompetence for himself. By the end of the war, he could admit to admiring 'the Burgher of the Transvaal and Orange River Colony': 'for some reasons I was almost sorry to see them go under'.[36] (That generosity did not extend to the 'Cape Colonial rebel', who was 'not at all a nice person',[37] and whose perfidy provides the occasion, in 'A Sahibs' War', for one of Kipling's most brutal stories of revenge.) Kipling's poetry notices the Boers only in 'Half-Ballad of Waterval' and 'Piet', and in each case the tone is respectful: after all, 'What *is* the sense of 'ating those | 'Oom you are paid to kill?'[38] The contrast with his attitude not only to the Russians, but also to the Germans in late 1918—he would call for the 'sword | Of justice' to be wielded against 'ancient sin' and 'Evil Incarnate' ('Justice')[39]—could hardly be more obvious. The Boer is enemy and brother, praised for his bravery and ingenuity, and pitied in defeat by captors who (in 'Half-Ballad of Waterval') recall how they were obliged to endure a similar misery earlier in the war:

> They'll get those draggin' days all right,
> Spent as a foreigner commands,
> An' 'orrors of the locked-up night,
> With 'Ell's own thinkin' on their 'ands.
> I'd give the gold o' twenty Rands
> (If it was mine) to set 'em free . . .

---

[34] Algernon Charles Swinburne, 'The Transvaal', in *The Poems*, vi (London: Chatto & Windus, 1904), 385.

[35] Kipling to William Alexander Fraser, 8 Jan. 1900, in *Letters*, iii. 9.

[36] Kipling to Edward Lucas White, 11 Nov. 1902, ibid. 112.   [37] Ibid.

[38] Kipling, 'Piet', in *Five Nations*, 199.   [39] Kipling, *Complete Verse*, 317.

For I 'ave learned at Waterval
The meanin' of captivity![40]

That depth of fellow-feeling, especially when combined with their contempt for military and political leaders, raises the question of why Kipling's soldiers choose to fight at all. It is a question which the rallying cry of 'The White Man's Burden', collected in *The Five Nations*, does not forestall, and which, in spite of Kipling's unshaken political certainties, his Boer War poems increasingly struggle to answer. Giving voice to his soldiers, Kipling explores the schism which would open still more damagingly during the Great War between what Robert Graves and Alan Hodge would come to characterize as 'the Fighting Forces' and 'the Rest'.[41] That later war confirms the importance of Kipling's ambition in his poetry to bridge the divide; it also confirms that, in this crucial respect, his warnings were ignored.

While making plain his own allegiances in the common soldier's fractured relationships with both the civilian and the General, Kipling resists the temptation to idealize. Like Tommy Atkins of *Barrack-Room Ballads*, he advocates nothing more than fair and equal treatment: 'We aren't no thin red 'eroes, nor we aren't no blackguards too'.[42] 'The Absent-Minded Beggar', Kipling's fund-raising poem for the families of Boer War servicemen, even concedes that Tommy's 'weaknesses are great', and that 'There are girls he married secret, asking no permission to | For he knew he wouldn't get it if he did'.[43] And yet, Kipling stresses, these are trivial misdemeanours compared with the far greater shame which would fall on a society failing to support the soldier's dependents while he was 'out on active service, wiping something off a slate'. (Appalled before long by its jolly propaganda, Kipling never collected 'The Absent-Minded Beggar', though the poem served its cause by raising £250,000.) Kipling's

[40] Kipling, *Five Nations*, 198.
[41] Quoted in Paul Fussell, *The Great War and Modern Memory* (Oxford: Oxford University Press, 1975), 89.
[42] Kipling, 'Tommy', 322.   [43] Kipling, *Complete Verse*, 372.

clear-sighted defence of Tommy Atkins allows his Boer War poetry to express unlikely sympathies, as in ' "Wilful-Missing" ', spoken by the British army's deserters who have taken their 'chance to cut the show'. The dramatic monologue excludes criticism, and pleads instead for the understanding that the men's torment cannot be understood:

> There is no need to give our reasons, though
> Gawd knows we all 'ad reasons which were fair;
> But other people might not judge 'em so,
> And now it doesn't matter what they were.[44]

Kipling grants the reader little opportunity to join the ranks of the 'other people' who would condemn the deserters by refusing the assurance that their reasons were 'fair'. 'What man can size or weigh another's woe?', the poem continues; its question may not command the severity of 'Judge not, that ye be not judged', but it still outflanks the judgemental by obliging a generous response.

' "Wilful-Missing" ' typifies Kipling's reluctance to censor the common soldier no matter how deleterious his behaviour. It is a poem of negative capability: when Keats describes how, in a room of people, each person's identity presses on him until he is 'in a very little time annihilated',[45] he describes what will become one of Kipling's greatest imaginative resources. As a Boer War poet, Kipling carries out these acts of sympathy and self-annihilation more successfully than Hardy, so that his dramatic monologues become worthy of the name. While Hardy writes disguised lyrics, and channels his own ethical and political predilections through the cipher of other people, Kipling's poems accommodate rather than manipulate. They immerse themselves in the tedium of relent-lessly 'foot—slog—slog—slog—sloggin' over Africa' ('Boots'),[46] or report the jokes told by men under bombardment ('The Instructor'),

---

[44] Kipling, *Five Nations*, 204–5.
[45] Keats to Richard Woodhouse, 27 Oct. 1818, in *The Letters*, ed. Maurice Buxton Forman (Oxford: Oxford University Press, 1935), 228.
[46] Kipling, *Five Nations*, 185.

or imagine enduring the vulnerable isolation of being posted into the Oudtshoorn ranges to guard a railway line ('Bridge-Guard in the Karroo'). These attempts to share the soldiers' experiences may never convince the anonymous poet of the Bloemfontein *Friend* that Kipling is doing more than faking up something—all dramatic monologues being, in a narrow sense, fake—but at the very least they offer a powerful championing of the underdog's interests.

Kipling's identification with, and support for, the British soldier against his undeserving nation ensure that the wilful-missing represent only the most immediately dangerous symptom of a widespread disillusionment. Not only are the generals inept, but the freedom promised by the South African landscape, and the brotherhood forged with foreign nationals, compare favourably with the smallness of life back home. Filled with pleas for Britain to prepare its defences, *The Five Nations* struggles to find reasons why anyone should bother. It is significant that 'Lichtenberg', expressing a Boer War soldier's homesickness, is voiced for an Australian. 'Smells are surer than sounds or sights | To make your heart-strings crack,' the soldier begins, before reporting how the smell of wattle suddenly and vividly evoked the glories of his distant nation:

> And I saw Sydney the same as ever,
>   The picnics and brass-bands;
> And the little homestead on Hunter River
>   And my new vines joining hands.
> It all came over me in one act
>   Quick as a shot through the brain—
> With the smell of the wattle round Lichtenberg,
>   Riding in, in the rain.[47]

Nostalgia is a deadly force, as violent and overpowering as that other ever-present danger, 'a shot through the brain'. Nowhere in *The Five Nations* does a British soldier experience anything comparable. The 'married man' looks forward to finishing his 'little bit' and

47 Kipling, *Five Nations*, 101–2.

going home 'to 'is tea',[48] but his are purely family reasons, bereft of patriotism. More often, the nostalgia is for South Africa herself, that 'woman wonderful' who, for all her 'drouth', 'plague', 'dust', and 'lies', can never be abandoned for long by the men she treats 'despiteful-wise', and who remains in their eyes 'most | Perfect and adorèd' ('South Africa').[49]

'One curses it but one comes back to it,'[50] Kipling acknowledged in 1907, having returned yearly to South Africa since the outbreak of the Boer War. Only after a new Liberal government in Britain had ceded control of the Transvaal to the Afrikaners did his affair end: to Duckworth Ford, later that year, Kipling wrote, 'I'm going down to the Cape ... about December (just to watch the corpse being (in)decently buried) and then I suppose I must hunt about for another country to love.'[51] Bitterly complaining that the British government had given away everything the Boer War had been fought for, Kipling never again visited South Africa. His soldiers are less easily dissuaded. The speakers of several poems in *The Five Nations* face the choice of remaining or returning, and their vacillations hint at the poverty of opportunities in their native land. Hardy in 'Drummer Hodge' had portrayed South Africa as threateningly alien, with its 'strange-eyed' and 'foreign' constellations, its linguistic oddities of 'kopje', 'veldt', and 'Karoo',[52] and its landscape's antagonistic colonization of the British dead. Kipling does not disguise its threats, but he limns a land which is magnificent and awe-inspiring in scale. 'Bridge-Guard in the Karroo', one of the strongest of his Boer War poems, harrows with fear and wonder:

> Sudden the desert changes,
>   The raw glare softens and clings,
> Till the aching Oudtshoorn ranges
>   Stand up like the thrones of kings—

---

[48] 'The Married Man', ibid. 188.   [49] Ibid. 149–52.
[50] Quoted in Lycett, *Rudyard Kipling*, 503.
[51] Kipling to Duckworth Ford, 16 Sept. 1907, in *Letters*, iii. 262.
[52] Thomas Hardy, 'Drummer Hodge', in *The Complete Poems*, ed. James Gibson (Basingstoke: Palgrave, 2001), 90–1.

> Ramparts of slaughter and peril—
> Blazing, amazing—aglow
> 'Twixt the sky-line's belting beryl
> And the wine-dark flats below.
>
> Royal the pageant closes,
> Lit by the last of the sun—
> Opal and ash-of-roses,
> Cinnamon, umber, and dun.[53]

The landscape embodies a terrible majesty which emphasizes the loneliness of vulnerable humans—here, the 'Details guarding the line'. They also serve who only stand and wait, and their posting amidst such a glorious conflagration is a reminder that the Boer is not the only, or even the most impressive, threat to the foreign army which must fight in and for South Africa.

The Five Nations never loses sight of a dangerously strange country—'bought by blood, | And by blood restorèd'[54]—even though the British speakers of Kipling's poems eventually make their peace with, and sometimes their home in, the landscape they might have feared. That price of blood is not forgotten: 'Half [her land] was red with battle,' Kipling notes in 'South Africa'; the epigraph of 'Bridge-Guard in the Karroo' situates the guards at the 'Blood River Bridge'; and in 'The Settler', as 'the deep soil glistens red', the speaker talks of neighbours atoning for 'the set folly and the red breach | And the black waste of it all'.[55] However, that last example also paints Kipling's vision for a future South Africa, one which does not forget the bloodshed of the past but which repairs wrongs as one-time enemies start 'Giving and taking counsel each | Over the cattle-kraal'.[56] The battle sites where bullets fell and shrapnel burst will become fruitful as trees are planted and wells dug. Revenge would be an indulgence condemned by 'the ungrazed upland, the untilled lea' and the 'fields forlorn', so neighbours must unite in

---

[53] Kipling, *Five Nations*, 113.   [54] 'South Africa', ibid. 151.
[55] Ibid. 149, 113, 153.   [56] Ibid. 153.

a spirit of reconciliation against a new and still more formidable antagonist:

> Here will we join against our foes—
> The hailstroke and the storm,
> And the red and rustling cloud that blows
> The locust's mile-deep swarm;
> Frost and murrain and floods let loose
> Shall launch us side by side
> In the holy wars that have no truce
> 'Twixt seed and harvest tide.[57]

Redness is no longer the product of man's, but of nature's, inhumanity to man, as rival factions are brought together in the face of this environmental challenge. 'The Settler' looks forward to a future enjoyed by the inheritors of this union ('After us cometh a multitude') who will, regardless of race, be sustained by the shared labour which produces 'our land's food'.[58] The rhyme 'multitude/food' stresses practical considerations. Nevertheless, the resolution is only problematically achieved, as the elements are tamed into 'a healing stillness' and a 'vast, benignant sky'. Reconciliation between warring humans may be possible, but reconciliation with nature looks more like wishful thinking.

The poem's repetitive use of the first person plural leaves no distinction between Boer and Briton: they are all settlers alike, and they must 'atone' and 'repair' together, for the sake of 'the living and the dead' as well as for 'the folk of all our lands'. (That phrase, like most contemporary and many subsequent debates about the Boer War, passes silently over the black Africans who belong among the 'folk' of the 'lands' but do not share in the ownership.) As a propitiative conclusion to the poems of war in the main section of *The Five Nations*, 'The Settler' prepares for the 'Service Songs' which immediately follow, and which pursue this hope of a peaceful and prosperous future for South Africa. After a short,

---

[57] Ibid. 154.   [58] Ibid. 155.

untitled dedicatory poem, the songs begin with 'Chant-Pagan', in which a dissatisfied soldier, having arrived home, decides to head back to South Africa: there is, he believes, 'a Dutchman I've fought 'oo might give | Me a job were I ever inclined'.[59] That dilemma is repeated in 'The Return', just before the hymnic solemnity of Kipling's 'Recessional', except that the speaker this time chooses to remain in England. The positioning of the poems implies a progression out of disenchantment and towards renewed fealty to the Empire's mother-nation. Yet the poems themselves prohibit that patriotic solace: 'The Return' answers any indifference to England with a rhetoric of blind faith which is everywhere challenged by the available evidence.

'Chant-Pagan' lays numerous charges against England, but they are all distilled into the complaint that 'there's somethin' gone small with the lot'.[60] After the Boer War, England appears to Kipling's irregular soldier a petty and prissy nation, with its absurdly deferential society and its ' 'ouses both sides of the street'.[61] Paul Fussell quotes Sassoon's observation that '[t]he man who really endured the [Great] War at its worst was everlastingly differentiated from everyone except his fellow soldiers'.[62] Fussell's insistence on viewing the Great War as an unprecedented and paradigmatic catastrophe ensures that the Boer War rates barely a mention in his work. Yet a poem like 'Chant-Pagan' illustrates, once again, the extent to which Kipling's poetry of the Boer War acts as a dress parade for—rather than a faking up of—the salient themes of the Great War. His soldier is no longer satisfied with the prospect of returning to a class-ridden society where he must touch his hat to the gentry and earn a living by mowing the squire's lawns. As Sassoon would later find, he is everlastingly differentiated from everyone at home, even to the point where he feels more kinship not only with his 'fellow soldiers' but with the enemy he once fought against. Just as England repels, so South Africa attracts, with the immensity of its 'valleys as big as

59 'South Africa', ibid. 162.   60 Ibid.   61 Ibid. 159.
62 Quoted in Fussell, *Great War and Modern Memory*, 90.

a shire' and its ' 'igh, inexpressible skies'.[63] Most of all, its severe
magnificence opens a direct relationship with the soldier's God, free
from obstructive intermediaries such as the parson who gets 'between'
the 'two sides of the lane' earlier in the poem. The religious language
used to describe South Africa in *The Five Nations*—its 'firmament',
its 'hosts of heaven', its plagues of 'pestilence' and locusts—is
confirmed in the soldier's plain-spoken desire to live 'Where there's
neither a road nor a tree—| But only my Maker an' me'.[64] In
contrast to this primitive glory, England is enclosed, its sunshine
'pale', and its breezes 'stale'—trite rhymes befitting triteness.

'Chant-Pagan' opens the 'Service Songs' with a persuasive denun-
ciation of both English society and the English landscape and climate.
Accordingly, it falls on 'The Return', the last of the Cockney-soldier
poems, to defend the nation's honour. The speakers of the poems
share a sense of having been transformed by their wartime experi-
ences. In 'Chant-Pagan', the soldier can never 'take on' with 'awful
old England again',[65] having seen what he has seen. 'The Return'
begins with the same problem: 'Peace is declared, an' I return | To
'Ackneystadt, but not the same'.[66] The Africanization of Hackney
and London ('Thamesfontein') does little to blur distinctions, as the
soldier exultantly remembers the personified South African landscape
he has left behind:

> Rivers at night that cluck an' jeer,
> Plains which the moonshine turns to sea,
> Mountains that never let you near,
> An' stars to all eternity . . .[67]

Also included are memories of burnt towns, starving dogs, and
dead comrades, all of which have contributed to 'The makin's of
a bloomin' soul'. Yet even this diversion into the distresses of war
cannot prevent a longing for the 'thousand Places left be'ind' and the
brotherhood and companionship among soldiers. Discharged and

[63] Kipling, *Five Nations*, 160.   [64] Ibid. 162.   [65] Ibid. 159.
[66] Ibid. 210.   [67] Ibid. 211.

back in England, the speaker must regretfully 'fall away | To do with little things again'.[68]

Only the chorus which ends the poem salvages some hope from the profound disappointment of serving a nation which may be guiltier than Kipling of faking up something:

> *If England was what England seems,*
> *An' not the England of our dreams,*
> *But only putty, brass an' paint,*
> *'Ow quick we'd chuck 'er! But she ain't!*[69]

This is potentially a dubious and, at worst, a self-deluding consolation. The speaker of 'The Return' decides not to follow his counterpart from 'Chant-Pagan' back to South Africa, purely on the basis that the real England is not 'what England seems' but rather 'the England of our dreams'. Nothing in the poem has encouraged that faith, especially as the stanza's protasis is more feelingly detailed than the rebuttal; nor is it clear, as the chorus steps out of italic in its final words, who is responsible for that stark unargued riposte. Earlier in *The Five Nations*, South Africa had been portrayed as a woman 'wonderful', 'perfect', and 'adorèd', attracting men who, despite their 'sore duresse', keep returning 'for orders'.[70] England is fortunate that, despite the dissatisfaction and whatever the cost, the nation can still inspire a similar fidelity in many of her ill-treated subjects. Watching army manœuvres over a decade later, in the summer of 1913, Kipling claimed to have felt 'the whole pressure of our dead of the Boer War flickering and re-forming as the horizon flickered in the heat'.[71] That the dead of one war haunt the doomed of the next becomes a provocative image for twentieth-century war poetry, with its grim implication that there is never an end to sacrifice.[72] Kipling's soldiers fight and die for an England of their dreams, which, he

[68] Kipling, *Five Nations*, 212–13.   [69] Ibid. 213.

[70] 'South Africa', ibid. 149–52.

[71] Quoted by George Shepperson, 'Kipling and the Boer War', in Gross (ed.), *Rudyard Kipling*, 86.

[72] See, e.g., Ted Hughes, 'Scapegoats and Rabies', in *Collected Poems*, ed. Paul Keegan (London: Faber, 2003), 187.

alleges, is nevertheless more real than the putty, brass, and paint of appearances. Quite why that dream should be believed is a question which will increasingly concern the poets of the Great War. Kipling's Boer War poetry, for all its best efforts, fails to include in its legacy a satisfactory answer.

3

Wilfred Owen's Concern

Do the poets of the First World War write well? Craig Raine thinks not. 'Wilfred Owen's tiny corpus is perhaps the most over-rated poetry in the twentieth century,' he insists, before explaining that Owen's work has been shown to advantage because 'the other poetry of the First World War is undistinguished and, therefore, an excellent foil'.[1] Raine finds posterity 'embarrassed' by the horrors of trench warfare, and consequently reluctant to discriminate in issues of aesthetic merit: rather than no poetry after Auschwitz, no lit. crit. after Passchendaele. Bedevilled with doubts over their reasons for valuing his poetry, even Owen's admirers voice reservations. Just as Raine acknowledges that Owen's 'life and death as a soldier make literary criticism seem pedantic and invalid', so Seamus Heaney concedes that his own occasional complaints may sound 'prissy', 'trivial', and 'nit-picking' compared with 'what lay behind [Owen's] words'. These critical self-effacements promote a hygienic distinction between art and life even while implying its near-impossibility. As Philip Larkin argues, 'the temporal accidents of [Owen's] lifetime . . . make independent critical assessment so difficult'.[2] It may not be negative criticism of Owen which is 'invalid', such concerns suggest, but the valorizing of a poet whose exemplary life needs to compensate for artistic shortcomings.

---

[1] Craig Raine, 'Wilfred Owen', in *Haydn and the Valve Trumpet* (London: Faber, 1990), 158.

[2] Philip Larkin, 'The War Poet', in *Required Writing: Miscellaneous Pieces 1955–1982* (London: Faber, 1983), 159.

The prosecution case against Owen was famously broached by W. B. Yeats, who omitted his poetry from the *Oxford Book of Modern Verse* (1936), and privately concluded that 'there is every excuse for him, but none for those who like him'.[3] That omission has been widely regretted, especially when set beside the mediocrity of some of Yeats's inclusions; but in recent decades it has occasionally attracted sympathy. In the cases of Rosenberg and Owen, Donald Davie maintains,

we see poets trying to respond to unprecedentedly harrowing and horrific experience, before they had had time to achieve technical mastery, and writing in circumstances that prevented their acquiring it. Both Rosenberg and Owen are in important respects *incompetent* writers, and although W. B. Yeats gave other reasons for excluding them . . . it is possible to think that he excluded them because of their incompetence. No one will deny that time and again the urgency of what they had to say overcame their incompetence in the saying of it, so as to produce irreplaceable poems . . . But it is surely wrong to infer that urgency of concern can at all times bypass the need for . . . learned mastery . . . Brooke and Owen (and Rosenberg and the wartime Gurney) belong in that history, of the poet's relations with his audience, not in the history of the art as such.[4]

Davie never explains what, beyond writing poetry and reading, might be the circumstances which allow the acquiring of 'technical mastery'; nor does he offer examples of the war poets' confidently alleged incompetence. His own various circumlocutions ('it is possible to think that . . . No one will deny that . . . it is surely wrong to infer that . . .') betray a rhetoric straining under its own special pleading and guilty of what it condemns. The passage voices a judgement more commonly encountered in the silent ignoring of war poetry which, as Davie reveals, must be consigned to the inferior history of reception and prevented from polluting the pure aesthetic line.

[3] W. B. Yeats to Dorothy Wellesley, 21 Dec. 1936, in Yeats, *The Letters*, ed. Allan Wade (London: Rupert Hart-Davis, 1954), 874.
[4] Donald Davie, 'Ivor Gurney Recovered', in *Under Briggflatts: A History of Poetry in Great Britain 1960–1998* (Manchester: Carcanet, 1989), 195–6.

'Anything, however small, may make a poem,' Edward Thomas noted; 'nothing, however great, is certain to'.[5] A glance at the soldier-poet anthologies published during the First World War confirms that 'urgency of concern' does not often 'produce irreplaceable poems', and that incompetent poets never do. Davie's distinction between urgency and 'learned mastery' forgets that Owen's urgency is a masterly effect of language. Ironically, it is Owen's 'Preface', seeming to concede the case, to which Davie's absent-mindedness is indebted:

This book is not about heroes. English Poetry is not yet fit to speak of them.
Nor is it about deeds, or lands, nor anything about glory, honour, might, majesty, dominion, or power, except War.
Above all I am not concerned with Poetry.
My subject is War, and the pity of War.
The Poetry is in the pity.[6]

Owen argues that the subject of War precludes a concern with Poetry, those two capitalized abstractions existing in an antagonistic relationship which may render the phrase 'War Poetry' oxymoronic. 'Above all I am not concerned with Poetry': that 'Above all' indicates a determined renunciation more than mere indifference. What Davie calls Owen's 'urgency of concern' is almost as much a concern for urgency as opposed to the aesthetic luxuries of the dilettante. Poetry creeps in only accidently, bound up with the 'pity of War' which is Owen's avowed focus.

Owen died in battle a week before the Armistice, aged 25; had he lived, he might not have published the 'Preface' in this form (if at all). Even so, its hostages to fortune are less vulnerable than some critics imagine. Owen, it must be admitted, shows little care to avoid the predictable retaliatory responses, as exemplified by C. H. Sisson: 'what right has a poet to say that he is not concerned with poetry?' (Despite

[5] Edward Thomas, quoted in Edna Longley, 'Introduction', in *Poetry in the Wars* (Newcastle: Bloodaxe, 1986), 12.
[6] Wilfred Owen, *The Complete Poems and Fragments*, ii: *The Manuscripts and Fragments*, ed. Jon Stallworthy (London: Chatto & Windus, Hogarth Press, and Oxford University Press, 1983), 535.

its debt to Owen, and because of different critical preconceptions about religious poetry and war poetry, T. S. Eliot's comment in 'East Coker' that 'The poetry does not matter' has met with considerably less resistance.[7]) For generations with a dwindling emotional investment in the sufferings of the First World War, Owen's urgency of concern may be sympathized with but no longer reciprocated. Those who are concerned with poetry will expect that, whatever the historical context, poets show a similar concern for their art; and Davie, finding Owen lacking in this regard, ejects him from the poetic tradition. However, the 'Preface' does not so straightforwardly support Davie's objections. Artfully camouflaging his artistry, Owen exploits an age-old suspicion of rhetoric to enhance his authority as witness: how can he stop to worry about poetry, he seems to ask, in the midst of such horror? The gesture is merely strategic, because Owen's mature work closes the discrepancy between poetry and truth—'That is why', the 'Preface' continues with the force of seeming tautology, 'the true Poets must be truthful.'[8] Owen's position rejects Touchstone's argument that the truest poetry is the most feigning: by being true to war, poets remain true to their art. Poetry, Owen believes, is capable of a truth beyond the range of other media: telling his sister in 1917 that Siegfried Sassoon's work is more 'perfectly truthfully descriptive of war' than 'Cinemas, cartoons, photographs, tales, plays', he clinches his argument: '*Now* you see why I have always extolled Poetry.'[9]

Owen may have always extolled Poetry, but the manner of his worship shifts significantly during his short writing life. His pre-war poetry cannot be accused of failing to make appropriate oblations. The earliest surviving poem, 'To Poesy' (1909–10), opens with the besotted teenage poet as supplicant, 'Stricken with love for thee, O Poesy'.[10] 'No man', he confidently boasts, 'Has loved thee with

---

7 T. S. Eliot, *The Complete Poems and Plays* (London: Faber, 1969), 179.

8 Owen, *Complete Poems and Fragments*, ii. 535.

9 Owen to Mary Owen, 29 Aug. 1917, in Owen, *Collected Letters*, ed. Harold Owen and John Bell (Oxford: Oxford University Press, 1967), 489.

10 Owen, *The Complete Poems and Fragments*, i: *The Poems*, ed. Jon Stallworthy (London: Chatto & Windus, Hogarth Press, and Oxford University Press, 1983), 3.

a purer love than mine', and he is prepared to perform any task in order to acquire 'power and skill' as the years advance. There follow poems about 'see[ing] fair Keats, and hear[ing] his lyre',[11] about a pilgrimage to Keats's house, and about seeing a lock of Keats's hair (indebted to Keats's 'On Seeing a Lock of Milton's Hair'). In 1912, Owen is still harping on Poesy: 'Speak to me, Poesy! Give me on this height | The one true message of thy thousand oracles' ('[Science has looked]').[12] His letters sound no less infected: playing Thomas to Keats's Christ, Owen tells his mother that W. M. Rossetti's biography of the poet 'guided my groping hand right into the wound, and I touched, for one moment the incandescent Heart of Keats'.[13] Such febrile declamation, and the younger self who luxuriated in it, are what Owen abjures in his 'Preface' when he abjures Poetry. This reproduces a pattern of dedication and renunciation first observed in his religious life, when after a crisis of faith in 1912–13 he writes to his mother, 'Murder will out, and I have murdered my false creed. If a true one exists, I shall find it.'[14] In poetry, as in religion, Owen is a disenchanted votary, never more tied to the gods of his youth than when he repeatedly assaults them. His statement that he is not concerned with Poetry becomes inherently contradictory; unconcern would be sealed with silence.

If the nature of Owen's development must complicate the account of a poet indifferent to his art, it does not altogether satisfy Davie's complaint that Owen lacked learned mastery. But nor is Davie's hauteur alive to the challenges posed to his own critical values by the poetry he dismisses. Owen's 'Preface' states from the outset that English poetry—even, it would seem, Sassoon's—is inadequate to the historical occasion: 'This book is not about heroes. English poetry is not yet fit to speak of them.'[15] Owen wants a new poetry which is fighting fit and able to brave the war. The debate is not

---

[11] Owen, 'Written in a Wood, September 1910', ibid. 7.   [12] Ibid. 35.
[13] Owen to Susan Owen, 17 Sept. 1912, in Owen, *Collected Letters*, 159.
[14] Owen to Susan Owen, 4 Jan. 1913, ibid.
[15] Owen, *Complete Poems and Fragments*, ii. 535.

between, as Davie contends, the 'amateurish' and the 'professionally accomplished',[16] but between conflicting ideas of what in such conditions the nature and value of poetic accomplishment ought to be. 'To praise a thing for its faultlessness is to damn it with faint praise,' Ivor Gurney writes from the trenches, noting that the reader of *King Lear* who feels as though 'he has been out all night on the empty uplands in a great storm' is moved by far more than artistic 'perfection'.[17] Like Gurney, Owen is obliged by his experiences to reject the kind of accomplishment sought by his juvenilia, and to require nothing less than the remaking of poetry: after his cousin, the poet Leslie Gunston, grumbles that one of Owen's poems had offended his 'musical ear', he replies, 'I suppose I am doing in poetry what the advanced composers are doing in music.'[18] It is a common theme among the century's best soldier-poets: three decades later, Keith Douglas responds to the desire of his friend and fellow poet J. C. Hall for a more 'musical verse' with the observation that 'I see no reason to be either musical or sonorous about things at present.'[19] What is sometimes criticized as failure of technique, in Owen as in Gurney and Douglas, is an ambitious and forceful new poetry which, attuned to its historical circumstance, necessarily affronts the old harmonies.

Feigning a lack of concern for poetry, Owen enacts the paradox that for true poets artistic truth must always incorporate some measure of transfiguration. This helps to distinguish his achievement from Sassoon's. Both poets use physical horrors to assault the myths of glory; both portray German soldiers as fellow sufferers; and both cast the warmongers of either side as the real enemy: Owen allows himself an indulgent fantasy when he wishes that 'the Bosche would have the pluck to come right in & make a clean sweep of the Pleasure

---

[16] Davie, 'Ivor Gurney Recovered', 196.
[17] Ivor Gurney to Marion Scott, 3 Aug. 1917, in Ivor Gurney, *Collected Letters*, ed. R. K. R. Thornton (Ashington and Manchester: MidNag/Carcanet, 1991), 294.
[18] Owen to Leslie Gunston, 12 Feb. 1918, in Owen, *Collected Letters*, 531.
[19] Keith Douglas to J. C. Hall, 10 Aug. 1943, in Douglas, *The Letters*, ed. Desmond Graham (Manchester: Carcanet, 2000), 295.

Boats, and the promenaders on the Spa, and all the stinking Leeds
& Bradford War-profiteers now reading *John Bull* on Scarborough
Sands'.[20] Yet for all the comparisons between the two poets, Owen
escapes the devastating compliment paid to Sassoon by Ivor Gurney:
'He is one who tries to tell Truth, though perhaps not a profound
truth.'[21] Owen's profound truth communicates the political and
historical realities of the First World War, but it subjugates such
designs to a more complex vision unsatisfied with merely being right.
He struggles to express his truth: 'The more I think of your ease
and rapidity in writing,' Owen tells Leslie Gunston with a contempt
masquerading as envy, 'the more I hope for an inimitable book next
time.'[22] He hopes, politely enough, but he knows better than to
expect. And to his mother, he notes:

> Leslie has been unfavourably reviewed by the *Times Literary Supplement*.
> Not attacked of course: one does not attack harmless civilians—They say
> he rimes with ease but has no originality or power.
>
> I rime with wicked difficulty, but a power of five men, four women, three
> children, two horses, and one candle is in me.[23]

Ease versus difficulty; technique versus power. These may be false
distinctions (the latter close to Davie's separation of competence
and urgency), but they illustrate Owen's consciously chosen route
to learned mastery: his is a difficult, an awkward, but also a harmful
and a powerful truth, well beyond Gunston's tiny range.

When Owen calls Gunston harmless, his insult is anything but.
Gunston appears limited and ineffectual, cut off from contemporary
reality, a relic of a bygone era. His poetry is all washed up: 'You
can hark back if you like, and be deliberately archaic,' Owen tells
him, 'but don't make yourself a lagoon, salved from the ebbing tide
of the Victorian age.'[24] Owen also values deliberate archaism, but

---

20 Owen to Susan Owen, 10 Aug. 1918, in Owen, *Collected Letters*, 568.
21 Gurney to Marion Scott, 23 Aug. 1917, in Gurney, *Collected Letters*, 307.
22 Owen to Leslie Gunston, 8 Jan. 1918, in Owen, *Collected Letters*, 526.
23 Owen to Susan Owen, 5 Jan. 1918, ibid. 526.
24 Owen to Leslie Gunston, 8 Jan. 1918, ibid. 526.

he combines this harking back with an insistence on progression ('Did Poetry ever stand still?'[25]). Not even fleetingly disconcerted by Gunston's criticisms of his work, he may have drawn reassurance from them: it can hardly be much of a revolution if the old guard fails to protest. 'Miners', the poem which jars Gunston's musical ear, is meant to achieve exactly that, by confronting harmless civilians who benefit unthinkingly from the sacrifice of others. It begins with the poet listening to the coals in his hearth. What they whisper is not the expected tale of their ancient creation, but the story of the miners' suffocating fates, which leads to consideration of those who 'worked dark pits | Of war':

> Comforted years will sit soft-chaired,
>   In rooms of amber;
> The years will stretch their hands, well-cheered
>   By our life's ember;
>
> The centuries will burn rich loads
>   With which we groaned,
> Whose warmth shall lull their dreaming lids,
>   While songs are crooned;
> But they will not dream of us poor lads,
>   Left in the ground.[26]

Jahan Ramazani interprets 'Miners' as ultimately evasive, with the poet at first confessing, and then eluding his confession, that 'he uses the dead for poetic gain': they are his 'elegiac fuel'.[27] Certainly, Owen is always concerned enough with poetry to weigh its human costs and benefits. Yet although the deaths of miners and soldiers may be considered a necessary price, those men have not been sacrificed so that Owen might write poems about them. The recognition of the elegist's exchange of human loss for artistic gain disturbs 'Miners', but only incidentally, as one amidst several much more brutal transactions: between the poor and the rich, the dead and the

[25] Ibid.   [26] Owen, *Complete Poems and Fragments*, i. 135–6.
[27] Jahan Ramazani, *Poetry of Mourning: The Modern Elegy from Hardy to Heaney* (Chicago: University of Chicago Press, 1994), 83.

living, the pained and the comfortable. Owen's pararhymes create a discordant duet between the groaning of soldiers and the crooning of comfortable dreamers, making them interdependent. The 'rooms of amber' in which such dreamers sit are founded on 'our life's ember': opulence—like amber itself—is a product of past lives. Owen lays bare the necessary suffering which makes luxury possible, and in so doing he writes one of the most politically radical poems of his age.

'Miners', dating from January 1918, is one of Owen's earliest experiments in pararhyme. Drawing comparisons with the advanced (presumably twelve-tone) composers, he overstates neither his challenge to traditional orthodoxies nor the effect of this pioneering new technique on subsequent generations of poets: as Davie should have known, the learned mastery of countless successors has involved learning and mastering pararhyme (of which there are many examples in Davie's own verse). From the start, Owen's readers have looked elsewhere for the source: 'you have found a new method and must work it yourself,' Robert Graves wrote to him; 'those assonances instead of rhymes are fine—Did you know that it was a trick of Welsh poetry or was it instinct?'[28] But cynghanedd, the Welsh form to which Graves alludes, does not exploit end-rhymes. Used systematically, Owen's pararhyming is a technique geared to his circumstance, rejecting the consonance of pure rhyme. When he conveys the *Times Literary Supplement*'s opinion of Gunston—'he rimes with ease but has no originality or power'—Owen implies a causal link: easeful rhyme is weak, the 'wicked difficulty' of pararhyme original and powerful.

Owen never completely abandons traditional techniques. Almost all the rhyming poems he writes during his last year neatly divide as either pararhymes ('Arms and the Boy', 'Exposure', 'Strange Meeting', 'Insensibility', 'A Terre', 'The Show') or pure rhymes ('Disabled', 'The Sentry', 'Smile, Smile, Smile', 'Spring Offensive', 'The Send-Off', 'The Next War'), and there is nothing inherently

---

[28] Robert Graves to Wilfred Owen, *c*.22 Dec. 1917, in Owen, *Collected Letters*, 595–6.

distinctive about each group in subject or form to explain Owen's choice. Only very rarely does he combine different rhyming techniques, as in 'Futility':

> Move him gently into the sun—
> Gently its touch awoke him once,
> At home, whispering of fields half-sown.
> Always it woke him, even in France,
> Until this morning and this snow.
> If anything might rouse him now
> The kind old sun will know.
>
> Think how it wakes the seeds—
> Woke once the clays of a cold star.
> Are limbs, so dear achieved, are sides
> Full-nerved, still warm, too hard to stir?
> Was it for this the clay grew tall?
> —O what made fatuous sunbeams toil
> To break earth's sleep at all?[29]

'Futility' recalls a tour of the 'advanced Front Line': 'The marvel is that we did not all die of cold. As a matter of fact, only one of my party actually froze to death.'[30] The poem sets warmth and movement against cold and *rigor mortis*, from its opening imperative to the recognition that the dead body is 'too hard to stir'. That same struggle is enacted in the poem's rhymes. Both stanzas pararhyme *ababccc*, but in each case the final triplet incorporates homophonic rhyme as well: 'snow / know'; 'tall / at all'. If Douglas Kerr's claim that pararhyme constitutes 'a broken promise to return' is right,[31] then the use of homophonic rhyme might be expected to signal closure—a kept promise, a moment of harmonic consolation to heal the dissonance. Instead, Owen's rhymes codify the poem's increasingly desperate scepticism as the 'wise old sun' dwindles to

[29] Owen, *Complete Poems and Fragments*, i. 158.
[30] Owen to Susan Owen, 4 Feb. 1917, in Owen, *Collected Letters*, 430.
[31] Douglas Kerr, *Wilfred Owen's Voices: Language and Community* (Oxford: Oxford University Press, 1993), 295.

'fatuous sunbeams', and 'tall and 'toil' must succumb entropically to 'at all'. (In a similar way, the sun might wake the corpse like 'seeds' or 'the clays of a cold star', but the determined reiteration of the verb—'awoke', 'woke', 'wakes', 'woke'—fails to discriminate between two crucially different kinds of waking.) Repetitions indicate no development towards greater knowledge, but merely a lack of movement, a perplexed and enervated echo forced to state the familiar questions over and over. 'Was it for this | That one, the fairest of all rivers, loved | To blend his murmurs with my nurse's song,' asked Wordsworth,[32] his self-disillusionment the waste product of Romantic egotism; 'Was it for this the clay grew tall?' asks Owen, concerned about much more than poetic failure. Another Romantic question informs Owen's concluding doubts about divine agency. William Blake's address to the tyger—'What immortal hand or eye | Could frame thy fearful symmetry?'[33]—considers what kind of creator might have framed the intricacies of the tyger's terrible magnificence; Owen's equally fraught argument from design considers what kind of creator (Owen asks 'what', not who, 'made fatuous sunbeams toil') might have framed the 'dear achieved', 'Full-nerved' soldier only to allow that investment to be squandered by his premature death.

'Futility' shows why Owen's best work, written by a self-styled Georgian who suffered shell-shock, cannot be simply dismissed as the product of shell-shocked Georgianism. Nor is Owen a derivative Romantic who pararhymes, despite Raine's magisterial flourish: '[Owen] has read, quite uncritically, too much bad Keats and worse Shelley, and so associates poetry with the merely poetic.'[34] Like Davie, Raine condemns Owen in terms indebted to his 'Preface', which by shrinking poetry (or, significantly, Poetry) to the poetic, silently makes room for the un-Poetical poetry with which Owen

---

[32] William Wordsworth, *The Fourteen-Book Prelude*, ed. W. J. B. Owen (Ithaca, NY: Cornell University Press, 1985), i. 35, ll. 269–71.
[33] William Blake, *Complete Writings*, ed. Geoffrey Keynes (Oxford: Oxford University Press, 1966), 214.
[34] Raine, 'Wilfred Owen', 158.

is concerned. Owen's relationship with his predecessors is much more complex than Raine allows: his work is not symptomatic of the Poetical, but it does, in passing, provide a diagnosis. The use in 'Futility' of Wordsworth and Blake reconfigures their questions for the trenches, creating an urgency of concern which, inspired by Romanticism, at the same time inevitably censures it. Owen's mature work punishes Romanticism by underscoring its indulgences and trumping its glorious illusions with the horror of modern warfare. 'I think it was [Czesław] Milosz,' Ted Hughes has written, 'who when he lay in a doorway and watched the bullets lifting the cobbles out of the street beside him realized that most poetry is not equipped for life in a world where people actually do die. But some is.'[35] Owen had already experienced the same revelation in the trenches. The clearest victim of his growing resistance to ill-equipped predecessors is Tennyson, a softer option for Owen than his beloved Keats and Shelley. In 1917, having finished reading a biography, Owen musters little sympathy for that poet's lifelong unhappiness: 'But as for misery, was he ever frozen alive, with dead men for comforters.'[36] Tennyson, Owen concludes, 'was always a great child. So should I have been, but for Beaumont Hamel.' Owen implies that he has been forced to grow up by the war, with irreversible effects on his understanding of poetic tradition and his place within it. The poet who, in pre-war years, could not read a life of Keats without crying,[37] was unlikely to spend his tears so idly in the midst of more pressing business. Nowhere does Owen attack Keats or Shelley with anything approaching the disdain reserved for Tennyson; their early deaths offer some protection against that response. Yet Owen's writings do reveal a shift from idolization to a more critical engagement, as might exist between equals. Graves and Sassoon, he tells his mother, are 'already as many Keatses'.[38] Almost

---

[35] Ted Hughes, 'Vasko Popa', in *Winter Pollen: Occasional Prose*, ed. William Scammell (London: Faber, 1994), 221.

[36] Owen to Susan Owen, 8 Aug. 1917, in Owen, *Collected Letters*, 482.

[37] Owen to Susan Owen, 9 Sept. 1912, ibid. 160.

[38] Owen to Susan Owen, 25 May 1918, ibid. 553.

all the numerous references to Keats and Shelley in the letters date from before active service in January 1917, and the few mentions thereafter convey little enthusiasm. Except when Owen reports that he has seen for sale a first edition copy of *Lamia, Isabella & etc.*, Keats disappears altogether. And just as Owen claims a greater range of emotional experience, both positive and negative, than Tennyson, so he finally comes to believe that he has surpassed Shelley in at least one respect: 'Serenity Shelley never dreamed of crowns me. Shall it last when I shall have gone into Caverns & Abysmals such as he never reserved for his worst daemons?'[39]

Owen's inspiration is often antiphonal, responding either explicitly or covertly to another text by delivering a severe corrective to old lies which pass themselves off as traditional wisdom. His borrowings become, increasingly, acts of hostility towards their source. 'Dulce et Decorum Est', with its Horatian title and its buttonholing of Jessie Pope ('My friend'[40]), offers the crudest example; if, as Heaney claims, the poem is overwritten, that overwriting can be only partially excused as a redressing of the jingoistic excess of Pope's recruitment poems and fantasies of glorious battle. Similarly, 'Anthem for Doomed Youth' takes its cue from a Prefatory Note in *Poems for Today: An Anthology* (1916). 'What passing-bells for these who die as cattle?' Owen begins, destroying the anthology's daydream of a poet going 'singing to lay down his life for his country's cause . . . to the music of Pan's flute, and of Love's viol, and the bugle-call of Endeavour, and the passing-bells of Death'.[41] The music of 'Anthem for Doomed Youth' comes instead from the 'shrill, demented choirs of wailing shells'.[42] Twice Owen fronts a poem with an epigraph from Yeats, on each occasion showing up the make-believe and afflatus of his source. 'S.I.W.' quotes a passage from *The King's Threshold* to compare two kinds of suicide, S.I.W. being the military abbreviation for a self-inflicted wound. '[T]hat man there has set his

---

[39] Owen to Siegfried Sassoon, 1 Sept. 1918, ibid. 571.
[40] Owen, *Complete Poems and Fragments*, i. 140.
[41] Quoted by Jon Stallworthy, in Owen, *Complete Poems and Fragments*, i. 99.
[42] Owen, ibid.

teeth to die,' the epigraph states. Owen literalizes Yeats's cliché into
sickening reality as he records the circumstances of a soldier's death:

> With him they buried the muzzle his teeth had kissed,
> And truthfully wrote the mother, 'Tim died smiling.'[43]

The adverb 'truthfully' hints at saccharining deceits or, here, equi-
vocations which usually accompany the accounts of death in battle.
Only the suicide dies with a smile on his face. While the Yeat-
sian epigraph ends, 'I cannot mourn him', that refusal to mourn
echoes through Owen's poem as a voice to be resisted: the official
prohibitions against suicide, and the attendant accusations of dis-
honour and dereliction of duty, are confronted at every point by
the particularities of the dead man's appalling life in the trenches.
Owen knows his enemy: when Yeats, denying Owen's achievement,
declares that 'passive suffering is not a theme for poetry',[44] he states a
position which 'S.I.W.' had already sensed and refuted two decades
previously.

Owen may claim that he is not concerned with Poetry, but his
aggression towards other texts suggests that the terms could just as
easily be reversed: Poetry shows no concern with him, nor with the
lives and deaths of millions of fighting men. This lack of concern
incurs losses on both sides. The Romantics who sustained his work
until 1917 now become vulnerable to his techniques of rebuttal and
one-upmanship, as experience ruthlessly points out the imaginative
failings of innocence. Keats's 'My heart aches, and a drowsy numbness
pains | My sense' ('Ode to a Nightingale'[45]) prompts the opening
of Owen's 'Exposure': 'Our brains ache, in the merciless iced east
winds that knive us'.[46] But as for aching, Owen might have asked,
was Keats ever frozen alive, with dead men for comforters? The pain

---

[43] Ibid. 161.
[44] W. B. Yeats (ed.), *The Oxford Book of Modern Verse* (Oxford: Clarendon Press,
1936), p. xxxiv.
[45] John Keats, *The Complete Poems*, ed. Miriam Allott (London: Longman, 1970),
525.
[46] Owen, *Complete Poems and Fragments*, i. 185.

dare not sleep or the 'twitching agonies' of those caught on the wires. Desmond Graham has argued that Owen uses Keats's poem to 'reveal and define the extremity of the negation brought about by the war'.[47] That negation becomes a curious kind of affirmation for Owen, whose work transcends downwards until it plummets into the underworld of 'Strange Meeting'. In its dialogue with 'Ode to a Nightingale', 'Exposure' manages more than a reiterated disappointment that circumstances prevent it from achieving the sensual awareness of Keats. Owen may be excluded from Keats's vision, but that vision is incorporated only to be mourned as illusory in Owen's. The soldiers' escapist dreams of home, where 'we drowse, sun-dozed, | Littered with blossoms trickling where the blackbird fusses', are also, via their Keatsian cadences, dreams of a lost poetic tradition killed off by the 'flickering gunnery' and the fastening frost. There is no hope of return, or of healing the breach: ghosts drag home to find, with a definitive repetition, 'Shutters and doors, all closed; on us the doors are closed'. The antistrophe may stress that the doors of Romantic perception are now closed on Owen, but he portrays the loss ambiguously, being unable entirely to regret its exposure of an idyllic tradition so ill-fitted to the war poet's reality.

'Ode to a Nightingale' is one of the things 'Exposure' exposes. Yet Keats's poem inspires Owen, even if by negative example, and the complexity of his engagement amounts to far more than the vigorous dismissal of Jessie Pope or the ironic use of Yeatsian epigraphs. While criticizing the Romantic tradition through attacks on carefully selected targets, Owen's poetry aims to become that tradition's unexpected fulfilment. There is no longer the slippage between language and experience which Owen detects in Tennyson and, to a lesser degree, in Keats and Shelley: 'Futility' matches Romantic inquisitions with a context capable of justifying and enriching their urgent concerns; 'Exposure' shows what it means to ache, to be drowsy and numb, to suffer from a pained sense.

---

[47] Desmond Graham, *The Truth of War: Owen, Blunden, Rosenberg* (Manchester: Carcanet, 1984), 64.

When Owen considers titling his first collection *With Lightning and with Music*—a phrase Shelley uses in 'Adonais' to describe Keats's art—he portrays himself as a latter-day Keats, evoking a lightning which is no longer entirely metaphorical. (Describing judgement day, 'The End' opens with a 'blast of lightning from the east'.[48]) And when the disabled soldier of 'A Terre' alludes to 'Adonais', it is to prove that Shelley's intellectual radicalism has become the commonplace wisdom of the British troops:

> Certainly flowers have the easiest time on earth.
> 'I shall be one with nature, herb, and stone,'
> Shelley would tell me. Shelley would be stunned:
> The dullest Tommy hugs that fancy now.
> 'Pushing up daisies' is their creed, you know.[49]

Whether this illustrates the success of Shelley's philosophy or its final debasement is left unanswered, although it is revealing of Owen's literary preferences that his soldier thinks of Shelley rather than the more famous lines from Wordsworth's 'A slumber did my spirit seal' which may provide Shelley's source: 'Roll'd round in earth's diurnal course | With rocks and stones and trees.'[50] Shelley had originally written about Keats-Adonais,

> He is made one with Nature: there is heard
> His voice in all her music, from the moan
> Of thunder, to the song of night's sweet bird;
> He is a presence to be felt and known
> In darkness and in light, from herb and stone,
> Spreading itself wher'er that Power may move
> Which has withdrawn his being to its own,
> Which wields the world with never-wearied love,
> Sustains it from beneath, and kindles it above.[51]

---

[48] Owen, *Complete Poems and Fragments*, i. 159.   [49] Ibid. 179.

[50] Wordsworth, *Lyrical Ballads and Other Poems, 1797–1800*, ed. James Butler and Karen Green (Ithaca, NY: Cornell University Press, 1992), 164.

[51] Shelley, *Poetical Works*, ed. Thomas Hutchinson (Oxford: Oxford University Press, 1967), 441.

Shelley's lines therefore endure a two-stage reduction, first into compact misquotation—'I shall be one with nature, herb, and stone'—and then into a euphemism with its own potency: 'Pushing up daisies'. Transforming his fallen comrades into Keatses, the dullest Tommy is a Shelley whose language, unconcerned with the bombastic verbiage of Poetry, nevertheless embodies a memorable poetry of its own. Romanticism has been distilled into army slang.

Douglas Kerr has convincingly argued that 'The blinded cripple in "A Terre" is the smashed remnant of a Wordsworthian tradition'—a natural philosopher in the mould of the leech-gatherer and the old Cumberland beggar. Even so, Kerr refuses to draw the obvious conclusion, and suggests that Owen's self-appointed task was to restore a debilitated tradition by testing 'where it was still alive and where it was atrophied'.[52] Owen, admittedly, announces nothing so grandiose as the death of Romanticism, yet concern for that particular patient is what his 'Preface' disclaims. Owen's 'Above all, I am not concerned with Poetry' makes no case that poetry should cease, but embodies a belief that what has been traditionally understood as poetry cannot survive the shock of contemporary events: poetry must change fundamentally, in directions which Owen tries to instigate, if it is to prove itself worthy of continuing concern. '[I saw his round mouth's crimson]' synchronizes the moment of lyrical consummation with the moment of death:

> I saw his round mouth's crimson deepen as it fell,
>   Like a sun, in his last deep hour;
> Watched the magnificent recession of farewell,
>   Clouding, half gleam, half glower,
> And a last splendour burn the heavens of his cheek.
>   And in his eyes
> The cold stars lighting, very old and bleak,
>   In different skies.[53]

---

52 Kerr, *Wilfred Owen's Voices*, 256.
53 Owen, *Complete Poems and Fragments*, i. 123.

So gorgeous is the language that it almost successfully camouflages its subject: the sudden and violent death of a young man in battle. The haemorrhage implied in the opening line contrasts starkly with the 'guttering, choking, drowning' of the gas victim in 'Dulce et Decorum Est', whose blood 'Come[s] gargling from the froth-corrupted lungs'.[54] Yet '[I saw his round mouth's crimson]' does not represent an unaccustomed indulgence in an upper-case Poetry. The poem reveals what dies with the soldier: the life-giving sun, the beneficent heavens, the consolation of the stars. What also dies is an elegiac tradition of which Shelley's 'Adonais' is, for Owen, the epitome. It is 'Adonais' from which Owen draws his diction and elemental metaphors and, more particularly, his image of a dying sun. Shelley describes great poets during their lifetime as suns, and the great poets of the past as 'immortal stars': in his poem's final lines, the soul of Keats-Adonais 'burn[s] through the inmost veil of Heaven', and 'like a star', it 'Beacons from the abode where the Eternal are'.[55] For Owen's dying soldier, these exalted gestures have diminished to the level of the body: the burning heavens are in his cheeks, and the stars coldly light in his eyes. The symbols of past poets are now 'very old and bleak', shining indifferently 'In different skies'. Owen's stars do not exist in an English heaven, and nor do they form strange-eyed constellations. They are merely obsolete and irrelevant to the war-dead. Fulfilling the tradition by closing it, Owen taunts Romanticism as glorious but hopelessly ineffectual: its light is going out.

Paradoxically, the evidence for Romanticism's continued survival can be found in Owen's eagerness to perform the autopsy. Like Hardy, whose darkling thrush sings amidst a landscape of broken Romantic symbols, Owen's poetry of loss must imaginatively revive that past which it defines itself against. Yet for all his influence on later generations of poets and readers, Owen writes a poetry of endings—the end of life, of the old lies, of patriotism, of God, of hope, of a poetic tradition, of civilization. 'The End' is a favourite

[54] Ibid. 140.   [55] Shelley, *Poetical Works*, 438, 444.

title, appearing twice in his drafts and fragments as well as heading a sonnet which judges that the Christian schema of death and rebirth provides only a spurious comfort. 'Shall Life renew these bodies? Of a truth, | All death will he annul, all tears assuage?',[56] Owen asks in the octave; the sestet resolutely decides not. (When Owen's mother chose these lines, as far as 'annul' and without the question mark, for her son's gravestone, she occluded the poem's meaning by reinstating consolation where Owen had found none.) His emphasis throughout his mature work on denial, rebuttal, and negation might wrongly be considered a limiting factor, which poets who endured similar conditions managed to surpass: as Graves told Owen in December 1917, 'For God's sake cheer up and write more optimistically—The war's not ended yet but a poet should have a spirit above wars.'[57] Graves's advice either responds to, or is answered by, a stanza in Owen's 'Apologia pro Poemate Meo', written around the same time:

> I, too, have dropped off Fear—
> Behind the barrage, dead as my platoon,
> And sailed my spirit surging light and clear
> Past the entanglement where hopes lay strewn . . .[58]

Owen's spirit sails above and (as 'Strange Meeting' indicates) sinks below wars, all the while living in their midst. His 'Apologia' describes a deliberate refusal of other poetic possibilities, and locates on the battlefield all the requisite subjects—God, fear, death, exultation, love, joy, hell—which are gathered together and intensified by war. War, for Owen, is poetry's consummation: it transforms rhetoric into reality, the illusory into the authentic. The true poets will be truthful because, finally, their experience exonerates their language.

---

[56] Owen, *Complete Poems and Fragments*, i. 159.
[57] Graves to Owen, c.22 Dec. 1917, in Owen, *Collected Letters*, 596.
[58] Owen, *The Complete Poems and Fragments*, i. 124.

4

In Pursuit of Spring: Edward Thomas and Charlotte Mew

'Now I know that Spring will come again'.[1] The most surprising thing about Edward Thomas's confidence is that it should require articulation. This being the opening line of a poem, 'March', the reader is given no clues to the poet's state of mind prior to his new understanding. Yet Thomas's need to assert the seemingly obvious is not unique. Writing in the month of her poem's title, Charlotte Mew opens 'May, 1915' with a similar sentiment: 'Let us remember Spring will come again'.[2] Whereas Thomas's line presents its foreknowledge of spring as a purely personal discovery, Mew implies that she and her readers need encouragement in a dispute between head and heart: we may not feel it under present circumstances, but a willed remembrance of the past assures us that spring will return in the future. This distinction occurs, nevertheless, within a context of strong correspondences. A reading of Thomas and Mew together discovers a coincidence of concerns which often find expression in mutually illuminating and startlingly congruous ways.

There is no evidence that Thomas and Mew ever met, or that they read each other's work. The opportunity briefly existed: Mew's first collection *The Farmer's Bride* was published in May 1916, eight months before Thomas left for France; but among his many writings

[1] Edward Thomas, *Collected Poems*, ed. R. George Thomas (Oxford: Oxford University Press, 1981), 7.
[2] Charlotte Mew, *Complete Poems*, ed. John Newton (Harmondsworth: Penguin, 2000), 77.

on contemporary poetry Thomas made no reference to Mew, and the posthumous publication of his *Poems* (1917), *Last Poems* (1918), and *Collected Poems* (1920) met with a reciprocal silence. Mew could not have known Thomas's 'March', which was written five months before 'May, 1915' but would remain unpublished for several years. The pairing of these poets is not, therefore, a story of influence in either direction. At first glance they seem to have grown out of opposing traditions—Mew's work steeped in the stock *fin-de-siècle* subjects of 'desire, guilt, death, prostitution and sainthood',[3] and looking back beyond them to female precursors like Emily Brontë and Christina Rossetti; and Thomas, the 'English empiricist',[4] learning from his American pragmatist friend Robert Frost, but also drawing on centuries of English nature writing in prose as well as poetry. However, despite the distance between their starting-points, and their very different maps of the terrain, Mew and Thomas converge towards the same destination. Thomas wants literature to 'make words of such a spirit, and arrange them in such a manner, that they will do all that a speaker can do by innumerable gestures and their innumerable shades, by tone and pitch of voice, by speed, by pauses, by all that he is and all that he will become';[5] Mew in her dramatic monologues aims to capture the 'cri de coeur' of her personae, according to the success of which 'one either has or has not the person', and she singles out for praise those examples in literature where 'one has not only the cry but also the gesture and the accent'.[6] Both poets seek to free poetry from its rhetorical paraphernalia, wanting to return it to its origins in the human voice: 'the best lyrics seem to be the poet's natural speech', [7] Thomas insists.

Their emphasis on the human voice is not the only sign of compatibility. Both turned to poetry late, after earlier ambitions as prose

---

[3] Angela Leighton, 'Charlotte Mew (1869–1928)', in Angela Leighton and Margaret Reynolds (eds.), *Victorian Women Poets: An Anthology* (Oxford: Blackwell, 1995), 646.

[4] Edna Longley, 'Edward Thomas and Robert Frost', in *Poetry in the Wars* (Newcastle: Bloodaxe, 1986), 44.

[5] Thomas, *A Language not to be Betrayed: Selected Prose*, ed. Edna Longley (Manchester: Carcanet, 1981), 159.

[6] Mew, quoted by John Newton, 'Notes', in Mew, *Complete Poems*, 108.

[7] Thomas, *A Language not to be Betrayed*, 63.

writers: *The Farmer's Bride*, the only poetry collection Mew published during her lifetime, appeared when she was 47, and contained just seventeen poems; Thomas wrote his first poem in his mid-thirties. Both left relatively small bodies of poetry: sixty-eight poems by Mew, 142 by Thomas,[8] in each case mainly short lyrics. Thomas's years as an active poet, from December 1914 until his death at the Battle of Arras in April 1917, overlapped Mew's most productive period, when between 1912 and 1915 she wrote much of her best work. Independently and simultaneously, they sought to produce a poetry which would respond to the challenges of war while never abandoning the source of their inspiration in the natural world. Their worries about the arrival of spring, in 'March' and 'May, 1915', reflect a poetry constantly negotiating between these opposing demands.

Both poets are finely attuned to seasonal change. To ask during which time of year one of their poems is set is to expect a precise answer. Ten of Thomas's poems reply even through their titles, two specifying not just the season or the month but the day, while others—'New Year', 'February Afternoon', 'March', 'April', 'July', 'October', 'November Sky'—hint that Thomas may have been sporadically (if not, perhaps, consciously) working towards a shepherd's calendar. Mew's titles reserve the highest exactness for two war elegies, 'May, 1915' and 'June, 1915'. In addition, her work repeatedly invokes the seasons as subject and metaphor: the title poem of *The Farmer's Bride* mentions, in its first stanza, summer, winter and 'Fall', and seven out of seventeen poems contain the word 'Spring'—a ratio fairly reflecting a preoccupation with the vernal throughout her poetry. The preoccupation is shared by Thomas, whose travel book *In Pursuit of Spring* (1914) prompted Robert Frost to recommend a new direction: 'I referred him to paragraphs in his book *In Pursuit of Spring* and told him to write it in verse form in exactly the same cadence.'[9] It should not be

[8] Thomas's *Collected Poems* includes 144 poems, of which two are cancelled versions.
[9] Robert Frost, quoted in Elizabeth Sergeant, *Robert Frost: The Trial by Existence* (New York: Holt, Rinehart & Winston, 1960), 136.

surprising, for a writer who so often resorts to organic metaphors in his descriptions of poetry,[10] that Thomas blossoms as a poet while pursuing spring. He and Mew take inspiration from all seasons, but it is spring in particular—its pursuit and promises, its glories and disappointments—to which their work most often returns.

Shelley asks in 'Ode to the West Wind', 'If Winter comes, can Spring be far behind?'[11] Seasonal cycles provide one of poetry's most well-worn tropes: spring follows winter, and analogically, rebirth follows death, renewal follows grief, inspiration follows desolation. Thomas subtly acknowledges his gratitude to Shelley in 'The Wind's Song': 'My heart that had been still as the dead tree | Awakened by the West wind was made free.'[12] However, Mew and Thomas cannot so easily assert the same traditional consolations. When they announce the inevitability of spring, they predict a better future; but by doing so, they draw attention to the sufferings of the present. If spring is near, it must still be winter: as Thomas admits later in 'March', 'though I knew that Spring | Would come again, I knew it had not come'. The title of Mew's poem obliges an even bleaker reading. Already, in May, the poet looks forward to next spring, the season this year having apparently failed to bring deliverance from the sufferings of winter. Thomas's 'March' may be indebted to passages from *In Pursuit of Spring*, but his prose more rationally acknowledges seasonal change: 'Spring would come, of course—nothing, I supposed, could prevent it.'[13] Contrast the poet of 'March', who 'now' knows but must have doubted before; or Mew's appeal to memory, because the current climate makes it so easy to disbelieve or forget. Their poetic portrayals of spring reveal a complication which soon becomes a crisis; and although the origins of that crisis can be traced back, in Mew's case, to pre-war writing, it is hastened, shaped and amplified by the Great War.

---

[10] See Thomas, *A Language not to be Betrayed*, 62–3.
[11] Shelley, *Poetical Works*, ed. Thomas Hutchinson (Oxford: Oxford University Press, 1967), 579.
[12] Thomas, *Collected Poems*, 101.
[13] Thomas, *In Pursuit of Spring* (London: Thomas Nelson and Sons, 1914), 15.

When T. S. Eliot opens another poem born out of that war's ruins with the belief that 'April is the cruellest month',[14] his overturning of an assumption about the benevolence of spring sounds familiar to readers of Thomas and Mew. Thomas on several occasions prompts himself to 'remember | What died into April' ('The Thrush');[15] while Mew, whose poetry provides an under-researched source for *The Waste Land*,[16] complains in one dramatic monologue, 'The Quiet House', that

> Red is the strangest pain to bear;
> In Spring the leaves on the budding trees;
> In Summer the roses are worse than these,
> More terrible than they are sweet . . .[17]

Debate about *The Waste Land* has often centred on whether it should be read as the fragmentation of a society or of an individual mind. Seasonal disruptions in the poetry of Mew and Thomas provoke similar doubts, as relationships and distinctions between inner and outer weather, and between natural history and human history, become unstable. Thomas's 'The Thrush', written in November 1915, nowhere mentions war overtly, but knowledge of what died into the previous April—the month of the first German gas attack at Ypres and the first landings at Gallipoli—ensures that the poet keeps a painful silence: loss on that scale requires no further elaboration.

The inability of Mew and Thomas to depend on the arrival or efficacy of spring indicates an emergency for traditional modes and tropes, which both poets find inadequate to the occasion of war. Jahan Ramazani has argued that the twentieth-century elegist 'tends not to achieve but to resist consolation, not to override but to sustain anger, not to heal but to reopen the wounds of loss'.[18] But the poetry of Mew and Thomas neither achieves nor resists consolation,

---

[14] T. S. Eliot, *The Complete Poems and Plays* (London: Faber, 1969), 61.

[15] Thomas, *Collected Poems*, 84.

[16] See Newton, 'Notes', in Mew, *Complete Poems*, 111, 112–13, 115.

[17] Mew, *Complete Poems*, 37.

[18] Jahan Ramazani, *Poetry of Mourning: The Modern Elegy from Hardy to Heaney* (Chicago: University of Chicago Press, 1994), p. xi.

charting instead the drama and cost of its failure. In 'May, 1915'
Mew evokes spring as healer, only to find that war's scars run too
deep for such remedies:

> Let us remember Spring will come again
> To the scorched, blackened woods, where all the wounded trees
> Wait, with their old wise patience for the heavenly rain,
> Sure of the sky: sure of the sea to send its healing breeze,
> Sure of the sun. And even as to these
> Surely the Spring, when God shall please
> Will come again like a divine surprise
> To those who sit to-day with their great Dead, hands in their hands, eyes
> in their eyes,
> At one with Love, at one with Grief: blind to the scattered things and
> changing skies.[19]

Although the rhymes skilfully conceal the extent of the problem, this
is a poem fractured across its middle. The first four and a half of the
nine lines may admit a prior doubt by asserting their faith, but they
now confidently affirm spring's power to regenerate the desolation
of war. The woods are 'sure' of spring, and 'wise' to be so, just as the
reader is encouraged to be sure by the opening line. However, the
poem's syntax exposes the awkwardness of establishing an equivalence
between the natural world and the human. 'And even as to these': the
phrase is as unpersuasive as the simile it flat-footedly introduces. The
next line switches from the authority of 'Sure' to the special pleading
of 'Surely', although the poet's descent from 'Sure' to 'Surely' proves
her no longer so sure. And to be at one with Love and at one with
Grief is to make the grim discovery that Love and Grief have become
synonymous. Even the promise of a divinely ordained spring may
not overcome the mourners' blindness to the 'scattered things and
changing skies' which make May sound decidedly autumnal.

'May, 1915' attempts and fails to impose spring as a means of
resolving grief. Typically, spring in Mew's work is haunted by death:
having met with things dying, the poetry cannot celebrate things

---

[19] Mew, *Complete Poems*, 77.

new-born. 'The Forest Road', a pre-war precursor of 'May, 1915', notes that there is no grief for the dead among the birds of the 'green Spring', but that, by contrast, the poem's speaker cannot recover from or forget about her own loss: 'But it shall not be so with you. I will look back'.[20] If the birds are all desire, Mew is all memory. In later poems Mew, like Thomas, aims to learn from the birds' example. Thomas's thrush, singing in November and in April alike, reminds him that some things are born in winter and die in spring; missing a loved one who was with her last year, in 'I so liked Spring' Mew's speaker determines to 'like Spring because it is simply Spring | As the thrushes do'.[21] Yet she protests too much: 'I'll not think of you,' she asserts, thinking of nothing but. 'The Trees are Down' (*c.*1922) laments a spring 'unmade' by the felling of 'the great plane trees at the end of the gardens', and this calls to mind

> one evening of a long past Spring
> Turning in at a gate, getting out of a cart, and finding a large dead rat in
>   the mud of the drive.
> I remember thinking: alive or dead, a rat was a god-forsaken thing,
> But at least, in May, that even a rat should be alive.[22]

Why should a dog, a horse, a rat, not have life? The pain felt at the death of a rat in May hints at the suffering present in 'May, 1915', where the dead are many thousands of young men. In these and other poems such as 'To a Child in Death', spring fails to heal, and even aggravates the wound. Death should be winter's vocation; but Mew finds that, in Thomas's words, 'Spring's here, Winter's not gone'.[23]

   Thomas's observation about the overlapping of winter and spring occurs in the last line of 'But these things also', a poem which makes a short inventory of spring's dead belongings: a patch of grass 'Long-dead that is greyer now | Than all the winter it was', and an empty snail shell. 'But these things also' is one of six examples where Thomas ends a poem with a line evoking spring; two others mention

[20] Ibid. 40.   [21] Ibid. 76.   [22] Ibid. 81.
[23] Thomas, 'But these things also', in *Collected Poems*, 42.

May, one April, and one the passing of winter. Across such a small body of poetry, the frequency indicates Thomas's consistent appeal to the revitalizing powers of spring, and in several poems ('The Huxter', 'April', 'Thaw') this gesture remains undarkened by loss or scepticism. However, Thomas is usually less certain of seasonal renewal. Decorating his study with posters which amused him, he found an advertisement for an indigestion mixture which promised that

SPRING IS COMING!

BRINGING DEBILITY[24]

This may be the source for the final line of 'Health': 'scarce this Spring could my body leap four yards'.[25] War turns absurdity into prophecy, as spring offensives deliver not only debility but death. No wonder Thomas's poetry fails to delight in even that most peculiarly English pursuit of spring—the listening for the first cuckoo. 'The cuckoo cry is Spring's | Most nearest token,' Ivor Gurney notes in a post-war poem.[26] The subject becomes, in Thomas's hands, a poem about the conjunction of spring and death and the inability of seasonal renewal to alleviate grief:

> And now, as you said, 'There it is' I was hearing
> Not the cuckoo at all, but my man's 'Ho! Ho!' instead.
> And I think that even if I could lose my deafness
> The cuckoo's note would be drowned by the voice of my dead.[27]

Thomas is not alone in linking the cuckoo's call with death. In a letter of June 1916, Gurney reports from the trenches that he had heard a cuckoo and been reminded of 'the old haunts of home', until a Welshman interrupted: ' "Listen to that damned bird", he said. "All through that bombardment in the pauses I could hear that

---

[24] Quoted in Helen Thomas, *Under Storm's Wing* (Manchester: Carcanet, 1988), 256.
[25] Thomas, *Collected Poems*, 61.
[26] Ivor Gurney, 'Spring's Token', in *80 Poems or So*, ed. George Walter and R. K. R. Thornton (Ashington and Manchester: MidNag/Carcanet, 1997), 48.
[27] Thomas, 'The Cuckoo', in *Collected Poems*, 28.

infernal silly 'Cuckoo, Cuckoo' sounding while Owen was lying in my arms covered with blood. How shall I ever listen again . . . !" He broke off, and I became aware of shame at the unholy joy that had filled my artist's mind.'[28] Gurney does not seem on this occasion to have converted his joy into poetry, but he did share the general anger at the simultaneity of war's destruction and the revitalizing powers of spring: 'O Curse the war, it is No Bon, and War in Spring is bad taste of the vilest description and radically damnable'.[29]

'The Cuckoo' is one of three poems by Thomas which pursue a connection between the cuckoo and death. In 'She dotes' the woman dotes on the birdsong of 'all that sing in May', hoping in vain that they will communicate something about her dead lover. After the many named birds, the cuckoo has the final word: 'she has slept, trying to translate | The word the cuckoo cries to his mate | Over and over'.[30] And in 'Melancholy' the poet describes how, caught in a summer storm, he heard all day long

> a distant cuckoo calling
> And, soft as dulcimers, sounds of near water falling,
> And, softer, and remote as if in history,
> Rumours of what had touched my friends, my foes, or me.[31]

This has been blamed for 'soften[ing] the reality of what it depicts',[32] but only because of a failure to spot the poem's source. Thomas refers to 'rumours of the war remote' in 'The sun used to shine';[33] the identity of those ominous mutterings in 'Melancholy' becomes certain when Thomas's indebtedness to Coleridge is recognized. The 'dulcimers' and the 'sounds of near water falling' come from a rewriting of 'Kubla Khan', and Thomas leaves potently unstated a parallel with Kubla himself: 'And mid this tumult Kubla heard

---

[28] Gurney to Catherine Abercrombie, ? June 1916, in *Collected Letters*, ed. R. K. R. Thornton (Ashington and Manchester: MidNag/Carcanet, 1991), 91.

[29] Gurney to Marion Scott, 18? May 1917, ibid. 259.

[30] Thomas, *Collected Poems*, 62.   [31] Ibid. 64.

[32] Michael Kirkham, *The Imagination of Edward Thomas* (Cambridge: Cambridge University Press, 1986), 36.

[33] Thomas, *Collected Poems*, 106.

from far | Ancestral voices prophesying war!'[34] War has become the undertone heard below the sounds of the natural world.

With its hidden allusion, 'Melancholy' proves the lengths to which Thomas will sometimes go to write war poems which avoid all overt reference to war. The voice of Thomas's war-dead calls loudly, and no less loudly for sometimes being inaudible. The continuity in his work between those poems which do and do not directly refer to the war ensures that war will be heard even in the silences. Like Picasso insisting that although he did not paint the war, the war was in everything he painted, Thomas writes the war into all his subjects. 'Roads', for example, describes the war-dead as revenants populating his native landscape:

> Now all roads lead to France
> And heavy is the tread
> Of the living; but the dead
> Returning lightly dance:
>
> Whatever the road bring
> To me or take from me,
> They keep me company
> With their pattering,
>
> Crowding the solitude
> Of the loops over the downs,
> Hushing the roar of towns
> And their brief multitude.[35]

The towns' multitude is 'brief', the reader grimly assumes, because of imminent depopulation: as Wilfred Owen explains in 'Smile, Smile, Smile', 'England one by one had fled to France, | Not many elsewhere now, save under France.'[36] The dead had drowned out the arrival of spring in 'The Cuckoo', which makes no mention of war;

[34] Samuel Taylor Coleridge, *The Collected Works*, xvi: *Poetical Works, Part One: Poems* (Reading Text), ed. J. C. C. Mays (Princeton: Princeton University Press, 2001), 513.

[35] Thomas, *Collected Poems*, 90.

[36] Wilfred Owen, *The Complete Poems and Fragments*, i: *The Poems*, ed. Jon Stallworthy (London: Chatto & Windus, Hogarth Press, and Oxford University Press, 1983), 190.

and in 'Roads', which does mention it, they drown out 'the roar
of towns'. Thomas, even when apparently silent on the subject of
war, implicates it in absences and dearths. His cherry trees strew 'the
grass as for a wedding | This early May morn when there is none to
wed' ('The Cherry Trees');[37] as in Mew's 'May, 1915', spring may
revitalize the trees, but there is no longer a guarantee that it will
assuage human suffering. The past becomes a pre-lapsarian age to be
defined against the present: previous autumns are recalled as times
before 'the war began | To turn young men to dung' ('Blenheim
Oranges').[38] An owl's sudden cry tells the poet 'what I escaped | And
others could not', those others being 'soldiers and poor' ('The
Owl').[39] 'What of the lattermath to this hoar Spring?',[40] Thomas
asks in 'It was upon', worrying about more than the prospect of a bad
harvest. A different kind of silence is heard at the end of 'March': 'a
silence | Saying that Spring returns, perhaps tomorrow'.[41] But even
here, the optimism is ghosted by a more naïve belief: as Michael
Longley, one of Thomas's most dedicated successors, states in his
poem 'The War Poets', 'everybody talked about the war ending | And
always it would be the last week of the war'.[42]

   The hope that the start of spring will mark the end of the war is
destined to be disappointed, and the season's plenitude accentuates
the loss. 'In Memoriam [Easter 1915]', Thomas's four-line elegy for
the war dead, confronts not only a seasonal but a religious failure:

> The flowers left thick at nightfall in the wood
> This Eastertide call into mind the men,
> Now far from home, who, with their sweethearts, should
> Have gathered them and will do never again.[43]

The poem gives and takes away. It opens with an image of abundance,
which calls to mind those men 'far from home' who can no longer

---

[37] Thomas, *Collected Poems*, 105.   [38] Ibid. 118.
[39] Ibid. 40.   [40] Ibid. 111.   [41] Ibid. 8.
[42] Michael Longley, 'The War Poets', in *Poems 1963–1983* (Harmondsworth:
Penguin, 1986), 168.
[43] Thomas, 'In Memoriam [Easter 1915]', in *Collected Poems*, 58.

fulfil Thomas's favourite image of lovers in a wood (see 'Lovers' and 'As the team's head brass'). Not until the shock of the final line does that distance from home become eschatological as well as geographical. The men are either dead already, or as good as dead: they will not be coming back. In its anastrophic delaying of the negative—'and will do never again' instead of the customary 'and will never do again'—the poem tantalizes by briefly imagining a replenished future, only to snatch that potential away with emphatic immediacy. The poem also grieves for something which dies with the men. Its title is unique among Thomas's work for the way it uses brackets: 'In Memoriam [Easter 1915]'. This risks sounding like an inability to decide between alternatives. Had Thomas stopped at 'In Memoriam', his poem would have directly challenged the scale of Tennyson's elegy for Arthur Hallam: Thomas's four lines eloquently mourn a generation; across 131 numbered sections Tennyson mourns an individual. Even the addition of the bracketed date, Easter 1915, does not disqualify the comparison. But it also raises a question about the relationship between the title's two halves. 'In Memoriam' announces an elegy, and Easter 1915 can be construed as the object of the elegizing. The religious journey towards an Easter rebirth is halted by times out of joint: this Easter there will be no resurrection, only death.

Mew writes a more overtly religious poetry than Thomas. Easter 1915 may have failed to deliver its promise of resurrection, but Mew's 'May, 1915' still places a shaken faith in divine providence: 'Surely the Spring, when God shall please, | Will come again like a divine surprise'.[44] 'The Cenotaph', another (and probably the latest) of Mew's war elegies, is tempted to find some divine recompense for the dead, although its mazy obscurities betray the strain on such hope. The poem begins with a recognition that the seasons are powerless to provide instant remedies: 'Not yet will those measureless fields be green again | Where only yesterday the wild sweet blood of wonderful youth was shed'. The Brookean 'wild sweet blood' may

---

[44] Mew, *Complete Poems*, 77.

have been lost 'only yesterday', but its poetic glories are long past. The flowers placed at the base of the cenotaph speak 'wistfully of other Springs' which the dead once enjoyed:

> In splendid sleep, with a thousand brothers
>   To lovers—to mothers
>   Here, too, lies he:
> Under the purple, the green, the red,
> It is all young life: it must break some women's hearts to see
> Such a brave, gay coverlet to such a bed!
> Only, when all is done and said,
> God is not mocked and neither are the dead.
> For this will stand in our Market-place—
>   Who'll sell, who'll buy
>   (Will you or I
> Lie each to each with the better grace)?
> While looking into every busy whore's and huckster's face
> As they drive their bargains, is the Face
> Of God: and some young, piteous, murdered face.[45]

Spring and death again coincide, and their juxtaposition breaks the syntax just as it breaks 'some women's hearts'. Mew brings the dead back to their 'little places': for lovers and mothers, the dead lie here at the cenotaph, as well as in war graves abroad. God and the dead search the consciences of the living (not least through the punishing rhyme: buy/I/lie), and peer into our impure motives: 'God is not mocked: for whatsoever a man soweth, that shall he also reap' (Galatians 6: 7). Yet the dead undergo no transformation, and reap no reward for their sacrifice: theirs (and Christ's) remains, in the unsparing final image, a 'young, piteous, murdered face', unregenerated by spring.

Women's war poetry of the period has been widely dismissed. A major anthology titled *Women's Writing of the First World War* fails to include a single poet—a circumstance which would be unthinkable if men were not omitted.[46] Jan Montefiore, one of the persuasive

---

[45] Ibid. 61–2.
[46] Angela K. Smith (ed.), *Women's Writing of the First World War: An Anthology* (Manchester: Manchester University Press, 2000).

champions of women's writing, condemns women's poetry of the
Great War as 'bad' for failing to 'transcend the chauvinist ideologies
and literary clichés of their time'.[47] However broadly justifiable that
complaint, Mew defies it: her work evokes only to reject the truisms
and easy consolations of her age. While so many contemporaries
make the reflex gesture towards a confident Christian salvation,
Mew often calls on God to intervene, yet without any expectation of
his doing so. 'Exspecto Resurrectionem', the twelve-line lyric which
ends the first edition of *The Farmer's Bride*, addresses the 'King who
hast the key', hoping that he will rescue the newly dead from the
coffin's 'narrow bed';[48] but if there is a response, it goes unreported.
Mew's poem 'The Forest Road', the title of which brings together
Thomas's two most common symbols, remains uncertain about the
likelihood of divine agency: 'I wish that God would take [your hands]
out of mine'; 'I wish I knew that God would stand | Smiling and
looking down on you when morning comes'.[49] Thomas, in 'Roads',
describes roads as 'wind[ing] on for ever',[50] and in 'Old Man' he is
taken back by the smell of the herb to 'an avenue, dark, nameless,
without end';[51] in another curious coincidence, Mew describes an
'infinite straight road stretching away | World without end'.[52] (Both
poems date from 1914; Mew's is the earlier, although not published
until 1916.) She lifts 'World without end' from Ephesians 21: 3
(or possibly from the 'Gloria'), but both she and Thomas use these
religious resonances antithetically: their roads never do lead to God
or to enlightenment, although they retain enough of their religious
symbolism to encourage fantasies that, as Thomas states, 'The next
turn may reveal | Heaven' (just as his enjambment does).[53] Mew's
longest and most brilliant poem, 'Madeleine in Church' (1914–15),
is a religious meditation which ends like Thomas's 'In Memoriam
[Easter 1915]' with an Easter associated with suffering and death

[47] Jan Montefiore, *Feminism and Poetry: Language, Experience, Identity in Women's Writing* (London: Pandora Press, 1987), 65 and 69.
[48] Mew, *Complete Poems*, 50.   [49] Ibid. 40.
[50] Thomas, *Collected Poems*, 89.   [51] Ibid. 9.
[52] Mew, *Complete Poems*, 40.   [53] Thomas, *Collected Poems*, 89.

but no rebirth. Madeleine remembers lying awake in bed, thinking about the crucified Christ's hands:

> He was alive to me, so hurt, so hurt! And most of all in Holy Week
> When there was no one else to see
> I used to think it would not hurt me too, so terribly,
> If He had ever seemed to notice me
> Or, if, for once, He would only speak.[54]

Christ never addresses the latter-day Magdalen who talks to and about him for over 200 lines. The child 'never quite believed that He was dead', but felt only the pain and none of the glory of Holy Week. The implication remains that the adult now does believe that Christ is dead, and with him the redemption offered by Easter. Christ, like the murdered war-dead in 'The Cenotaph', becomes defined by suffering rather than glory.

It is not Mew's conclusion, but how she reaches it, which marks an important difference from Thomas. Mew's sometimes frenzied religious explorations search for answers to questions that Thomas considers hardly worth asking. His prose book, *In Pursuit of Spring*, records a journey begun on Good Friday, and like John Donne before him, Thomas rides westwards—though on a bicycle, and untroubled by theological speculations. He most nearly approaches a 'religious humour' on Easter Sunday, but his is merely an 'unconscious imitation', as he repeats some verses of George Herbert 'with a not wholly sham unction'. Even that mood is destroyed by his double, the 'Other Man', atheistically praying, 'with unction exaggerated to an incredibly ridiculous degree', to be delivered from 'Parents, Schoolmasters, and Parsons, from Sundays and Bibles, from the Sound of Glory ringing in our ears, from Shame and Conscience, from Angels, Grace, and Eternal Hopes and Fears'.[55] God, in Thomas's poetry, features hardly at all; and the real, and rival, forces of his universe are night and the sun. 'In Memoriam [Easter 1915]' finds among the war-dead the grave of the Christian world-view. In

---

[54] Mew, *Complete Poems*, 49.   [55] Thomas, *In Pursuit of Spring*, 121–2.

'February Afternoon', as men 'strike and bear the stroke | Of war', God sits aloft, 'stone-deaf and stone-blind'.[56] It is pointless to expect intervention from such an enfeebled figure. A later poem, 'The Dark Forest', does offer an ambiguous restitution by bringing the dead back home to pick flowers in the wood, but theirs is an entirely separate and non-Christian afterlife with which communication is impossible:

> The forest foxglove is purple, the marguerite
> Outside is gold and white,
> Nor can those that pluck either blossom greet
> The others, day or night.[57]

These dead may not be 'far from home', but they are beyond the living. Even though the poet reports on its botany, the forest comes to stand for death's unknowable realm. Religious consolation is again tantalizing but out of reach: 'overhead | Hang stars like seeds of light | In vain'. Rather than accessing a world of light, the dead are consigned to a 'dark' and 'deep' forest, and those seeds of light will never germinate into effulgence.

War poems tend to concern themselves not so much with the timeless as with the specificities of time and place. By inserting in their titles a precise historical reference, Thomas's 'In Memoriam [Easter 1915]' and Mew's 'May, 1915' and 'June, 1915' enlist with a sizeable group of poems: Brooke's *1914*; Rosenberg's '1914' and 'Spring 1916'; Owen's '1914'; Meynell's 'Summer in England, 1914'; Yeats's 'Easter, 1916'; Gurney's 'Spring. Rouen, May 1917' and 'Sonnets 1917'; Blunden's 'Vlamertinghe: Passing the Château, July, 1917'. Several of these poets write other poems mentioning dates in the titles, but the cluster around the war years is conspicuous and continues into the next generation: Auden's poetry offers as examples 'Spain 1937' and 'September 1, 1939'. This practice is a bearing witness in important times, writing a history beyond official versions. It may also suggest that the poem's sentiments are

---

[56] Thomas, *Collected Poems*, 91.   [57] Ibid. 116.

provisional or transitory like a journal entry—not for all time, but of an age. In Mew's case, 'May, 1915' represents a significant retitling, the poem having been known in manuscript as 'Spring 1915'. One of her editors, John Newton, has suggested that 'Mew could well have changed the poem's title after writing "June, 1915" '.[58] Whether that hypothesis is true or not, the title 'June, 1915' advertises the poem as a sequel, which rehearses and seeks to redress the pain of the previous month.

'May, 1915', like Thomas's 'In Memoriam [Easter 1915]', had mourned a season which brought death but no sign of human renewal. 'June, 1915' is Mew's tentative attempt to re-establish in the natural cycles a hopeful analogue for the processes of human suffering and recovery. Yet the cost is devastatingly high:

Who thinks of June's first rose to-day?
    Only some child, perhaps, with shining eyes and rough bright hair
                    will reach it down
In a green sunny lane, to us almost as far away
    As are the fearless stars from these veiled lamps of town.
What's little June to a great broken world with eyes gone dim
From too much looking on the face of grief, the face of dread?
    Or what's the broken world to June and him
Of the small eager hand, the shining eyes, the rough bright head?[59]

Hands, eyes, to-day, great, grief, sun—this recapitulates many of the words and images of its predecessor, but leaves to their misery those who mourn. In 'May, 1915' their only hope had been divine intervention; now even that possibility is no longer broached. And whereas Mew had grouped 'us' separately from 'those who sit to-day with their great Dead', the later poem situates 'us' on the other side of grief in the 'great broken world': the blindness of grief has spread. Like June's first rose, that blindness has its roots in *Paradise Lost*: 'Thus with the year | Seasons return; but not to me returns | Day, or the sweet approach of even or morn, | Or sight of vernal bloom,

58 Newton, 'Notes', in Mew, *Complete Poems*, 123.
59 Mew, *Complete Poems*, 77–8.

or summer's rose.'[60] Mew measures a gap between the rose of the 'green sunny lane' and the dimmed broken world which is as unbridgeable as the distance Thomas charts between his soldiers and their home. The unpicked flowers of Thomas's poem are left to a new generation, and it is only in that generation that Mew can heal the breach between the seasonal and the human cycles. Abandoning any hope for the adult realm, 'June, 1915' proposes as restorative a shining childlike vision: if 'little June' is of no importance to the broken world, then the broken world is of no importance to the child who delights in little June. Even this refuge, though, is impermanent. The child gathers rosebuds while he may; but as Mew's rewriting of Herrick must lead her to suspect, if summer comes, autumn cannot be far behind.

[60] John Milton, *Paradise Lost*, ed. Alistair Fowler (London: Longman, 1971), iii. 40–3, 145.

5

Ivor Gurney's Memory

'I must go over the ground again,' Edmund Blunden confesses in the 'Preliminary' to his memoir *Undertones of War*, as he recalls his earlier attempts in poetry and prose to give a truthful account of his wartime experiences. Remembering, for Blunden, involves reliving and reconnoitring. Only death will bring release from that inexorable task:

A voice, perhaps not my own, answers within me. You will be going over the ground again, it says, until that hour when agony's clawed face softens into the smilingness of a young spring day; when you, like Hamlet, your prince of peaceful war-makers, give the ghost a '*Hic et ubique?* then we'll change our ground,' and not that time in vain.[1]

Explicitly and allusively, the answering voice condemns the haunted survivor to a lifetime of such remembrance. 'Remember me,' insists the ghost of King Hamlet, to which his son vows obedience for as long as 'memory holds a seat | In this distracted globe'. Blunden must acquiesce in that same single-mindedness, which his writing is powerless to purge or satisfy. He reports not long before his death in 1974: 'My experiences in the First World War have haunted me all my life and for many days I have, it seemed, lived in that world rather than this.'[2] The war poet who survives war is both Prince Hamlet and his spectral father, self-divided and self-haunted, inhabiting two realms at once. Death alone can bring the peace of reconciliation.

---

[1] Edmund Blunden, *Undertones of War* (London: Penguin, 1937), p. xii.
[2] Quoted in Paul Fussell, *The Great War and Modern Memory* (Oxford: Oxford University Press, 1975), 256.

Blunden does not present with the symptoms of what Paul Fussell has diagnosed as 'the lunacy of voluntary torment',[3] whereby survivors willingly revisit their battlefields in memory. No more choosing to be haunted than Hamlet, he suffers a torment imposed by external circumstances and supported by a compelling inner voice which both is and is not his own. Ivor Gurney anticipates a similar destiny in 'Memory, Let All Slip', albeit a destiny which this time even death may not prevent:

> Memory, let all slip save what is sweet
> Of Ypres plains.
> Keep only autumn sunlight and the fleet
> Clouds after rains,
>
> Blue sky and mellow distance softly blue;
> These only hold
> Lest I my pangéd grave must share with you.
> Else dead. Else cold.[4]

Like Blunden's inner voice, Gurney's memory is separated from himself, potentially with its own disruptive volition. Gurney also shares Blunden's identification with Hamlet's predicament, and his letters are dotted with passing allusions to the play.[5] 'My Hamlet mind revolves its usual course,'[6] he tells his friend and favoured correspondent, the music critic Marion Scott, in January 1917—the year the poem was written—and the following month he states that 'my mind is Hamlet's a wavering self-distrustful one'.[7] The source for the self-distrustfulness of 'Memory, Let All Slip' could hardly be more famous. Gurney's archaism, 'pangéd', has its origins in Hamlet's reference to 'the pangs of disprized love' (III. i. 72) in his 'To be or not to be' soliloquy; and just as Hamlet fears bad dreams

---

[3] Quoted in Paul Fussell, *The Great War and Modern Memory*, 328.

[4] Ivor Gurney, *Collected Poems*, ed. P. J. Kavanagh (Manchester: Carcanet, 2004), 33.

[5] See Gurney, *Collected Letters*, ed. R. K. R. Thornton (Ashington and Manchester: MidNag/Carcanet, 1991), 36, 110, 127, 198, 288.

[6] Gurney to Marion Scott, 11 Jan. 1917, ibid. 184.

[7] Gurney to Marion Scott, 7 Feb. 1917, ibid. 202.

after death, so Gurney fears bad memories. In each case, oblivion seems the preferable fate.

Hamlet swears that his father's commandment 'all alone shall live | Within the book and volume of my brain, | Unmixed with baser matter' (I. v. 102–4). Gurney, however, refuses to succumb to the dictations of memory, and looks forward to a future free of war's hauntings: 'All I want is—guerre fini, soldat fini; and to go home without burden of any thought save music, and hard swot for a time.'[8] His wartime poetry dreams of the day when 'winds of Joy shall cleanse the stain of war' ('The Immortal Hour');[9] trenches will be filled in as 'Once more joyful faces' turn back to England ('De Profundis');[10] days of pain will 'Somewhere reflower', and the sun 'Draw out of memory all bitterness' ('Song of Pain and Beauty');[11] living and dead returning to England will immediately be 'paid in full' by their nation's 'royal grace and dignity' ('Spring. Rouen, May 1917');[12] the beauty of the dead will be renewed 'In other forms', thereby ensuring that 'The new clear joy shall make all darkness clear' ('Afterwards').[13] And so on: borrowing traditional, and often clichéd, tropes of renewal, Gurney seeks escapism by repeatedly striving to convince himself that the consolations for which he most yearns await him. Yet there are occasional hints that the ghost may not be so easily exorcized. 'Camps' acknowledges that even 'lapped deep in sunshine and ease, | We are haunted for ever by the shapes of wars.'[14] Preparing for peace, therefore, the poet must consciously intervene to disrupt the processes of memory formation. In this respect Gurney is not alone: 'I remember things I'd best forget,' writes Siegfried Sassoon in 'A Night Attack';[15] similarly, 'I try not to remember these things now',[16] Wilfred Owen admits in 'The Sentry', claiming to

---

[8] Gurney to Marion Scott, 24 Aug. 1918, ibid. 443.

[9] Gurney, *Severn & Somme and War's Embers* (Ashington and Manchester: Mid-Nag/Carcanet, 1987), 75.

[10] Ibid. 105.　　[11] Ibid. 42.　　[12] Ibid. 44.

[13] Ibid. 25.　　[14] Ibid. 63.

[15] Siegfried Sassoon, *The War Poems* (London: Faber, 1983), 42.

[16] Wilfred Owen, *The Complete Poems and Fragments*, i: *The Poems*, ed. Jon Stallworthy (London: Chatto & Windus, Hogarth Press, and Oxford University Press, 1983), 188.

abjure the very incidents which prompt and are preserved by his work. Poetic rhythms, as powerful means of keeping time, render self-defeating the poet's effort to forget. So, in 'Scots', Gurney evokes some dead soldier-friends who 'Are now but thoughts of blind pain, and best hid away. . .':[17] the poem acts against the stated desire of its author, forcing to the surface memories better buried. The urgency and impossibility of that active need for concealment (forgetfulness commonly being a passive process) are the subject of 'To his Love', not Gurney's best poem, but perhaps his best known:

> You would not know him now . . .
> But still he died
> Nobly, so cover him over
> With violets of pride
> Purple from Severn side.
>
> Cover him, cover him soon!
> And with thick-set
> Masses of memoried flowers—
> Hide that red wet
> Thing I must somehow forget.[18]

'To his Love' discovers more than it covers over, as the poem crosses the fault line separating commemoration from memory. Gurney attempts to observe the rites of official remembrance while withstanding a panicked reaction to the wounded corpse. The poem's unexceptional opening stanzas had sought the traditional elegiac consolations of a pastoral landscape by recalling the dead man to his native environment, where once he walked among sheep in the Cotswolds and sailed along the Severn. Gurney's ellipses eloquently disclose the strains of denying a more grievous truth, which can be hidden neither by aureate assertions of nobility and pride nor by those 'memoried flowers': rather than being 'Full of or fraught with memories' in the rare sense offered by the *OED*, they are distractions strategically deployed by a mind uncertain of how to bury what it has witnessed.

17 Gurney, *Severn & Somme and War's Embers*, 31.   18 Ibid. 76.

Gurney's is a memorial poetry. '[H]e wrote several [poems] called "Memory",'[19] notes P. J. Kavanagh, and the word, its derivatives and associates, are scattered, sometimes thickly, throughout Gurney's poetic output. In most of his wartime work, the poet's relationship with memory remains benign and simple, if not simplistic. Gurney's 'Preface' to his first volume, *Severn & Somme* (1917), assures the reader that although 'these verses were written in France', the poet's 'images of beauty'

> were always of Gloucester, county of Cotswold and Severn, and a plain rich, blossomy, and sweet of airs—as the wise Romans knew, who made their homes in exile by the brown river, watching the further bank for signs of war.[20]

Gurney's wartime poetry dwells on the power of the Gloucestershire landscape to sustain the soldiers through memory. Casting their wistful glances towards home, *Severn & Somme* and its successor, *War's Embers* (1919), are only occasionally able to accommodate the immediate experiences of trench warfare. Memories of war may need to be purged in case they linger in the grave, but the poet's *locus amoenus* provokes no such fears: 'whether I die or live [Gloucester] stays always with me—being in itself so beautiful, so full of memories'.[21] Gurney asserts the connection frequently enough to imply a tautology: all his memories are of beauty, and only in memory can beauty be found. Back in his native environment, it is often memory which bestows beauty. 'What are the streets that have no memories?,' he asks with some puzzlement in 'Thoughts of New England', unfavourably comparing the relatively recent and uprooted communities across the Atlantic with Gloucester's haunted and 'historied ground of Roman or Danes'.[22] Memorable places have memories of their own: 'Do not forget me quite, | O Severn meadows,'[23] Gurney had

---

[19] P. J. Kavanagh, 'Introduction', in Gurney, *Collected Poems*, p. xxv.
[20] Gurney, *Severn & Somme and War's Embers*, 20.   [21] Ibid.
[22] Gurney, *Rewards of Wonder: Poems of Cotswold, France, London*, ed. George Walter (Ashington and Manchester: MidNag/Carcanet, 2000), 39.
[23] Gurney, 'Song: "Only the Wanderer"', in *Severn & Somme and War's Embers*, 36.

pleaded from France, seeking a reciprocal relationship. His request is an attempt at immortality; as he concludes in 'The Tax Office', 'The earth has such memory—nothing dies, nothing in thought does die.'[24]

This being the case, Gurney after the war sets himself the task of remembrance—although still not, initially, remembrance of the trenches. 'Memory, Let All Slip', a poem with the ambition of forgetting the unnamed horrors of Ypres, spends several of its eight lines seeking to retain the 'sweet' glories of the skyscapes there. Amidst the natural world, Gurney regrets only that he cannot record everything, and imagines death as a release from necessarily having to 'grieve again | Because high Autumn goes beyond my pen | And snow lies inexprest in the deep lane'.[25] When the poet fails to memorialize, beauty escapes and is forgotten. Conversely, he believes that his successes keep beauty alive. 'O Tree of Pride', written in 1918, describes the poet's duty to preserve the fleeting majesty of summer as a comfort during winter months spent by the fireside:

> For memory passes
> Of even the loveliest things, bravest in show;
> The mind to beauty most alert not know
> How the August grasses
> Waved, by December's
> Glow, unless he see deep in the embers
> The poet's dream, gathered from cold print's spaces.[26]

Memory cannot be relied on unless provoked and enriched by poetry. Shelley's image of the fading coals may lie behind the poem's lines, but Gurney shares nothing of Shelley's disappointment at the gap between inspiration and the printed word. Rather, the wonder of poetry is that its 'cold print' should hold in its spaces the warm embers of the 'poet's dream'.

[24] Gurney, *Rewards of Wonder*, 32.
[25] Gurney, 'Moments', in *Collected Poems*, 65. A different version appears in *80 Poems or So*, ed. George Walter and R. K. R. Thornton (Ashington and Manchester: MidNag/Carcanet, 1997), 128.
[26] Gurney, *Collected Poems*, 41.

Despite the title of his second volume, war's embers prove to be a different matter. If Gurney's wartime poetry is often prospective in its outlook, dreaming of a future peace, the poems he writes in the years immediately after the war attempt to enjoy that peace by eliding any unsettling memory. *80 Poems or So*, the book he finished in 1922 (although it would not appear for another 75 years), remains silent about the war. There is nothing more conspicuous than a passing reference in 'Valley Farm' to fertile land once covered with water: 'If War should come here only then might one | Regret water receding'.[27] As Donald Davie has argued, the valley must be 'inundated afresh, and removed from man's dominion, if that dominion eventuates in what Gurney had seen in wartime France'.[28] However, the poem's touch is lighter than Davie's elaboration, and as the volume's only mention of war, it implies that Gurney has successfully trained his memory to forget. 'Now are the hills born new in sparkling light,' he begins one poem, as night 'goes from thoughts of men'.[29] It is a hymn to the peace which, so fondly imagined in his wartime poetry, has finally been realized.

Gurney assured Marion Scott in August 1915 that 'Great poets, great creators are not much influenced by immediate events; these must sink in to the very foundations and be absorbed.' Rupert Brooke, by contrast, 'soaked it in quickly and gave it out with as great ease'.[30] The same damning verdict deserves to fall on Gurney's own wartime poetry, itself influenced by Brooke. *80 Poems or So*, written immediately after the war, stumbles over the opposite problem: for all the poems' quiet strengths, purgation has become more important than absorption. If, as Gurney believes, great poetry is born out of memory, the forgetfulness of the volume must constitute a lesser achievement. Only when he returns in 1922 to his wartime experiences does Gurney begin to write unforgetting

---

[27] Gurney, *80 Poems or So*, 90.
[28] Donald Davie, 'Ivor Gurney Recovered', in *Under Briggflatts: A History of Poetry in Great Britain 1960–1988* (Manchester: Carcanet, 1989), 198–9.
[29] Gurney, ' "Now are the hills born new in sparkling light" ', in *80 Poems or So*, 104.
[30] Gurney to Marion Scott, 3 Aug. 1915, in *Collected Letters*, 29.

and unforgettable poetry. That value judgement has nothing to do with an implicit hierarchy of subject-matters, but derives from Gurney's new, more complex and troubled, attitude to memory, which becomes not merely a solace but a weapon of aggression and defiance. Dispensing with the need for self-protection, Gurney is no longer prepared to let anything slip, whatever the cost. It is no coincidence that this poetic revisiting of wartime experiences should exist alongside an increasingly angry disillusionment with the nation for which Gurney had fought. 'Brown Earth Look', a poem written around the same time as this renewed interest in the war, still musters the old belief that 'Peace with its sorrow blots out the agonies of strife'.[31] Although sorrow had not been presaged by Gurney's earlier work as it gazed into an idyllic future, the poem remains just about hopeful of the continuing ability of peace to offer refuge. More typical is 'Old Dreams', from the same notebook, in which the dream of 'return to a sunlit land' cruelly rhymes with the eventuality: 'tangles of fate one does not understand, | And as for rest or true ease, where is it or what is it'.[32] England 'likes sin too well' ('War Poet'),[33] its leaders lost in corruption 'While the cheated dead cry, unknowing, "Eadem Semper!"' ('What's in Time').[34] Failing so dismally to provide the promised consolations, peace reawakens memory of war and of promises broken. 'Mist on Meadows' deplores the fact that England 'takes as common' the soldiers' 'vast endurance',[35] and does not honour them. Still more resentfully, the irregular sonnet 'Strange Hells' turns from the camaraderie and courage of the Gloucester regiment in the trenches to a less heroic post-war fate:

> Where are they now on State-doles, or showing shop-patterns
> Or walking town to town sore in borrowed tatterns
> Or begged. Some civic routine one never learns.
> The heart burns—but has to keep out of face how heart burns.[36]

---

[31] Gurney, *Collected Poems*, 156.   [32] Ibid. 166.   [33] Ibid. 213.
[34] Ibid. 328.   [35] Ibid. 173   [36] Gurney, *Rewards of wonder*, 82.

One critic has claimed that Gurney at this time became 'unable to distinguish the past from the present', and began 'writing war poetry as though the war was still on'.[37] This travesties a poet indignantly aware that to forget the past would be to conspire with the injustices of the present. By bringing his wartime memories to bear on an amnesiac nation, Gurney points up the shamefulness of the soldiers' treatment. That curious 'begged' relates to the 'tatterns'; but its positioning seems to pursue the Gloucesters' passive suffering into a post-war society where even the active assertion of begging is denied them. Compare Falstaff, considering the ruins of his own men: 'there's not three of my hundred-and-fifty left alive, and they are for the town's end, to beg during life' (*I Henry IV*, v. iii. 35–6). Yet, while Falstaff reduces 'honour' to an airy word, Gurney uses it frequently and unironically as a reminder of mutual obligations. The soldiers have been 'begged', and gave generously; now that they themselves are reduced to begging, those who owe them so much prove notably less forthcoming.

Gurney's complaints about his own plight grow increasingly desperate during the same period—a period which includes his inability to keep a steady job or get his poetry published, his declining mental health and consequent suicide attempts, and, in December 1922, his enforced committal to the City of London Mental Hospital at Dartford (where he would spend the final fifteen years of his life). Even before his incarceration within the asylum's 'intolerable ... four walls',[38] Gurney grieves for a lost companionship, finding 'the old earthly rewards' of 'Poetry, friends, music' replaced by 'the restless searching, the bitter labour, | The going out to watch stars, stumbling blind through the difficult door'.[39] A wretched isolation returns in 'Afterwards', when Gurney's failed attempts to befriend a group of men in a pub leave him 'Hurt with the thought that he who sang longing and wrath | Of soldiers, should in the friendly Inn, be

---

[37] E. L. Black, quoted by George Walter, 'Introduction', in *Rewards of Wonder*, 1.
[38] Gurney, 'To God', in *Collected Poems*, 197.
[39] Gurney, 'The Not-Returning', in *Collected Poems*, 168.

kept dumb, apart'.[40] This comes from a poet who, during the war, had looked forward to the 'joy' of being 'able to go into the nearest Cotswold inn and drop into conversation with the nearest man!'[41] A wartime poem, also called 'Afterwards', had dreamt of a time after the war when men, walking the paths once walked by their dead friends, would feel 'a presence near, | Friendly, familiar, and the old grief gone'.[42] The later poem consciously and bitterly dispels that delusion by giving the unfriendly men the 'looks' of fallen comrades.

Once in the asylum, Gurney calls for those comrades to release him from his continuing imprisonment: 'Why have you dead ones not saved me—You dead ones not helped well?' ('O Tan-faced Prairie Boy');[43] and in 'Farewell', seeking to be either 'dead or free happy alive', he reminds them that 'I lay with you under the unbroken wires once'.[44] This desperation at having been abandoned produces an extraordinarily plangent lyric, 'It Is Near Toussaints':

It is near Toussaints, the living and dead will say:
'Have they ended it? What has happened to Gurney?'
And along the leaf-strewn roads of France many brown shades
Will go, recalling singing, and a comrade for whom also they
Had hoped well. His honour them had happier made.
Curse all that hates good. When I spoke of my breaking
(Not understood) in London, they imagined of the taking
Vengeance, and seeing things were different in future.
(A musician was a cheap, honourable and nice creature.)
Kept sympathetic silence; heard their packs creaking
And burst into song—Hilaire Belloc was all our Master.
On the night of all the dead, they will remember me,
Pray Michael, Nicholas, Maries lost in Novembery
River-mist in the old City of our dear love, and batter

---

[40] Gurney, *Best Poems and The Book of Five Makings*, ed. R. K. R. Thornton and George Walter (Ashington and Manchester: MidNag/Carcanet, 1995), 53.
[41] Gurney to Marion Scott, 23 Mar. 1917, in *Collected Letters*, 232.
[42] Gurney, *Severn & Somme and War's Embers*, 25.
[43] Gurney, *Best Poems and The Book of Five Makings*, 44.
[44] Gurney, *Collected Poems*, 266.

At doors about the farms crying 'Our war poet is lost',
'Madame—no bon!'—and cry his two names, warningly, sombrely.[45]

The poem embodies *in extremis* a failure in Gurney's work to distinguish between the inspired and the incompetent; a similar unevenness in his musical compositions may have prompted Sir Charles Stanford's comment that, of all his pupils—including Bliss and Vaughan Williams—Gurney was potentially 'the biggest of them all, but the least teachable'.[46] 'It Is Near Toussaints' lapses into doggerel ('remember me/Novembery'), distorts word order to deliver rhymes ('His honour them had happier made'), and indulges in the blandest of imprecations ('Curse all that hates good') as it ignores the basic lessons. That the poem survives these calamities is testament to the strenuous force of a poetic language which is, in Geoffrey Hill's phrase, 'wrought from impediment'.[47] Gurney's impediment here is the control he exerts over memory—which collapses momentarily as the poet taunts himself with thoughts of how his account of mental breakdown ('breaking') was misunderstood by his fellow soldiers as revolutionary fervour ('taking | Vengeance'). The irrupting frustration of these memories forces syntax to break as well, and places the poet beyond the ameliorative effects of commemoration. The poem is set during a period of remembrance: the Armistice, on 11 November 1918, came less than a fortnight after Toussaints, and ' "Have they ended it?" ' implies a date around that time. Gurney refers to Toussaints (into which he merges All Saints' and All Souls' Night) in at least eight of his published poems, its importance residing in the belief that, if 'nothing in thought does die', the remembrance of the dead is a way of keeping them alive. Yet as the poem dances between tenses and nations, Gurney's own voice becomes lost in time and place. He belongs with neither living nor dead, who have more in common than either group has with

45 Ibid. 267.
46 Quoted in Jon Stallworthy, *Anthem for Doomed Youth: Twelve Soldier Poets of the First World War* (London: Constable, 2002), 146.
47 Geoffrey Hill, 'Gurney's Hobby', F. W. Bateson Memorial Lecture, *Essays in Criticism*, 34/2 (April 1984), 120.

the poet. Caught in an unmapped and obscure destiny, denied the consolations of the revenants, he is the lost soul, looked for in vain amidst the farmhouses of France and his native Gloucester as the dying fall of the poem's final dactyls fades into silence.

Gurney's living death enhances the importance of memory. As P. J. Kavanagh argues, his asylum poems inhabit the past, 'for as far as he is concerned he has no present'.[48] The point is made most explicitly at the start of another of his poems, titled 'Memory': 'They have left me little indeed, how shall I best keep | Memory from sliding content down to drugged sleep?'[49] The trajectories remain the same: memory slides, as once it might have let all slip. However, the contentment of 'drugged sleep' is almost exactly what Gurney had previously chosen in preference to less comforting memories of Ypres. His wavering, self-distrustful Hamlet mind, opting for death and oblivion over bad dreams, has been replaced by a potentially violent desire to resist death and oblivion through memory: 'my blood in its colour even is known fighter', Gurney warns, gathering the bodily resources which will support him in his struggle. Abandoned by living and dead, he uses memory to assert a besieged identity, as well as to excoriate the nation which has betrayed him. The self-styled 'War poet'—'First war poet', he insists—refuses to forget the experiences which validate his calling: 'War told me truth, I have Severn's right of maker, | As of Cotswold: war told me: I was elect'.[50] Gurney's pride is audible; but so is the belligerence of a poet who will continue to assert his 'right' and his 'truth' regardless of the enemies besetting him.

Gurney grows nostalgic for that truth of war, even in its grim drudgery. 'This is not happy thought, but a glimpse most strangely | Forced from the past',[51] he admits in 'Riez Bailleul', as he remembers mending reserve posts behind the line. The forcing of unpleasant memory operates to 'hide this pain and work myself free | From

---

[48] Kavanagh, 'Introduction', p. xxxiv.   [49] Gurney, *Collected Poems*, 264.
[50] Gurney, 'While I Write', in *Collected Poems*, 262.   [51] Ibid. 203.

present things'. Other poems sound a similar note, as Gurney determines to 'work out . . . crazes of my untold pain | In verse which shall recall the rightness of a former day'.[52] 'First poem', a rhyming quatrain which opens *The Book of Five Makings* (finished in 1925, published in 1995), wonders:

> O what will you turn out, book, to be?
> Who are not my joy but my escape from the worst
> And most accurst of my woe? Shall you be poetry,
> Or tell truth, or be of past things the tale rehearsed?[53]

To which the following poems tacitly answer: all of the above. Gurney writes several poems which suggest that he observes his own inspiration (and, by extension, his own memory) with a fascinated detachment. His is not quite the 'voluntary lunacy' described by Fussell, because his return to the battlefields provides a relatively sane sanctuary from the still greater lunacy—personal, institutional, national—of the present. In 'December 30th',[54] Gurney claims that he writes 'to keep madness and black torture away'. But he recognizes the potential perversity of his preoccupations, and sometimes it is his writing which causes the pain. '[T]his memory | Will not pass,' Gurney declares unspecifically, describing memory as a 'grinding' from which the cadences of poetry offer only a little ease: 'The pain is in thought, which will not freely range.'[55] Returning to the same preoccupations, the same places, and the same incidents, sometimes over a dozen times, Gurney's poetic *opus* can seem like a vast hall of mirrors—or, as he more despairingly figures it, like a floor which must be continually 'swept or rubbed' without a 'moment's respite' as the sufferer cries out 'in the Most Holy Name | Of God for Pity'. Ultimately, Gurney accepts pain as the price worth paying for the art which is born out of it. In 'Looking There', he states, 'if my thoughts hurt, I must leave my writing', but he ends the poem with the need for perseverance: 'Misery drowns in many ways and I take

---

[52] Gurney, 'The Last of the Book', in *Best Poems and The Book of Five Makings*, 140.
[53] Ibid. 91.   [54] Gurney, *Collected Poems*, 278.
[55] Gurney, 'There Is a Man', in *Collected Poems*, 195.

this | To hurt a heart with making past remembrance—and to get work done.'[56] A later poem, 'War Books', recalls the poet's work in the trenches: 'Out of the heart's sickness the spirit wrote. | For delight, or to escape hunger, or of war's worst anger'.[57] Here, the paradoxes created by Gurney's grammar bear as much relevance to the conflicting motivations of later war poems. As Desmond Graham notes, 'The spirit wrote, the sentence somehow says, to escape war's worst anger and about war's worst anger.'[58] In the asylum, Gurney writes painfully about pain to 'work [himself] free' from pain.

Gurney's poetry moves from the desire to forget to the urgency of remembering. His work explicitly addresses the questions of *why* and *how* he remembers, but an early hint of *what* he remembers comes from a letter to Marion Scott in October 1916. Sending her a conventionally Brookean triolet, 'Serenity' — 'Nor steel nor flame has any power on me, | Save that its malice work the Almighty Will' — he adds a destructive piece of self-criticism: 'Which is all very well; but what about Mud and Monotony? And Minnies and Majors?'[59] His work after 1922 achieves the all-inclusiveness which the narrow range of neither his wartime poetry nor his *80 Poems or So* can incorporate. Gurney's war is burdened by fear, and broken by moments of kindness and companionship and by sudden extreme danger. But, despite everything, it is a war he can never regret, not least because of its imaginative opportunities. War 'bores' him,[60] he complains to Marion Scott, apparently forgetting how a fortnight earlier he had told her that 'War's damned interesting. It would be hard indeed to be deprived of all this artists [*sic*] material now.'[61] After news of Francis Ledwidge's death causes Gurney to mourn a 'life so wastefully spent', his second thoughts revise that routine denunciation of waste: 'the fire may not have been struck in [Ledwidge and other poets]

[56] Gurney, 'Looking There', ibid. 169.
[57] Gurney, 'War Books', ibid. 258.
[58] Desmond Graham, ' "Out of the heart's sickness": Ivor Gurney as a Poet of War', *The Ivor Gurney Society Journal*, 7 (2001), 9.
[59] Gurney to Marion Scott, 10 Oct. 1916, in *Collected Letters*, 155.
[60] Gurney to Marion Scott, 22 June 1916, ibid. 103.
[61] Gurney to Marion Scott, 7 June 1916, ibid. 87.

save for the war'.[62] Wartime conditions bring unexpected pleasures: ' "This is right marching, we are even glad to be here, | Or very glad?" ', Gurney remembers his regiment asking itself in 'Towards Lillers', although 'This was war; we understood'.[63] The accuracy of the memory is confirmed by the ambivalences of his wartime letters. In one letter, after having 'gone through a strafe', Gurney is left feeling 'exalted and exulting only longing for a nice blighty'; he is 'tired of this war', and yet 'would not willingly give up such a memory of such a time'; 'It was a great time,' 'But O to be back out of it all!'[64] The war also brings relief for Gurney from fear of mental illness: his 'sickness', he approvingly observes, is 'caused by real surroundings now, not by imaginary'.[65] Cold comfort is better than no comfort. In his later work, those remembered wartime sufferings can seem more manageable and more justifiable than the asylum's 'torture'.

While Owen's work dwells on the extremities of war—its physical and emotional devastations—and Sassoon meets the illusions of glory with an equal and opposite disillusion, Gurney remains faithful to what he calls, in another context, 'small trifles'.[66] His memory takes pleasure in the minutiae of trench life, evoking the hardships and indigences endured by the body, only to delight the more in their abeyance. Poems recall the luxury of warm straw after a long march, or tobacco which 'kept heart and soul together, and the mud out of thinking',[67] or 'café-au-lait as princes know it' made by a kind woman to revive 'Lousy, thirsty' soldiers.[68] A roll-call in 'Laventie' even alchemizes trench rations into poetry—'Maconachie, Paxton, Tickler, and Gloucester's Stephens; | Fray Bentos, Spiller and Baker'—before offering a more mouth-watering inventory of possible purchases from 'small delectable cafés' in the town: 'vin,

---

62 Gurney to Marion Scott, 18 Aug. 1917, ibid. 305.
63 Gurney, *Collected Poems*, 177.
64 Gurney to Marion Scott, 18 Aug. 1917, in *Collected Letters*, 305.
65 Gurney to Marion Scott, 8 Aug. 1917, ibid. 297.
66 Gurney, 'The Escape', in *Collected Poems*, 170.
67 Gurney, 'Tobacco', in *Rewards of Wonder*, 27.
68 Gurney, 'La Gorgues', ibid. 65.

rouge-blanc, chocolats, citron, grenadine'.[69] Gurney's wartime letters to Marion Scott again confirm the emphasis: during a particularly dangerous strafe, 'I had time to wish I had chocolate, and wonder whether so much baccy was good for me.'[70] In the midst of another strafe, he incurs the wrath of his sergeant-major for seeking him out to ask 'where the biscuits and cheese were'.[71] Gurney's appetites may sound like evidence of a relapse into the pre-war mental illness manifested in his obsessive eating of cream buns; and if he exaggerates the account of his predilections to entertain Marion Scott, they nevertheless indicate that food has become a comfort and an avoidance strategy (much like the memory tests in the less successful of Gurney's later poems). Even this reveals a truth about war rarely noticed by other soldier-poets. Owen, an officer, must slip into unconvincingly Kiplingesque Cockney dialect to talk about eating: 'I'm longing for a taste of your old buns. | (Say, Jimmie, spare's a bite of bread)'.[72] Geoffrey Hill's accusation that Owen has a 'blankness respecting articulacy among the other ranks' may be overstated;[73] but Owen's limitations in this respect are undeniably shown up by Gurney. Gurney's egalitarian memory gives him greater range in both voice and subject-matter than his contemporaries (over many of whom, of course, he holds the considerable advantage of having survived). That range is never more humorously illustrated than in his Byronic rhyming of 'Sarsparilla' and 'glad gorilla',[74] or at the end of 'Serenade': 'True, the size of the rum ration was still a shocker | But at last over Aubers the majesty of the dawn's veil swept.'[75]

The mind's ability to distract itself in the midst of extreme danger is no mere gourmandizing, but the necessary tactic of seeking imaginative refuge in a more pleasurable world. Whether that refuge is found in rum, chocolate, tobacco, cheese and biscuits, or in

---

[69] Gurney, 'Laventie', ibid. 34–5.
[70] Gurney to Marion Scott, 22 June 1916, in *Collected Letters*, 104.
[71] Gurney to Marion Scott, 5 July 1916, ibid. 115.
[72] Owen, 'The Letter', in *Complete Poems and Fragments*, i. 137.
[73] Geoffrey Hill, 'Isaac Rosenberg, 1890–1918', Warton Lecture on English Poetry, *Proceedings of the British Academy*, 101 (1999), 215.
[74] Gurney, 'Masterpiece', in *Collected Poems*, 214.   [75] Ibid. 240.

cerebral matter, makes little immediate difference. 'I might be a good soldier could I forget music and books,'[76] Gurney confides to Marion Scott, yet music is the expediency which helps him survive in 'The Silent One':

Who died on the wires, and hung there, one of two—
Who for his hours of life had chattered through
Infinite lovely chatter of Bucks accent;
Yet faced unbroken wires; stepped over, and went,
A noble fool, faithful to his stripes—and ended.
But I weak, hungry, and willing only for the chance
Of line—to fight in the line, lay down under unbroken
Wires, and saw the flashes, and kept unshaken.
Till the politest voice—a finicking accent, said:
'Do you think you might crawl through there; there's a hole;' In the afraid
Darkness, shot at; I smiled, as politely replied—
'I'm afraid not, Sir.' There was no hole, no way to be seen,
Nothing but chance of death, after tearing of clothes.
Kept flat, and watched the darkness, hearing bullets whizzing—
And thought of music—and swore deep heart's deep oaths.
(Polite to God—) and retreated and came on again.
Again retreated—and a second time faced the screen.[77]

Gurney remains unequalled among soldier-poets in the degree of self-scrutiny performed by his memory. If the man described earlier in the poem, who steps over the wires and dies, is 'a noble fool'—still he died nobly?—the poet leaves conspicuously unstated the verdict on his own ignobly wise survival 'under unbroken | Wires'. It is only the line which breaks, and the possibility of a double meaning is endorsed by Gurney's talk of 'fight[ing] in the line': he wants to live so that his poetry can do the fighting. (The poet's own 'breaking', as reported in 'It Is Near Toussaints', may also ghost the poem.) Fulfilling the ambition it describes, 'The Silent One' fights not only by stressing the absurdity of

---

[76] Gurney to Marion Scott, ? June 1916, in *Collected Letters*, 102.
[77] Gurney, *Best Poems and The Book of Five Makings*, 49–50. I have added a full stop after 'clothes', following the version in *Collected Poems*, 250.

battle, but also through its psychological precision. The screen is a thin boundary separating a world where speech ends as the silent one hangs dead on the wires, and a world of insanely finicking manners where lives are preserved and lost according to the ability to resist the expected etiquettes. Just as Gurney retreats and comes on again, so do words like 'line', 'afraid' (conflating fear with a gracious refusal), and the unchanging 'darkness'. The word most closely interrogated is 'polite', which becomes contaminated with connotations of *politesse* by the finicking accent, before being restored to courtesy in the parenthetical 'Polite to God'. One kind of politeness is a class-bound performance, obscene in the circumstances and yet life-saving for the poet who must duplicitously mirror it. The other, embodied in the 'deep heart's deep oaths', shares Owen's sense that '[t]here is a point where prayer is indistinguishable from blasphemy. There is also a point where blasphemy is indistinguishable from prayer.'[78] Gurney's oaths are as 'deep'—another word which comes on again—as the finicking accent is shallow.

'The Silent One' stands apart as unusual in Gurney's work for its concentration on an extreme moment, and the reference to 'death, after tearing of clothes' remains peculiar enough to hint at the visceral panic in its imagining. Other near-fatal incidents are presented more jauntily and in passing. Several poems mention a shell landing near enough to blunt Gurney's razor while he is shaving, and their wry unconcern matches his account from the trenches: 'A whizzbang missed me by inches over my head and exploded ten yards from me—and the impression it gave and gives me now is chiefly of the comic.'[79] 'The Retreat' enjoys a similarly mordant humour as it recalls, first, Gurney's failed attempts to shoot some well-fed Germans, and then his injury sustained under machine-gun fire near Vermand:

---

[78] Wilfred Owen to Susan Owen, 18 Feb. 1918, in *Collected Letters*, ed. Harold Owen and John Bell (Oxford: Oxford University Press, 1967), 534.
[79] Gurney to Marion Scott, 21? June 1916, in *Collected Letters*, 101.

suddenly my arm went blazing with bright ardour of pain;
The end of music . . . I knelt down and cursed the double
Treachery of Fritz to Europe and to English music . . . [80]

Gurney's comical zeugma, as he instantly fears for his post-war musical career (and so for the future of English music), tells another truth about war rarely divulged by contemporary truth-telling poets. One reason is his rank as 'Common Private'. Gurney shows no ambition beyond surviving the war and returning home to continue his work. In 'Of Grandcourt' he remembers a friend's suggestion that they should volunteer for the front line. The friend has reason to be keen—'he was Lance Corporal and might be full Corporal'—but having turned him down, Gurney reveals his own priorities: 'Stars looked as well from second as from first line holes.'[81] Unable to take the war entirely seriously, Gurney is, he admits to Marion Scott, 'not a soldier' but a '*dirty civilian*'.[82] This confirms a critical distance from the military world he is forced to inhabit, and the stress, for a poet so attentive to bodily comforts, falls on 'dirty'. When Gurney sees a company of exhausted Canadian soldiers, 'Vermin-eaten, and fed beastly', almost the first thing he notices is, with an inflationary emphasis, their 'Faces infinitely grimed in'.[83]

Gurney shows the most extraordinary powers of recollection through his litany of place-names. In an unpublished poem, 'Reference Map of the Civil War', Gurney (in the words of his editors, Thornton and Walter) 'savours the names on the map and balances the exotic and distant against the familiar, where "of Severn country I know the names even of stiles" '.[84] Maps hold a talismanic fascination for Gurney, as an *aide-mémoire* as well as a prompt to the imagination: like the postcards of German towns discovered nailed to trees in what were once enemy-held positions, their purpose is to stimulate

---

[80] Gurney, *Collected Poems*, 347.
[81] Gurney, *Best Poems and The Book of Five Makings*, 42.
[82] Gurney to Marion Scott, 5 July 1916, in *Collected Letters*, 115.
[83] Gurney, 'Canadians', in *Rewards of Wonder*, 43.
[84] R. K. R. Thornton and George Walter, 'Introduction', in *Best Poems and The Book of Five Makings*, 5.

'memory's rewards'.[85] Having visited him in the asylum armed with her dead husband's Ordnance Survey map of Gloucestershire, Helen Thomas describes how Gurney 'trod, in a way we who were sane could not emulate, the lanes and fields he knew and loved so well, his guide being his finger tracing the way on the map'.[86] The distinction that Gurney's visitor draws between the sane and the insane may be nothing more, in this case, than the difference between routine memory and a genius for recollection and re-creation all the more passionate for lingering over what has been lost.

Gurney makes the exile's complaint in 'The High Hills' that 'memory is poor enough consolation | For the soul hopeless gone';[87] poor it may be, but it is his only consolation. He therefore delights in the kind of information listed by Ernest Hemingway: 'the concrete names of villages, the numbers of roads, the names of rivers, the numbers of regiments and the dates';[88] and although he does not share Hemingway's credo that, for the war poet, abstract words such as 'honor' are obscene by comparison, as the poet of place-names Gurney is pre-eminent. He maps his wartime experiences in the same way that he maps Gloucestershire, dwelling on the cadences of the proper nouns: a not noticeably unusual example ends with reference to 'Robecq, Merville, Riez Bailleul in the North France Autumn', and also mentions, in its previous twenty-four lines, Ypres, Arras, La Gorgues, Aveluy, Buire-au-Bois, and Creçy.[89] Names, for Gurney, not only conjure a physical reality, they become that reality. When the poet hopes for a Blighty which will allow him a large pension and the opportunity of 'tramping' round the English countryside, he imagines that

the first walk I shall take shall be Dymock, Newent, Ross and into Wales, to end at Chepstow after meeting names met in Malory; names known it

[85] Gurney, 'Chaulnes', in *Best Poems and The Book of Five Makings*, 137.
[86] Helen Thomas, quoted in Stallworthy, *Anthem for Doomed Youth*, 151.
[87] Gurney, *Collected Poems*, 181.
[88] Quoted in Fussell, *The Great War and Modern Memory*, 21.
[89] Gurney, 'Of Trees Over There', in *Rewards of Wonder*, 53.

would seem a thousand years ago in some forgotten life stronger in charm than their realities of houses and trees, almost.[90]

That final 'almost' puts a brake on Gurney's enthusiasm, but only reluctantly and as an afterthought. It may be the names, or the forgotten life, which possess the strong charm, or it may be the connection between them. Names embody a similar sorcery in Gurney's war poetry, distancing his work from more nebulous armchair generalizations about the glory of war or the horrors of the trenches. 'As to the attitude taken by certain writers to the present time and to their land', Gurney assured Scott in 1917, 'this usually represents what they wish to think, and on some rare occasions actually do.'[91] Except on 'rare occasions' of its own, Gurney's wartime poetry does not evade that dismissal, but his remembered names in later work place a protective emphasis on the contingencies of time and place. 'Gloucesters smothered regrets in cards, I could not: | Being full of actualities and wonderful images,'[92] he writes in 'October in Exile': the actualities filling Gurney's memory allow no smothering of the sometimes regrettable, sometimes exultant, truths told to him by war.

'Mostly I remember,'[93] Gurney begins 'Gifts and Courtesy', as he launches into a catalogue aria of his wartime experiences; thirty-six poems later in the *Rewards of Wonder* manuscript, a similar ransacking of memory concludes with the line, 'But of Buysscheure, the mill and St. Omer I remember most'.[94] Gurney's memory lets nothing slip: his rage to remember is, *inter alia*, an attempt to ward off the ravages of oblivion—both his own and that of events and places. In 'Robecq—A Memory', it is only through his conscious recollection that the town survives: 'Robecq that's swept away now, so men tell | Is but the faintest hint of what once was well'.[95] Gurney's memory preserves more than that faintest

[90] Gurney to Marion Scott, 18 May 1917, in *Collected Letters*, 261–2.
[91] Gurney to Marion Scott, 8 Aug. 1917, ibid. 297.
[92] Gurney, *Best Poems and The Book of Five Makings*, 94.
[93] Gurney, *Rewards of Wonder*, 54.
[94] Gurney, 'Buysscheure', ibid. 80.   [95] Ibid. 91.

past as it resists more recent destructions. Yet resistance ends in defeat: Gurney reports dolefully in 'I Would Not Rest', one of his last poems, 'Ashes my reward at end'.[96] War's embers have finally been extinguished; after 1925 Gurney stops writing about war as suddenly as he had (re-)started in 1922. The poems continue for four more years, but they are, as Kavanagh bluntly puts it, 'bloodless': 'It is as though the long struggle to remember, to live sanely, to celebrate his comrades, his native place, himself, went up in one quick flash, scattered, and that was the end.'[97] 'The Wind', written in early 1929 and possibly Gurney's final poem, records his lapse into blankness:

> All night the fierce wind blew,
> All night I knew
> Time, like a dark wind, blowing
> All days, all lives, all memories
> Down empty endless skies—
>
> A blind wind, strowing
> Blind leaves of life's torn tree
> Through blank eternity:
> Dreadfully swift. Time blew.
> All night I knew
> The outrush of its going.
>
> At dawn a thin rain wept.
> Worn out, I slept
> And woke to a fair morning.
> My days were amply long, and I content
> In their accomplishment—
> Lost the wind's warning.[98]

'The Wind' is a last farewell from the far shore of forgetfulness. The concluding stanza seems to promise rebirth into a 'fair morning', but the rain's grief hints at the scale of the loss. For all its attention to waking, the poem records a defeat in the battle to stop memory,

---

[96] Gurney, *Collected Poems*, 298.   [97] Kavanagh, 'Introduction', p. xxxv.
[98] Gurney, *Collected Poems*, 317.

however painful it may have been, from sliding content down to drugged sleep. Peace may bring contented oblivion, but the price of that contentment is Gurney's art. As memories are let go, so at last is poetry.

6

W. H. Auden's Journeys to War

Much of W. H. Auden's poetry of the late 1930s is defined by journeys to and from war. Although his decision to stay in New York after the outbreak of the Second World War attracted imputations of cowardice and betrayal, until then Auden had actively sought war zones. Civil war in Spain and the Sino–Japanese War had provided opportunities to witness what he perceived as the early skirmishes in a global struggle against fascism: '[I]n a crucial period such as ours,' he wrote shortly before setting off for Spain, 'I do believe that the poet must have direct knowledge of the major political events.'[1] That belief, he freely admitted, was a result of his having been 'seduced' by the example of Wilfred Owen.[2] Only in the crucible of war would Auden find the necessary testing-ground for a poetry burdened from the start by the knowledge that it was written *entre deux guerres*. 'Still I drink your health before | The gun-butt raps upon the door,'[3] Louis MacNeice addresses Auden at the end of their *Letters from Iceland*. The sentiment is so clearly identifiable as Audenesque that it lends itself to satire: William Empson's 'Just a Smack at Auden' opens and closes with the jolly fatalism of 'Waiting for the end, boys, waiting for the end'.[4] Listening for the rap of the gun-butt, waiting

---

[1] W. H. Auden, quoted in Humphrey Carpenter, *W. H. Auden: A Biography* (London: HarperCollins, 1981), 207.

[2] Auden, quoted in Richard Davenport-Hines, *Auden* (London: Heinemann, 1995), 163.

[3] Auden, 'Epilogue', in W. H. Auden and Louis MacNeice, *Letters from Iceland* (London: Faber, 1937), 261.

[4] William Empson, *The Complete Poems*, ed. John Haffenden (Harmondsworth: Penguin, 2000), 81–2.

for the end, Auden is ready and eager to answer the calls from Spain and China.

Each of Auden's wars (including the Great War, which ended when he was 11) profoundly affected his poetry. But his treatment of them eschews specifics: the world, Auden argued in 1939, 'has no localized events', and all people 'In all their living are profoundly implicated'.[5] 'Spain', later re-titled 'Spain 1937', puts the matter more melodramatically, with the voice of life stating that ' "I am your choice, your decision: yes, I am Spain" '.[6] Every war, no matter how distant, is everyone's war. This involvement could lead to an egotistical appropriation, heard in Christopher Isherwood's gratitude (before he and Auden left for the Sino-Japanese War) that China, unlike Spain, would not be 'crowded with star literary observers', and in Auden's boyish hope that 'We'll have a war all of our very own'.[7] But Auden's poetry understands the dangers of becoming a tourist in other people's griefs. Informed by localized events, it expresses them in an abstract language which does not limit the applicability of the lessons learnt. His Spanish Civil War poem, 'Spain 1937', plays off the title's stipulations of time and place against a broad perspective which erodes their significance. The poem in its final form mentions Spain once, and describes its geography in just one stanza out of twenty-three, as it ranges over 'Yesterday', 'To-day', and 'To-morrow'. Rather than being the pivotal moment in history, 'To-day' is a 'struggle' striving to bring about a future characterized as bland and faintly absurd: 'To-morrow the enlarging of consciousness by diet and breathing'. To a poet who could mock W. B. Yeats's supernatural world as 'Southern Californian',[8] that kind of consciousness seems better left unenlarged. The voice of life in the poem refers to the possibility of building 'the Just City',

---

[5] Auden, 'Commentary', in W. H. Auden and Christopher Isherwood, *Journey to a War* (London: Faber, 1939), 292.

[6] *The English Auden: Poems, Essays and Dramatic Writings 1927–1939*, ed. Edward Mendelson (London: Faber, 1977), 211.

[7] Auden, quoted in Carpenter, *W. H. Auden*, 225.

[8] Auden, quoted in Lucy McDiarmid, *Saving Civilization: Yeats, Eliot, and Auden between the Wars* (Cambridge: Cambridge University Press, 1984), p. xiii.

but in practice the struggle is foolishly aspirational: even the victors (whomever, from the uncertain perspective of 1937, they may yet turn out to be) are likely to discover that the promise of tomorrow disappoints.

Only 'Spain 1937' and the unusually spiritless prose report, 'Impressions of Valencia' ('The pigeons fly about the square in brilliant sunshine, warm as a fine English May'9), offer explicit evidence of the 'direct knowledge' sought by Auden. Put crudely, this may seem like a meagre artistic return on so much experience, but the Spanish Civil War is important for Auden's art because it teaches him that there is a kind of poetry he should not write. 'Spain 1937' musters so little political enthusiasm that a modern reader untutored in the poem's contexts would find it hard to deduce the colour of its sympathies. In the 1960s Auden would denounce the earlier version, 'Spain', as 'trash' which he was 'ashamed to have written'.10 (He also dropped 'Spain 1937' from his *Collected Poems*.) His shame has chiefly to do with the poet's weakness for apothegms. Never one to forgive the achievements of his younger self, Auden came to misinterpret his poem's conclusion, 'History to the defeated | May say Alas but cannot help or pardon', as a 'wicked doctrine' which equated 'goodness with success'.11 Still more controversial was a stanza quickly revised after publication:

> To-day the deliberate increase in the chances of death,
> The conscious acceptance of guilt in the necessary murder;
>   To-day the expending of powers
> On the flat ephemeral pamphlet and the boring meeting.12

Critics disagree over whether Auden would have read George Orwell's famous assault—'It could only be written by a person to whom

    9 Auden, *Prose and Travel Books in Prose and Verse*, i: *1926–1938*, ed. Edward Mendelson (Princeton: Princeton University Press, 1996), 383.
    10 Auden, quoted by Robin Skelton in *Poetry of the Thirties*, ed. Robin Skelton (Harmondsworth: Penguin, 1964), 41.
    11 Auden, 'Foreword', in *Collected Shorter Poems* (London: Faber, 1966), 15.
    12 Auden, 'Spain', in Skelton (ed.), *Poetry of the Thirties*, 136.

murder is at most a *word*'[13]—before he removed 'necessary murder' in revision. These debates hint at what is most significant about the poem: not quite Marvellian in the balancing of commitments, it none the less enacts a crisis in Auden's political confidence. Killing in war may be 'necessary', but even for the most apparently noble of causes it is still branded as 'murder'. That is why Orwell's criticism seems especially unjust: 'The Hitlers and the Stalins find murder necessary,' Orwell points out, 'but they don't speak of it as murder.'[14] Auden *does* acknowledge and weigh up the moral cost—he knows what murder is, and he refuses to disguise it with euphemisms. There is a bluntness about 'necessary murder' which makes its circumspect revision to 'The conscious acceptance of guilt in the fact of murder' seem regrettably evasive. Murder is a price which must be paid, the original version asserts, even if only to arrive at an untroubled society of breathing techniques, of walks by the lake, of 'exchanging of tips on the breeding of terriers'. Banal liberty is better than oppression. Tellingly, Auden revises the terrier-breeders out of the poem along with references to 'Madrid' and 'a people's army', and those changes work with the new impersonality of 'the fact of murder' to conceal doubts and costs which had formerly been confronted. The final version takes a small step back from courageous complication to blind conviction.

'I did not wish to talk about Spain when I returned [to England],' Auden would recall decades after the event, 'because I was upset by many things I saw or heard about.'[15] Prominent among those 'things' was the 'treatment of priests'—a coy allusion to a violent anticlericalism which led to the summary execution of several priests and the burning of almost all the churches in Barcelona by Republican sympathizers. Disillusioned by what he saw as the corruption and growing cruelty of Spanish Republicanism, Auden chose to fall silent,

---

[13] George Orwell, *Inside the Whale* (London: Victor Gollancz, 1940), 169.

[14] Ibid. 170.

[15] Auden, quoted by George Mills Harper, ' "Necessary Murder": The Auden Circle and the Spanish Civil War', in Vereen Bell and Laurence Lerner (eds.), *On Modern Poetry: Essays Presented to Donald Davie* (Nashville: Vanderbilt University Press, 1988), 68.

later explaining that 'It is always a moral problem when to speak. To speak at the wrong time may do great harm … If the Republic had been victorious, then there would have been reason to speak out about what was wrong with it.'[16] Auden cannot help or condemn the defeated; but that taciturnity makes his achievement something less than the war poetry he seeks to emulate, because it opts to preserve his political fidelities at the cost of experience. The defence that 'Any disillusionment of mine could only be of advantage to Franco'[17] conveniently ignores his often-voiced belief during the late 1930s that poetry makes nothing happen. The deadly contrast is with André Gide, who in 1937 had been fiercely attacked at a Writers' Conference in Madrid for having undermined communism by criticizing Stalin's regime. When Stephen Spender disapprovingly reported the delegates' behaviour, Auden agreed that 'Exigence is never an excuse for not telling the truth'.[18] Spain would help him articulate his poetic task 'to warn of excesses and crimes against humanity whoever commits them';[19] but practice proved more difficult than theory. By Auden's standard, his own suppressing silence was a moral failure, vulnerable to accusations of having put 'exigence' first.

That failure arises out of confused motives. Caught between the rival claims of the reporter and the partisan, Auden's imagination is paralysed when observations collide with preconceptions. His tinkering with the text and the title of 'Spain' suggests a continuing annoyance which will grow, thirty years later, into outspoken rejection. Auden can neither leave the poem behind nor make it right; it lives with him as a permanent rebuke. The Spanish Civil War also has a more subtle influence on his poetry, because his shock at the violent anti-Catholic sentiment in Barcelona awakens

---

[16] Auden, quoted in Edward Mendelson, *Early Auden* (London: Faber, 1981), 196.
[17] Ibid.
[18] Auden, quoted in Stephen Spender, *The Thirties and After: Poetry, Politics, People (1933–75)* (London: Macmillan, 1978), 31.
[19] Auden, quoted in John Fuller, *W. H. Auden: A Commentary* (London: Faber, 1998), 292.

a religious sensibility which will gradually oust politics from his later poetry: 'I could not escape acknowledging that, however I had consciously ignored and rejected the Church for sixteen years, the existence of churches and what went on in them had all the time been very important to me.'[20] But as a war poet, Auden remained dissatisfied by his experiences in Spain; and it is a measure of that dissatisfaction that within a year he should travel as far as China for what Humphrey Carpenter has called 'a second chance'.[21] Having been commissioned to write a travel book about an Asian country, Auden and Isherwood found that the outbreak of war between China and Japan, in July 1937, had made the decision for them. The war superficially replayed some of the political divisions of the Spanish Civil War, as an uneasy left-wing alliance fought to resist a fascist aggressor: 'Here [in China] danger works a civil reconciliation,' Auden wrote rather optimistically, and 'Interior hatreds are resolved upon this foreign foe.'[22] Despite his championing of the Chinese cause, Auden allowed himself a more observational role. He may have argued that everyone was implicated, but the fact that he and Isherwood had a war 'all of [their] very own' suggested that distance brought detachment. (In fact, they were not alone: while William Empson could not 'pretend all these passions about backing freedom against fascism',[23] he had stayed at his teaching job in China after the outbreak of war, at considerable risk to his safety.) Unburdened by expectations, this time Auden had no thought of becoming a soldier, driving an ambulance, or broadcasting propaganda. Any hope of emulating Owen had been banished: Auden now argued that 'there is only one field in which the poet is a man of action, the field of language'.[24]

Echoing the sentiment of the century's best soldier-poets, Empson wrote from China that it is not 'shameful to aver | A vague desire

---

[20] Auden, quoted in Carpenter, *W. H. Auden*, 210.   [21] Ibid. 225.

[22] Auden, 'Commentary', in *Journey to a War*, 290.

[23] Empson, quoted in John Haffenden, *William Empson*, i: *Among the Mandarins* (Oxford: Oxford University Press, 2005), 502.

[24] Auden, 'The Public v. the Late Mr. William Butler Yeats', in *English Auden*, 393.

to be about | Where the important things occur'.[25] Auden and Isherwood pursued that same 'vague desire', and having arrived at what they hoped would be the centre of the war, Isherwood recorded their sense of satisfaction: 'Today Auden and I agreed that we would rather be in Hankow at this moment than anywhere else on earth.'[26] Yet Auden and Isherwood were victims of circumstance, comically unable to find the war that was being fought all around them. Their disclaimer in the 'Foreword' to their collaborative project, *Journey to a War*, does not inspire confidence that the book will reveal any Owenite truths:

This was our first journey to any place east of Suez. We spoke no Chinese, and possessed no special knowledge of Far Eastern affairs. It is hardly necessary, therefore, to point out that we cannot vouch for the accuracy of many statements made in this book. Some of our informants may have been unreliable, some merely polite, some deliberately pulling our leg.[27]

The tone of self-deprecation reflects crucial differences between the wars in Spain and China. Spain required clear moral and political commitments. Yeats may have asked how he could possibly fix his attention on 'Roman or on Russian | Or on Spanish politics' while being distracted by a pretty girl,[28] but that was a calculated insult to the all-too-serious preoccupations—as well as, perhaps, the prevailing sexuality—of the new intelligentsia. (Auden and his generation, Yeats had already concluded, were 'not worth the blade of grass God gives for the linnet'.[29]) Even after realizing that he had been misinformed about the nature of the struggle in Spain, Auden knew that too much was at stake for nonchalant talk of legs having been pulled. But in China, he and Isherwood were able to remain disengaged, consciously presenting themselves as 'lunatic English

---

[25] Empson, 'Autumn on Nan-Yüeh', in *Complete Poems*, 97.

[26] Isherwood, in *Journey to a War*, 49.

[27] Auden and Isherwood, *Journey to a War*, 13.

[28] Yeats, 'Politics', in *Yeats's Poems*, ed. A. Norman Jeffares (Basingstoke: Macmillan, 1989), 472.

[29] Yeats, 'A General Introduction for my Work', in *Essays and Introductions* (London: Macmillan, 1961), 526.

explorers'.[30] Auden would later recall that 'Spain was a culture one knew. One could understand what was happening, what things meant. But China was impossible to know.'[31] That impossibility might have been expected to bring freedom from obligation, but Auden's contribution to *Journey to a War* is surprisingly earnest. Where Isherwood portrays himself as alternately confused, amused, scared, and entertained by events which often border on the farcical, Auden shuns the contingencies of his experience in favour of a panoramic poetry.

'Auden should not be blamed for drawing what he sees into a wider world view,' Tim Youngs has argued.[32] However, the relationship of 'what he sees' to the 'wider world view', and the relative significance he assigns to each, are complex matters which may indeed warrant blame. Auden's view can become so wide as to blur important details, not least in a pontificating tendency to present his own beliefs as general truths. ('It is always silly to generalize,'[33] he self-defeatingly announces.) The biggest annoyance in his poetry of the late 1930s is its weakness for the first person plural: 'We | Wish international evil'; 'You were silly like us'; 'The windiest militant trash | Important Persons shout | Is not so crude as our wish'.[34] Auden likes to speak windily for at least a generation, if not for humankind, and shuts out dissenting voices which might object to his coercion. Isherwood's prose account in *Journey to a War*, full of the vagaries and oddities of his and Auden's experiences, sits curiously alongside a poetry which avoids the lyric 'I' altogether. The pronoun appears rarely, and then only as part of a quotation of other authors; and, as in 'Spain 1937', Auden always hides amidst a collective 'we' to present his own beliefs and fears. The war of *Journey to a War* is, for Auden, a generic war; he would later publish its sonnet sequence separately as 'Sonnets

---

[30] Isherwood, in *Journey to a War*, 104.

[31] Auden, quoted in Carpenter, *W. H. Auden*, 239.

[32] Tim Youngs, 'Auden's Travel Writings', in Stan Smith (ed.), *The Cambridge Companion to W. H. Auden* (Cambridge: Cambridge University Press, 2004), 79.

[33] 'W. H. Auden Speaks of Poetry and Total War', in *Prose*, ii: *1939–1948*, ed. Edward Mendelson (Princeton: Princeton University Press, 2002), 153.

[34] *English Auden*, 249, 242, 246.

from China', but the original title, 'In Time of War', stays truer to his universalizing impulse. ('Sonnets from China' is also a misnomer because all but one of the poems were written after Auden's return to England, and few make specific reference to the Sino–Japanese War.) This tendency towards authoritative pronouncements is both the strength and the limitation of the sequence. Shorn of local detail, the sonnets can seem more vacuous than vatic, and Auden might have wondered, as he wondered of his accompanying verse commentary, whether they were the work of a 'prosy pompous old bore'.[35] Yet at their most effective, their distant bird's-eye view befits a modern technological warfare which is itself long-distance and impersonal: 'A telephone is speaking to a man'.[36] One of Auden's most brilliant early poems had opened by asking the reader to 'Consider this and in our time | As the hawk sees it or the helmeted airman'.[37] Now that 'our time' has become a 'time of war', Auden in sonnet XV portrays that transcendent perspective as dehumanizing, with the airmen seeing 'The breathing city as a target which ‖ Requires their skill'.[38] Auden's own 'skill' lies in embodying, but knowing the moral dangers of, the airman's view which his poem professes to loathe but to which he himself is always drawn.

After its foreword and dedicatory sonnet, *Journey to a War* opens with six poems by Auden which explore the metaphysics of journeying ('The Voyage', 'The Ship', 'The Traveller') and some of the notable staging-posts on the way to China ('The Sphinx', 'Macao', 'Hongkong'). Separated from these poems by the whole of Isherwood's prose account and by his own photographic record, Auden's sonnet sequence 'In Time of War' charts a more historical (and, for that matter, prehistorical) journey. 'Spain 1937' had begun with a 'Yesterday' of 'all the past'—the spreading of commerce, 'the diffusion | Of the counting-frame and the cromlech', the building of cathedrals—leading as if inexorably to the struggle of 'To-day'. 'In

[35] Auden, quoted in Fuller, *W. H. Auden*, 244.
[36] Auden, 'In Time of War', in *Journey to a War*, 274.
[37] Auden, 'XXX', in *English Auden*, 46.   [38] Auden, in *Journey to a War*, 273.

Time of War' casts back even further, finding the source of war in a creation myth, before exploring in unhurried fashion such subjects as the loss of Eden, the acquiring of language, the beginnings of agriculture, and the secularization of the Church. Not until the fourteenth sonnet (halfway through the sequence of twenty-seven) does Auden produce anything that might recognizably be classed as a war poem, when he arrives at a future which is suddenly and painfully present in 'Yes, we are going to suffer, now'.[39] This must raise concerns over coherence: the first thirteen sonnets do not obviously belong to a sequence titled 'In Time of War', except in the loose sense that several presage war by locating the seeds of conflict in the human psyche. 'War,' Auden would write in 1942, 'is an overt eruption of tensions and malaises which have long been present, and to which the poet has, or should have, long been sensitive.'[40] So sonnet XII registers the dying out of the legendary world of kobolds and dragons, and the people's mistaken belief that they are now 'safe' in a more rational world:

> Only the sculptors and the poets were half sad,
> And the pert retinue from the magician's house
> Grumbled and went elsewhere. The vanquished powers were glad
>
> To be invisible and free: without remorse
> Struck down the sons who strayed into their course,
> And ravished the daughters, and drove the fathers mad.[41]

This is not Auden at his most accomplished. The rhyme 'sad/glad' sounds as uninspired as Hardy's 'sadly/gladly' (in 'At the War Office, London'[42]), even allowing for the additional rhyme of 'mad'; and 'course' is chosen only for the rhyme with 'remorse' and (awkwardly) 'house', when 'strayed into their *path*' would be more natural. Several sonnets are blighted by similar infelicities of rhyme and rhythm, which Auden makes ingenious efforts to rectify in later

---

[39] Ibid. 272.   [40] 'W. H. Auden Speaks of Poetry and Total War', 152.
[41] Auden, in *Journey to a War*, 270.
[42] Thomas Hardy, *The Complete Poems*, ed. James Gibson (Basingstoke: Palgrave, 2001), 89.

editions. For this and other reasons, Edward Mendelson's claim that 'In Time of War' is 'Auden's most profound and audacious poem of the 1930s, perhaps the greatest English poem of the decade'[43] seems eccentric: the contention that Auden wrote the decade's most important poetry may be defensible, but the first half of the sequence falls substantially short of his best work. Only in the second half, when Auden turns his attention not just to how but to where 'we' have arrived, and where 'we' might go from here, does Mendelson's enthusiasm begin to look explicable.

It is a relief to arrive at the immediacy of sonnet XIV, and the timely reminder provided by 'Yes, we are going to suffer, now' that Auden is the great poet of opening lines. That sonnet is also noteworthy for a new, religious kind of moral vocabulary in Auden's work. 'It is time for the destruction of error,'[44] he had written, scarily, in 1929. Whereas error can encompass sin, *faux pas*, oversight, and mistake, Auden's poetry of the Sino–Japanese War for the first time resorts to a less ambiguous condemnation. The 'Commentary' dismisses those who 'have accepted *Pascal*'s wager and resolve | To take whatever happens as the will of God, | Or with *Spinoza* vote that evil be unreal'.[45] The younger Auden, flirting with Marxism albeit never quite a card-carrier, might have been amongst those who considered evil to be unreal, but by the late 1930s his experiences in Spain and China had changed his mind. Sonnet XIV of 'In Time of War' associates evil with human nature:

> Behind each sociable home-loving eye
> The private massacres are taking place;
> All Women, Jews, the Rich, the Human Race.
>
> The mountains cannot judge us when we lie:
> We dwell upon the earth; the earth obeys
> The intelligent and evil till they die.[46]

In the final line, Auden risks an extraordinary zeugma—'The intelligent and evil'—without clarifying the nature and extent of the

---

[43] Mendelson, *Early Auden*, 348.   [44] Auden, in *English Auden*, 40.
[45] Auden, in *Journey to a War*, 297.   [46] Ibid. 272.

relationship between those groups. Genocide, he has already averred, is carried out in the minds of each of us, as a 'private' mental process unique to humankind. (All other creatures, the first sonnet noted, 'knew their station and were good for ever'.[47]) Intelligence leads to evil, allowing us to 'lie' and to conduct our concealed 'massacres'. The switch from 'we' to 'they' does not extricate the poet or anyone else: 'they' are all of human—as opposed to animal—life.

'In Time of War' and the poems written immediately after name 'evil' with striking regularity. 'Evil is always personal and spectacular,'[48] Auden notes in his 'Commentary', and almost immediately retracts half that assertion in 'Herman Melville' from March 1939: 'Evil is unspectacular and always human.'[49] The best-known usage occurs in 'September 1, 1939', where 'error' returns but not at the expense of evil: 'I and the public know | What all schoolchildren learn, | Those to whom evil is done | Do evil in return.'[50] That belief in the reciprocity of evil is already expressed in sonnet XIV, as 'the sky | Throbs like a feverish forehead' and 'pain' is visited (in the form of an air-raid) on the cruel fantasists below;[51] and it is expressed, too, in the dedicatory poem for E. M. Forster, in which 'we | Wish international evil'.[52] The problem, Spain leads Auden to believe, is integral to human nature. It is not a political but a moral (and potentially religious) problem when fundamental evil starts to spring up on opposite sides of the world; as sonnet XVI insists, 'maps can really point to places | Where life is evil now: | Nanking; Dachau'.[53] Evil can be geographically pinpointed, 'now', in the present; it is a current way of 'life' for its perpetrators and their victims. The sequence has already alleged that evil is everywhere, and that we all commit atrocities behind 'each sociable home-loving eye'. The only difference at Nanking and Dachau is that it has become externalized and politicized as fascism. The abrupt four-syllable line stresses those locations, though it may also draw

---

[47] Ibid. 259.   [48] Ibid. 298.
[49] Auden, *Collected Poems*, ed. Edward Mendelson (London: Faber, 1976), 251.
[50] Auden, in *English Auden*, 245.   [51] Auden, in *Journey to a War*, 272.
[52] Ibid. 11.   [53] Ibid. 274.

breathing space from the fact that evil has not yet spread to fill a line of pentameter.

Apart from a passing mention of the 'Eighteen Provinces' in sonnet XIII, Auden's allusion to the Rape of Nanking at the end of sonnet XVI is the first time the sequence explicitly refers to China; and even there, it is balanced against a reference to a concentration camp in Nazi Germany. Auden makes the same comparison in his 'Commentary', while adding Italy as a third home for the violent and murderous who tempt with the 'brazen offer' of certainty:

> Now in that Catholic country with the shape of Cornwall,
> Where Europe first became a term of pride,
>
> North of the Alps where dark hair turns to blonde,
> In Germany now loudest, land without a centre
> Where the sad plains are like a sounding rostrum,
>
> And on these tidy and volcanic summits near us now,
> From which the Black Stream hides the Tuscarora Deep,
> The voice is quieter but the more inhuman and triumphant.[54]

The passage sounds like a despatch from the front, locally involved and globally knowledgeable. In fact, Auden wrote the 'Commentary' in Birmingham, many thousands of miles from the Tuscarora Deep off the coast of Japan. Having seen fascism at first hand, he is entitled to feel the continuing proximity and threat of his enemy. Less excusable is his failure to notice—as Gide had at least glimpsed—the millions of victims of Stalin's Terror. In Yeats's terms, Auden selectively fixes his attention on Roman and on Spanish but not on Russian politics. He would later rue his omitting of the Russian régime from the 'enemies of life':[55]

our great error was not a false admiration for Russia but a snobbish feeling that nothing which happened in a semi-barbarous country which had experienced neither the Renaissance nor the Enlightenment could be of any importance: had any of the countries we knew personally, like France, Germany or Italy, the language of which we could speak and where we

---

[54] Auden, in *Journey to a War*, 295.   [55] Ibid. 298.

had personal friends, been one to have a successful communist revolution with the same phenomena of terror, purges, censorship etc, we would have screamed our heads off.[56]

Auden is kind to call this an 'error', when he might have chosen a more severe label. And even his self-flagellating honesty may be partly disingenuous: if a genocide on that scale, even in what was perceived as a 'semi-barbarous country', had been carried out by fascists rather than communists, it is unlikely to have been met with silence. China may also qualify, by these 'snobbish' standards, as 'semi-barbarous'. Auden's uncomprehending distance from its culture and customs ensures that he screams his head off primarily because he wants Japanese atrocities in China to rouse Europe from its appeasing slumber. Remembering his Great War predecessors, he argues that art 'makes us more difficult to deceive';[57] and 'Commentary', by reporting events from the Far East, is his most determined attempt to help readers become less deceived by the tempting lies and the 'humbugs full of vain dexterity' who are 'our leaders'.[58] The terrifying example of China, Auden stresses in a call to arms, shows what will happen if we lack the 'courage to confront our enemies'.[59]

That is why Auden's poems most closely connected with the Sino–Japanese War present the conflict as one in which the West is directly involved. What Auden called his 'Sassoon sonnet',[60] XVIII, commemorates the sacrifice of a Chinese soldier, who 'turned to dust in China that our daughters || Be fit to love the earth'.[61] *Our* daughters will not be raped—'Disgraced before the dogs'—thanks to an otherwise unexceptional man from the other side of the world, of whose war we may know almost nothing. And while the battle is being fought on our behalf, and with so much resting on its outcome, Auden describes a popular culture in sonnet XXII which is oblivious

[56] Auden, quoted in Davenport-Hines, *Auden*, 157. I am grateful to Nick Cohen for drawing my attention to this passage.

[57] Auden, quoted in Mendelson, *Early Auden*, 350.

[58] Auden, in *Journey to a War*, 297.   [59] Ibid. 298.

[60] Auden, quoted in Fuller, *W. H. Auden*, 239.

[61] Auden, in *Journey to a War*, 276.

not only to events in China but, dismayingly, in Spain and Austria as well:

> Think in this year what pleased the dancers best:
> When Austria died and China was forsaken,
> Shanghai in flames and Teruel retaken,
>
> France put her case before the world; 'Partout
> Il y a de la joie.' America addressed
> The earth: 'Do you love me as I love you?'[62]

The references in the final tercet are to songs by Charles Trenet and Cole Porter. They are weighed against the cataclysms of the previous tercet—which reports the invasion of Austria by Hitler, the destruction of Shanghai by the Japanese, the paucity of foreign support for China, and the fall of Teruel to Franco—as if equivalent. The poem criticizes whole nations for this state of affairs: it is France which 'put[s] her case before the world', and America which 'addresse[s] | The earth', each pursuing an isolationist policy which celebrates the very things that fascist expansionism will destroy. Auden also answers the nonchalance of Yeats—a poet whose later work is greatly preoccupied with 'what pleased the dancers best'—by implying that if he does value 'that girl standing there', he had better fix his attention urgently on 'wars and war's alarms'.[63] We are all implicated, but Auden despairs that only he seems to have noticed.

'If artists during the last ten years turned themselves into journalists and committeemen for the Spanish or Chinese cause,' Auden would muse in 1942, 'it was because, however inefficient they might be, they saw that the fate of every individual was involved in all these causes at a time when the politicians, the public, the efficient men of action, were still indifferent.'[64] Those 'artists' are of course one artist: Auden himself. He had already diagnosed the problem of indifference, albeit on an individual rather than an international level, in sonnet XVII, which establishes the impossibility of imagining

[62] Auden, in *Journey to a War*, 280.   [63] Yeats, 'Politics', 472.
[64] 'W. H. Auden Speaks of Poetry and Total War', 152.

another's pain. Visiting a military hospital at Shang-kui, Auden and Isherwood had been 'upset' at the appalling conditions they found there.[65] However, Isherwood's two paragraphs of description in no way prepare for Auden's honest account of the limits of sympathy. Those who suffer are 'remote as plants',[66] Auden admits, drawing attention not only to their unrelated distance from the healthy but also to their perceived loss of human qualities: they are vegetable and apart. Neither remembered nor imagined, suffering can only exist in the experience of it:

> For who when healthy can become a foot?
> Even a scratch we can't recall when cured,
> But are boist'rous in a moment and believe
>
> In the common world of the uninjured, and cannot
> Imagine isolation. Only happiness is shared,
> And anger, and the idea of love.

The idea of love, not love itself. Humans are only capable of sharing an idea of the ideal, along with the most instinctive of emotions: happiness and anger. Small wonder that popular songs, as sonnet XXII argues, 'employ | The elementary language of the heart'[67] and ignore the complexities of international suffering. Consequently, Auden must make his appeal to selfish motives. 'We are compelled to realize that our refuge is a sham,' he maintains in 'Commentary'.[68] Few in the West may care about dead Chinese soldiers, but only by stopping the dance and starting to resist fascism — individually and internationally — can we avoid the same fate.

The final sonnets of the sequence vacillate between hope and resignation. Sonnet XXV, set in Shanghai under Japanese occupation, notes that only the brass bands 'foretell | Some future reign of happiness and peace'.[69] That slightly offhand imprecision cannot quite believe in a happy and peaceful future. The brass bands are Auden's version of Hardy's darkling thrush, proclaiming some

---

[65] Auden, in *Journey to a War*, 94.   [66] Ibid. 275.   [67] Ibid. 280.
[68] Ibid. 291.   [69] Ibid. 283.

blessed hope whatever the evidence to the contrary. However, despite his earlier cynicism, Auden in sonnet XXVI finds grounds for optimism in the 'little workshop of love'[70]—out of which comes a product capable of showing, even in times of disaster, 'a steady profit'. Finally, in sonnet XXVII, Auden portrays humanity as yearning for an unattainable golden age. 'But we are articled to error,'[71] he writes severely, preparing for the elaboration of 'September 1, 1939':

> the error bred in the bone
> Of each woman and each man
> Craves what it cannot have,
> Not universal love
> But to be loved alone.[72]

A selfish private love which can never be attained is preferred erroneously to 'universal love'—hence the potency of cheap music even while China, Austria, and Spain fall. No longer does 'In Time of War' make mention of imagined genocides: to be 'articled to error' is to be self-deceived, rather than evil. Mendelson comments that 'the hope for change persists faintly in the word *articled*: one is articled to apprenticeship, but for a fixed and finite term'.[73] That seems to be an unsupported hope. The journey to war ends with humanity 'Wandering lost upon the mountains of our choice', not so much free to fall as obliged to roam without direction: 'We live in freedom by necessity'. Lost in the demanding landscape of our own freedom, we are responsible for our situation but by nature incapable of saving ourselves from it.

In later years Auden dropped his 'Commentary' from the *Collected Poems* and spoke disparagingly of it as 'too New Deal'.[74] Post-war American Auden's opinions of pre-war English Auden are notoriously unreliable, and only by pretending that the call to intervene against fascism is in some enigmatic way akin to Roosevelt's interventionist economic policy can the phrase seem justified. There are more

---

[70] Auden, in *Journey to a War*, 284.   [71] Ibid. 285.
[72] *English Auden*, 246.   [73] Mendelson, *Early Auden*, 200.
[74] Auden, quoted in ibid. 200.

persuasive reasons for criticizing 'Commentary', which follows its title too closely as it explicates and expands on the themes of 'In Time of War'. Only in the final lines, when Auden overhears 'the voice of Man' as he had overheard in Spain the voice of life, does the poem exceed its brief, by proposing the wisdom that *'It's better to be sane than mad'* and *'It's better to sleep two than single'*.[75] But these are desperately impoverished observations. Like 'Spain 1937', 'Commentary' is successful in articulating only what it is fighting against; attempting a positive vision for the future, it soon descends into triteness. Auden the war poet is a Christian in the making, or at least in the searching. He requires a belief system which gives ultimate meaning to the struggle and the pain, and none of his poems from the late 1930s can deliver that meaning. The consummation would not come until 'Memorial for the City', written after Auden had travelled to unreconstructed Germany at the end of the Second World War to interview civilians for the US Strategic Bombing Survey. While it opens in what looks like familiar territory—'On the right a village is burning, in a market-town to the left | The soldiers fire, the mayor bursts into tears, | The captives are led away'[76]—the poem soon enters strange land. 'We are not to despair,' its first section ends, before Auden takes the reader on a journey across the history of Christendom and through the weakness of the flesh to a final image of resurrection: 'As for Metropolis, that too-great city ... I shall rise again to hear her judged.' Nothing in the poems of Spain and China could have sounded remotely like that. Yet hindsight allows Auden's modern readers to appreciate the logic of what few could have foreseen: that the 'Just City' of 'Spain 1937' would be attainable, if at all, only as the City of God. Even so, the most memorably prophetic lines in 'Memorial for a City' offer no religious consolation: 'our past is a chaos of graves,' Auden acknowledges, 'and the barbed-wire stretches ahead | Into our future till it is lost to sight.'

---

[75] Auden, in *Journey to a War*, 300; italics original.
[76] Auden, *Collected Poems*, 592.

7

Sky-Conscious: Poetry of the Blitz

> The sky is darkening like a stain,
> Something is going to fall like rain
>   and it won't be flowers.
>
> Auden, 'The Witnesses'

Auden's 'The Witnesses', written during late 1932, looks skywards for presentiments of danger.[1] There is ample cause: the assumption of security under an English heaven had been destroyed during the Great War by air raids which killed more than 1,000 civilians and caused widespread panic among the population. As Edward Thomas told his friend Robert Frost in 1915, 'All the talk now is of Zeppelin's [*sic*] coming to London. Everyone buys respirators against poison bombs.'[2] The American speaker of Frost's 'The Bonfire', written the following year, uses aerial attack as a bogeyman to scare children who think that war is only for men:

> 'Haven't you heard, though,
> About the ships where war has found them out
> At sea, about the towns where war has come
> Through opening clouds at night with droning speed
> Further o'erhead than all but stars and angels,—
> And children in the ships and in the towns?'[3]

---

[1] Auden, 'The Witnesses', in *The English Auden: Poems, Essays and Dramatic Writings*, ed. Edward Mendelson (London: Faber, 1977), 130.

[2] Edward Thomas to Robert Frost, 1 June 1915, in Matthew Spencer (ed.), *Elected Friends: Robert Frost and Edward Thomas to One Another* (New York: Handsel Books, 2003), 60.

[3] Robert Frost, 'The Bonfire', in *Collected Poems, Prose, & Plays*, ed. Richard Poirier and Mark Richardson (New York: Library of America, 1995), 127.

The sense of death proved to be most in apprehension. The poison bombs never fell, and compared with the losses sustained in mainland Europe, where 58,000 British soldiers were injured or killed on the first day of the Battle of the Somme alone, the numbers of fatalities caused by German raids over England attracted relatively little attention from poets and novelists. Rudyard Kipling's famous revenge fantasy, 'Mary Postgate' (1915), stands out as one of the few Great War texts to engage meaningfully with the new threat from the air. But by the late 1930s, and with the added stimulus of Guernica's annihilation by the *Luftwaffe* in April 1937, writers had new and sufficient reason to revisit fears of aerial attack. As Mark Rawlinson notes, 'The invasion-scare literature of the pre-1914 period . . . had been supplanted between the wars by fantasies and prophecies of airborne destruction; gas and germ warfare, and high explosive.'[4] The new enemy of nightmares came out of the sky, not the sea. Nor did the world of rational discourse allay anyone's fears. One pre-war government estimate put casualties from a sixty-day raid over Britain at two million, one-third of whom would be killed.[5] An Air Raid Warden service, established in 1937 as a result of such dire warnings, recruited 200,000 volunteers in the London area within a year; and even before the outbreak of war, gas masks were distributed against the possibility of chemical attack. Something, very soon, was going to fall like rain.

A male character in one of Elizabeth Bowen's wartime stories risks the prediction that the Blitz 'will have no literature' because it 'does not connect with the rest of life'.[6] In one sense, he is already wrong before the first bomb drops. So widely awaited is the Blitz that the foreboding colours everyday activity, and colours, inevitably, the poetry of the period. British aeroplanes which 'rove through our skies', above the idyllic setting of Anne Ridler's 'Ringshall Summer', 'serve to warn | Us to expect the locust soon':[7] they are still 'our

---

[4] Mark Rawlinson, *British Writing of the Second World War* (Oxford: Clarendon Press, 2000), 69.

[5] Quoted, in ibid. 70–1.   [6] Elizabeth Bowen, quoted in ibid. 83.

[7] Anne Ridler, 'Ringshall Summer', in *Collected Poems* (Manchester: Carcanet, 1994), 42.

skies', although the possessive pronoun's insistence is provoked by the knowledge that the swarm is coming to take them from us. The bucolic sublimities of a quintessentially English countryside, enjoyed by Ridler for more than 100 lines, allow only a temporary refuge from her closing realization that 'Jerusalem is not above all wars';[8] Blake's green and pleasant land, so often saved by its island status, has never been more menaced. It is the wait, the knowing what will come but not knowing exactly when, which proves unbearable. 'Death could drop from the dark | As easily as song,'[9] Isaac Rosenberg had written as he heard the larks singing above the trenches, his joy tempered by a simultaneous acceptance of death's nearness and facility. That dual consciousness invades Ridler's poem, where appreciation of the landscape becomes all the more intense because it is perceived to be imperilled. Ridler notices how the sunshine makes 'catastrophe seem unreal',[10] but must finally concede that 'wilder and more skilful eyes | Could see it now, and in these places'.[11] Hers is a reluctant acknowledgement that the sense of looming devastation has contaminated the natural world, interfusing pleasure and fear.

Nowhere more urgently does Blitz poetry recognize that truth than in its frequent and sometimes frantic readings of the skies. Ridler describes how, early in the day, 'the air's thin silky blue | Only the finest sun lets through', and draws a contrast with 'the wide-meshed air of evening'.[12] Her image of the sky as a net harbours an anxiety over what might be let through on future occasions: the adjective 'wide-meshed' promises little in the way of effective security. When the bombers finally arrive in 'For this Time', Ridler complains of a covenant broken: 'the firmament on high, | Noah's peace-promising sky, | Is given over to an enemy'.[13] That the sky now promises war implicates God in the violence, although the poet's religious

8 Anne Ridler, *Collected Poems*, 45.
9 Isaac Rosenberg, 'Returning, we hear the larks', in *The Poems and Plays*, ed. Vivien Noakes (Oxford: Oxford University Press, 2004), 139.
10 Ridler, *Collected Poems*, 42.   11 Ibid. 45.   12 Ibid. 43.
13 Ibid. 45.

sensibility soon hurries her back to a more orthodox faith in a divine guardian: 'Where should we turn unless Lord to Thee?' A source of hope as well as danger, beauty as well as conflict, protection as well as destruction, the sky becomes the most complex image in Blitz poetry, to be fought over, refashioned, and reclaimed.

Alice Coats's 'Sky-Conscious' expresses, sometimes inadvertently, the task facing the poet of the Blitz:

> Now we are forced to contemplate the sky,
> So long before an unregarded roof—
> Now charged with such significance, the proof
> Of potencies whereby we live or die;
>
> Frescoed with searchlights, shells and flares and stars,
> Trellised with trailing fumes of alien flight,
> Lit with false dawn of fires, and all the bright
> Ferocious constellations of our wars.
>
> In these we read the portents of our end
> And turn in fear to scan the skies again,
> For dooms like those the gods were used to send
> Whose rule no longer sways their old domain—
>
> Jove's superseded thunderbolts at rest,
> Aurora and Apollo dispossessed.[14]

Rarely has a sonnet seemed so long-winded. Taking no chances, Coats says most things at least twice: 'Now we are forced to contemplate the sky' pairs with 'And turn in fear to scan the skies again'; the 'proof' (to rhyme with 'roof') of 'potencies whereby we live or die' is insufficiently differentiated from 'the portents of our end'; and the conjunctive repetition in 'Frescoed with searchlights, shells and flares and stars' is driven purely by the needs of scansion. Yet, dwelling on these and other stylistic gaucheries (the awkward internal rhymes of 'whereby/die' and 'forced/before', or the ponderous iambics of the third quatrain) would be purposeless without a recognition

---

[14] Alice Coats, 'Sky-Conscious', in Catherine Reilly (ed.), *Chaos of the Night: Women's Poetry and Verse of the Second World War* (London: Virago, 1984), 29.

that the poem is strangely instructive in some of its deficiencies. 'Frescoed with searchlights', 'Trellised with trailing fumes'—Coats's attempts at metaphor make failed connections between the bombing and what Bowen's character calls 'the rest of life'. Her final claim that the Blitz is 'like', but has 'superseded', Jove's thunderbolts is the act of an exhausted imagination, even if the image shares with Ridler's 'For this Time' and many other Blitz poems the awareness that the skies are also the heavens. Coats delineates the dilemma faced by writers who, like the soldiers of the Western Front before them, must find a language adequate to their predicament as they wrestle with the necessity of creating a new literature; but despite encapsulating changed circumstances in the simple rhyme 'sky/die', Coats lacks the resources to make a significant poetry of the Blitz.

The aerial bombardment endured by many English cities after September 1940 imposed an egalitarian warfare which, like Auden's rain, did not discriminate between civilian and military targets. Keith Douglas, viewing the home front from North Africa, might still sneer at poets back in England who had 'no experiences worth writing of', or who wrote 'very involved verses with an occasional oblique or clever reference to bombs or bullets'.[15] But that made the mistake of pursuing a now-outmoded Great War suspicion of ignorant warmongers. War was for everyone. As William Golding admitted in reference to the doodlebug attacks of 1944, 'To come home on leave from a peaceful crossing of the Atlantic and hear your wife describe how she had been chased down the High Street of a provincial town by a flying bomb was to have the whole concept of the heroic fighting man stood on its head.'[16] One effect of turning so many civilians into witnesses and potential victims was to distribute the war poet's authority across the population: introducing his anthology of Second World War poetry, Brian Gardner observes that a book 'could have

[15] Keith Douglas, 'Poets in This War', in *The Letters*, ed. Desmond Graham (Manchester: Carcanet, 2000), 351.
[16] William Golding, 'Crabbed Youth and Age', in *A Moving Target* (London: Faber, 1982), 102.

been produced on the Blitz ... alone'.[17] The firmament might not previously have been quite so unregarded as Coats maintains, but the Blitz guaranteed that no one now could be denied an interest in the battles played out above their heads. In his study of Blitz literature, Adam Piette points out: 'The apocalypse falls from the empty sky into the waiting imagination, which claims it for its own.'[18] Nevertheless, that communal 'imagination' is in reality countless individual imaginations, each of which (people's lives being equal but imaginations not) must struggle to connect and communicate with the Blitz. Of the many called to contemplate the sky, only a few succeed in making that connection and draw a persuasive artistic meaning from the arbitrary nature of what they witness. Those poets accept that the defunct mythology of Jove's thunderbolts has been long since superseded. But Coats's negative conclusion represents a defeat which they refuse to accept in their search for new myths and metaphors capable of accommodating the terrible beauty of the Blitz. Elizabeth Bowen's character senses that 'One's feelings seem to have no language for [the bombing]'.[19] It is the job of the poets to calibrate expression against these experiences. As the 'familiar compound ghost' haunting T. S. Eliot's Blitz poem, 'Little Gidding', puts it, 'last year's words belong to last year's language'.[20]

The apocalypse falls from the sky not just into awaiting imaginations but into awaiting myths, of which Babylon, Siloam, Revelation, the Inferno, and the Purgatorio provide several of the most prominent examples. But this *is* last year's language. When in a prose account Louis MacNeice depicts the sky, during a savage seven-hour raid on London, as 'an imitation of Sodom and Gomorrah',[21] his

[17] Brian Gardner, 'Introductory Note', Brian Gardner (ed.), in *The Terrible Rain: The War Poets 1939–1945* (London: Methuen, 1966), p. xxiii.

[18] Adam Piette, *Imagination at War: British Fiction and Poetry 1939–1945* (London: Papermac, 1995), 46.

[19] Quoted in Rawlinson, *British Writing of the Second World War*, 83.

[20] T. S. Eliot, 'Little Gidding', in *The Complete Poems and Plays* (London: Faber, 1969), 194.

[21] Louis MacNeice, 'The Morning after the Blitz', in *Selected Prose*, ed. Alan Heuser (Oxford: Oxford University Press, 1990), 117.

comparison draws attention to problems raised by these imaginative flights from immediacy. Metaphor might be expected to make sense of the unfamiliar by coupling it to the familiar. Instead, the Blitz sky, which many of MacNeice's readers will not have seen, is compared with something which none of MacNeice's readers will have seen. Mood music drowns out accurate description. MacNeice finds a precedent for the unprecedented only by masking the unbiblical fact of real bombs falling out of enemy aeroplanes on to real civilians. Nor does he clarify the extent of the relationship between the bombed modern capital and the ancient cities destroyed as a result of their moral abomination. Poems by Ridler and Coats worry about the possibility of divine retribution as a destructive fire rains down from the skies; and Cyril Connolly, watching the bombardment from his top-floor flat, accepts with ill-disguised anti-capitalistic glee that ' "It's a judgement on us" '.[22] In MacNeice's case, that possibility of a deserved punishment (whether divinely ordained or not) vies with a suspicion that his passing reference to Sodom and Gomorrah offers nothing more than a shorthand means of expressing the thoroughness of the urban wreckage.

By providing a ready-made vehicle for interpreting and incorporating contemporary events, myth risks depriving them of their particularity. The result can be a poetry which, rather than contemplating the sky or offering via myth an understanding of it, imposes on its chaos a safer and more comforting vision. The period's most complete artistic creation of a redeemed world neglectful of immediate circumstances is Eliot's 'Little Gidding', which finds salvation by Christianizing the Blitz. The German bomber initially appears as 'the dark dove with the flickering tongue';[23] later, the image metamorphoses into 'The dove descending' which 'breaks the air | With flame of incandescent terror'.[24] Already the dove has become more religious symbol than enemy aircraft. D. H. Lawrence, watching a Zeppelin raid on London during the Great War, had seen it 'high, high, high,

---

[22] Cyril Connolly, quoted in Piette, *Imagination at War*, 41.
[23] Eliot, 'Little Gidding', 193.   [24] Ibid. 196.

tiny, pale, as one might imagine the Holy Ghost far, far above'.[25] Eliot must contend with the added difficulty of the aeroplanes' darkness and plurality, and his tone is less playful than Lawrence's, but the metaphor remains the same. His imagery conjoins the descent of the Holy Spirit on the disciples at Pentecost ('a sound from heaven as of a rushing mighty wind . . . And there appeared unto them cloven tongues as of fire' (Acts 2: 2–3)) with its descent as a dove at Christ's baptism (Luke 3: 22). In the poem's final lines, the 'tongues of flame' are accommodated to a glorious Christian consummation, where what was divisive and dangerous will be ecstatically reconciled: 'the tongues of flame are in-folded | Into the crowned knot of fire | And the fire and the rose are one'.[26] (The image is later developed by Stephen Spender, who, following Eliot, describes himself as 'A prophet seeking tongues of flame' as he walks through burning ruins in 'Rejoice in the Abyss'.[27]) Yet, however sophisticated Eliot's transubstantiations may seem, as wicked German bomber turns almost imperceptibly into charitable Holy Spirit, and destructive conflagrations become purifying religious fires, 'Little Gidding' shares with greatly inferior poetry an inability to find metaphors appropriate to the Blitz. Seamus Heaney, normally among the more celebratory of critics, pays the poem a lethal compliment when he observes how effectively 'the beauties of the poetic heritage' keep at bay 'the actual savagery of wartime experience'.[28] Heaney is over-generous in arguing that 'one of the triumphs of the poem' is to make its religious faith seem 'provisionally tenable'. The single laboured image allowing the poem to open on to the consolations of Christianity is its description of the bomber as the 'dark dove with the flickering tongue'. If that image fails, it invalidates the poem's theological resolution. And it does fail; even apart from the difficulty over the serpentine 'flickering tongue',

[25] D. H. Lawrence, *Kangaroo* (London: Martin Secker, 1923), 242.

[26] Eliot, 'Little Gidding', 198.

[27] Stephen Spender, *Collected Poems 1928–1953* (London: Faber, 1955), 136.

[28] Seamus Heaney, 'The Impact of Translation', in *The Government of the Tongue: The 1986 T. S. Eliot Memorial Lectures and Other Critical Writings* (London: Faber, 1988), 43.

Eliot's 'dark dove' remains uncompelling. His choice of adjective solves the problem with colour, and may recall that the black dove is a symbol of widowhood in ancient Egyptian mythology. But the obstructive facts—that the bomber is mechanical and metallic, vastly bigger and heavier, has fixed wings, and drops high explosives rather than liquid siftings—squash the one tiny encouragement that both aeroplanes and doves fly. 'The flames are no longer metaphorical,' writes Herbert Read in 1941.[29] Eliot, like the many contemporaries considered in Piette's detailed account of fire imagery in Blitz writing,[30] does his best to return them to that state. 'Little Gidding' is a poem which cannot bear very much reality; it must conscript its metaphors in order to achieve a bogus deliverance.

For Eliot, suffering has a larger and spiritually beneficial purpose. 'Those who knew purgatory here shall know | Purgation hereafter,'[31] the ghost consoles in an early draft of the poem's second part. That promise of eschatological restitution seems fluent to the point of glibness, and Eliot's cutting of the phrase reflects an artistic decision to intimate rather than state so plainly. Other, explicitly religious remakings of the Blitz follow Great War predecessors by finding parallels between human suffering and that of the crucified Christ—again, with an implied hope of redemption through pain. Spender's 'Air Raid Across the Bay at Plymouth' trips off the metaphor ('Man hammers nails in Man, | High on his crucifix'[32]) without heeding the potential complication of cruciform aeroplanes 'High' in the skies. And Edith Sitwell, by way of Marlowe's Faustus, sees Christ's blood (and not German bombers) streaming in the firmament ('Still Falls the Rain'[33]). Both poems fail to settle difficulties with altitude: lifted up on the cross, Christ belongs at least as much to the world of the bombers as to the passive victims below

[29] Herbert Read, quoted in Piette, *Imagination at War*, 40.
[30] Adam Piette, 'Fire', ibid. 39–81.
[31] Eliot, quoted in Helen Gardner, *The Composition of Four Quartets* (London: Faber, 1978), 187.
[32] Spender, *Collected Poems 1928–1953*, 130.
[33] Edith Sitwell, in Reilly (ed.), *Chaos of the Night*, 114–15.

him, and the blood which in Sitwell's poem falls from his 'wounded Side' seems to join with the 'Rain' (literal rain and the terrible rain of bombs) in an unlikely downpour. Only in Ruth Pitter's 'The Cygnet' does a poet bring Christian symbols, with their pledge of redemption, more tacitly to bear on what she calls, borrowing from *The Waste Land*, 'broken images of sorrow'.[34] Now the dove is no longer an enemy aeroplane but an uncomplicated harbinger of peace after the 'huge air' has been 'darkly defiled by wicked creatures'. The air appears

> in the white morning as beautiful,
> Dove-breasted smoky air over the dreadful
> Gap-toothed black scribbled skylines such as madness
> Might scrawl in dungeons . . .[35]

The dove and the darkness, forced together by Eliot in 'Little Gidding', are here sundered; and the image of a brooding bird which might yet bring new life is fleetingly implied rather than asserted. Pitter's technique is to understate her Christian optimism by using imagery which is primarily natural rather than religious: hope spreads as a kind of seed dispersal, 'sown by fury | In strange far meadows and small secret places';[36] and the poem's references to 'filth' and 'pollution' present the bombardment as an ecological warfare, corrupting the natural world in a way predicted by Ridler in 'Ringshall Summer' (which inhabits a strikingly similar landscape). It is the rain, heaven-sent, which will redeem:

> Water shall bless them, water out of heaven
> Washing from earth the stains of wicked creatures;
> Soul of the ermine dying of pollution,
> The martyred ermine dying and exhaling
> Back the unmingled purity of water,
> Absolving our corruption; incrupted
> Even though slain, exhaling into heaven
> And redescending in continual pardon.[37]

---

[34] Ruth Pitter, *Collected Poems* (London: Enitharmon, 1996), 156.
[35] Ibid. 157.   [36] Ibid. 159.   [37] Ibid.

Pitter may be describing the cycle of evaporation, condensation, and precipitation, but now she banishes scientific vocabulary with a theological lexis: 'bless', 'heaven', 'martyred', 'Absolving', 'incorrupted', 'pardon'. Just as nature is tainted by war, so God will act through nature to cleanse the 'blood-guilt of the wicked creatures' and 'Restore our innocence'. (Pitter loses control of the syntax, so that it is the soul of the ermine, bizarrely, which seems to redescend from heaven bringing pardon.) Whereas Eliot and Sitwell transfigure the bombing into a religious intervention, for Pitter the line is clear between nighttime evil and daytime hope, the weeping fire and the weeping rain, the wicked creatures overhead and the innocents below. It is less clear whether her moral distinctions can withstand the fire-bombing of German cities by Allied aircraft later in the war. (Dresden alone, even by the most conservative estimates, suffered 25,000 fatalities.) Pitter meets those obliterations with complete silence.

If the imposing of religion and morality fails to do justice to the complexities of the Blitz, other poets remain undistracted by such matters as they enjoy the *son et lumière* spectaculars apparently performed for their benefit. E. J. Scovell, writing 'In a Safe Area' without view of the aerial battles, wonders how to train her imagination not to take pleasure 'In all appearances this gold October | While London's refugees | Bestrew our streets like leaves'. Her qualms are over-nice: as she anxiously experiences the autumnal beauties of her peaceful university town, those who live under a more minatory sky find ample opportunity to relish its pyrotechnic effects. Looking forward to a time when 'the round sky is swept of wars | And keeps but gentle moon and stars', Rachael Bates provides an etiolated exception as she rejects a creative engagement with the Blitz in favour of the twee and clichéd. More common are poets who look back from Bates's peaceful future to a time before the round sky was swept of wars: fifty

38 Ruth Pitter, *Collected Poems*, 160.
39 E. J. Scovell, *Collected Poems* (Manchester: Carcanet, 1988), 83.
40 Rachel Bates, 'How Sweet the Night', in Reilly (ed.), *Chaos of the Night*, 11.

years after the event, Geoffrey Hill recalls how as a child he saw Coventry destroyed, 'huge silent whumphs | of flame-shadow bronzing the nocturnal | cloud-base of her now legendary dust'.[41] The poet witnesses what has since become 'legendary', his phanopoeia owning up to a recognition of the scene's awful magnificence. Even Ruth Pitter in 'The Cygnet', complaining that the music of the spheres has been drowned out by the bombardment, almost succumbs to visual delights:

> The fiery tears are falling; red and silver,
> They change and drift and wane, stars of disaster;
> Gold clusters, like the sparks in burning paper,
> Silently glimmer, then from haunted darkness
> Leaps their long shuddering voice of formal horror . . .[42]

The passage fluctuates between the artist's thrilled appreciation of exploding colours and the moralist's disapproving interventions. On this occasion it is to the detriment of the poem that the moralist ultimately wins; and those bland empty phrases—'stars of disaster', 'haunted darkness', 'formal horror'—symptomize a work which chooses to avert its gaze rather than acknowledge its own disturbing reaction to the Blitz. The poem's final stanza speaks of 'far secret places', 'the bright signature of love', 'the sacred river | Of life', 'anger and pollution', and 'dreary days and nights of terror',[43] as 'The Cygnet' gives up the fight and lapses almost entirely into magniloquent evasions. Yet for all Pitter's resolve to channel the reader's comprehension, it is that after-image of a brilliant night sky which survives the belletrist phraseology.

Pitter's evasions represent an understandable reluctance to accept the gorgeousness of a display which brings such daunting human costs. Knowing of innocent deaths, she permits herself only to deplore. For writers more willing to disclose what Louis MacNeice calls the 'enlivening' effects of the destruction,[44] there are other

---

[41] Geoffrey Hill, *The Triumph of Love* (Harmondsworth: Penguin, 1999), 3.
[42] Pitter, *Collected Poems*, 158.   [43] Ibid. 161.
[44] MacNeice, 'The Morning after the Blitz', in *Selected Prose*, 118.

strategies for excusing or disguising their aesthetic indulgence. MacNeice reports how, at 4 a.m. during a heavy raid on London, he found his neighbour 'standing on his doorstep, smoking his pipe and looking down the hill with a connoisseur's detachment'.[45] The neighbour's presence in the narrative acts at first to draw attention away from MacNeice's own Neronic inclinations, then to provide reassurance that it is common and natural to gorge on the feast of the senses served up by the Blitz:

There was a violent crackling and hissing from the fire downhill, and a rich autumn smell of burning wood. And beyond my house the sky was a backcloth for opera or ballet, a sumptuous Oriental orange-print mottled with bursts of black and rolling like water so as sometimes to bury the moon—a half-moon that looked very clean and metallic in this welter of colour.[46]

The fire, MacNeice finds, is 'very beautiful',[47] 'infinite' in its variety, and it manages 'subtleties never attained by any Impressionist painter'.[48] (The task for the writer is to achieve what the painter allegedly cannot, and capture the Blitz in all its beauty and terror.) As he wanders through the ruins the morning after a raid, he pauses to consider that 'People's deaths were another matter—I assumed they must have been many';[49] but the closest he comes to casualties are 'Shop-window dummies lolling amid wreckage' and 'houses without eyes, without teeth, without bowels'.[50] Concerned primarily with the vast amounts of prose fiction inspired by the Blitz, Mark Rawlinson makes a persuasive case that 'war's delight of the senses' veils atrocity, driving out 'thoughts of soft flesh'.[51] Yet MacNeice avoids this rule because he does not so much occlude the sight of broken bodies—there are no bodies left for him to see—as reinscribe their presence in his descriptions of damaged shops and houses. His

---

[45] MacNeice, 'The Morning after the Blitz', in *Selected Prose*, 117.
[46] Ibid. 118.
[47] MacNeice, 'London Letter [1]: Blackouts, Bureaucracy & Courage', ibid. 103.
[48] MacNeice, 'London Letter [5]: Reflections from the Dome of St. Paul's', ibid. 134.
[49] MacNeice, 'The Morning after the Blitz', ibid. 118.   [50] Ibid. 119.
[51] Rawlinson, *British Writing of the Second World War*, 78.

metaphors serve as pointed reminders, while he picks among now-sanitized ruins, that more than dummies had lolled amidst the wreckage, and more than houses had been disembowelled during the bombardment. That knowledge, nevertheless, does little to temper MacNeice's admiring wonder at the 'fantasy of destruction'. His best-known poem of the Blitz, 'Brother Fire', addresses the fire 'Jumping the London streets' as an 'enemy and image of ourselves', its thoughts echoed in 'ours': ' "Destroy! Destroy!" '[52] The plurals, 'ourselves' and 'ours', constitute a safety device: just as he had incriminated his neighbour, so now MacNeice spreads responsibility for this delight in the violent spectacle of the Blitz across an imaginative community which includes his readership.

MacNeice stares at ruin with an ardour which, although he ascribes the same enthusiasm to them, is rarely, if ever, found among his contemporaries. Derek Mahon comes close four decades later when his chiliastic reveries lead him to hope that soon the air raid sirens will sound again, as 'Radiant warplanes come | Droning up the Thames', 'Their incandescent flowers | Unfolding everywhere'.[53] The disarming beauty of the image (perhaps remembering, and certainly opposing, Eliot's 'in-folded' tongues of flame) conveys the poet's excitement at imminent devastation, enhanced by his nuclear-age certainty that 'Next time will be the last'. Mahon also takes issue with Auden's 'The Witnesses': what falls like rain is the one possibility that Auden had explicitly ruled out—'flowers'. To reconfigure bombs as flowers is to grant the prospect of a different kind of avoidance: 'Little Gidding', for example, concludes that 'all shall be well' as soon as the harmonious union of 'the fire and the rose' is achieved.[54] By comparison, Mahon's image works because it gestures ironically to a wishful thinking which it knows to be inapt. Beauty and atrocity (like the pleasure and fear of Ridler's 'Ringshall

52 MacNeice, 'Brother Fire', in *Collected Poems,* ed. E. R. Dodds (London: Faber, 1979), 196.

53 Derek Mahon, 'One of These Nights', in *The Hunt by Night* (Oxford: Oxford University Press, 1982), 50.

54 Eliot, *Complete Poems and Plays*, 198.

Summer') become conterminous partners which cannot be resolved into Christian faith.

The metaphor of unfolding flowers had been more fully explored in one of the most extravagant poems of the Blitz. Margery Lawrence's 'Garden in the Sky' comes with a footnote in which the author professes, with Coleridgean embellishment, that the poem was written in London, at midnight during one of the air raids of October 1941. Deeply uneven, and bemused by a delighted response to what should be merely horrifying, 'Garden in the Sky' begins by surrendering itself to euphoria:

> There is a monstrous garden in the sky
> Nightly they sow it fresh. Nightly it springs,
> Luridly splendid, towards the moon on high.
> Red-poppy flares, and fire-bombs rosy-bright
> Shell-bursts like hellborn sunflowers, gold and white
> Lilies, long-stemmed, that search the heavens' height . . .
> They tend it well, these gardeners on wings!
>
> How rich these blossoms, hideously fair
> Sprawling above the shuddering citadel
> As though ablaze with laughter.[55]

Lawrence's indebtedness to Thomas Campion—'There is a Garden in her face | Where Roses and white Lillies grow'[56]—imports rather than subverts his celebration of physical beauty. And, like Campion, Lawrence relishes the task of justifying her unlikely conceit. Adjectives and adverbs such as 'monstrous', 'luridly', 'hellborn', and 'hideously' make some effort to qualify the poet's admiration, but what dominates is a dazzling natural pageant. 'Civilian life', Susan Stewart remarks in relation to Homer, must necessarily be 'bound up with the pastoral and domestic worlds to which war is counter.'[57] But the challenge of the Blitz for the English poetic imagination

[55] Margery Lawrence, 'Garden in the Sky', in Reilly (ed.), *Chaos of the Night*, 74.
[56] Thomas Campion, 'There is a Garden in her Face', in *The Works*, ed. Walter R. Davis (London: Faber, 1969), 174.
[57] Susan Stewart, *Poetry and the Fate of the Senses* (Chicago: University of Chicago Press, 2002), 304.

is that this traditional contrast (which, despite Marvell's 'Nymph Complaining of the Death of her Fawn', had survived even the Civil War) has finally been demolished. As a consequence, 'gardens' are suddenly found to rhyme with 'air-raid wardens'.[58] No longer a retreat, the garden has been transformed into a war zone; and with reciprocal logic, Lawrence connects with the Blitz by describing the war zone as a garden. But she fails to sustain her ingenuity, and by the time that blossoms have begun to sprawl 'As though ablaze with laughter', the poem has become more concerned with Grand Guignol than gardens. Those poppies, sunflowers, roses, and lilies are soon dismissed as weeds. And in the third stanza Lawrence makes the seemingly obligatory genuflection to a Christian world-view, which remembers a 'Silent and cool' garden where 'Mary trailed her skirts amidst the dew | Of ageless planets, hand-in-hand with You | And Sleep and Peace walked with Eternity'. As if admitting to the anti-climax of such an orthodox ending, Lawrence adds an italicized rhyming couplet to bring the poem back to its opening line: '*But here I sit, and watch the night roll by. | There is a monstrous garden in the sky!*' That final exclamation mark betrays the source of the poem's excitement and astonishment, compared with which Lawrence's dutiful rehearsal of a plaintive Christianity seems insipid.

The ability to see a garden in the sky is as nothing to the star-gazing search for heavenly messages during the Blitz. Stephen Spender watches 'The dead of all pasts float on one calm tide | Among the foam of stars',[59] their purpose being to impart a cryptic wisdom summed up in the poem's title, 'Rejoice in the Abyss'. Elsewhere, Spender finds the stars less communicative, as their 'remote frozen tongues speak | A language of mirrors, Greek to Greek, | Flashing across space, each to each' ('Explorations').[60] Christian symbolism, even when resisted, is never far away from Spender's poetry, and in 'June 1940' a dead soldier regrets not having a 'Star whose rays

---

[58] Gardner, 'Introductory Note', in *Terrible Rain*, p. xix.
[59] Spender, *Collected Poems 1928–1953*, 136.   [60] Ibid. 149.

point a Cross to believe in'.[61] Later poets' re-imaginings are equally determined in their pursuit of a stellified significance. Craig Raine, for example, detects 'Bombers above and the braille of stars'[62]—a metaphor which, despite its visual and tactile infelicities, Simon Armitage recruits for the depiction of civilians in their garden shelters 'under a Braille of stars'.[63] (Further in his poem, Armitage confuses matters by making the unlikely claim that 'The stars took the shape of a Swastika once'.) The stars speak or encode a language alien to an audience which believes it has detected, but frustratingly cannot manage to decipher, the hidden meaning of the Blitz. Searchlights become part of this persistent mission. They build towers 'With beams and scaffoldings of light' (in Sylvia Lynd's 'The Searchlights'),[64] as if striving to create a second Babel capable of communicating with God. For Spender, similarly, they are 'Jacob ladders'—an image which brings the promise of ascent into, or descent of, revelation; and if not theological, then mathematical, proof is sought, as the searchlights 'Experiment with hypotheses | On the blackboard sky' ('Air Raid Across the Bay at Plymouth').[65]

That these quests for meaning are themselves ill-starred is signified by the extraordinarily provisional nature of metaphor in poetry of the Blitz: bombs are flowers (or explicitly not flowers), rain, seeds, filth, fiery tears; the sky is a net, a roof, a plaster surface to be frescoed, a backcloth for an opera or ballet, a garden, a cloud river, a tent; enemy planes are locusts, dark doves, the Holy Spirit, gardeners on wings; stars are frozen-tongued, braille, foam, a swastika, painted decorations, crucifixes. Sylvia Lynd's poem describes searchlights as, amongst other things, scaffoldings of light, water-lily flowers, a Harlequin's wand, and a grey stone forest. Each metaphor represents

    [61] Spender, *Collected Poems 1928–1953*, 133.
    [62] Craig Raine, '1941: Fire-watching', in *History: The Home Movie* (Harmondsworth: Penguin, 1994), 258.
    [63] Simon Armitage, 'Extracts from May the 8th 1945', *The Guardian*, 7 May 2005, accessed at <http://books.guardian.co.uk/review/story/0,,1477330,00.html> on 27 June 2005.
    [64] Sylvia Lynd, 'The Searchlights', in Reilly (ed.), *Chaos of the Night*, 81.
    [65] Spender, *Collected Poems 1928–1953*, 129–30.

an attempt not only to connect with the Blitz, but to grant poetic import and assert poetic authority by taming the absurdity of its phenomena. The undertaking seems particularly urgent, and potentially inexhaustive, because it is impossible: terrifying in its unpredictability, the Blitz will not conform to the impositions of its poets. As Louis MacNeice puts the problem, 'sometimes I say to myself "This is mere chaos, it makes no sense," and at other times I think "Before I saw wartime London I must have been spiritually colour-blind." ' [66] 'I find that I vacillate as to the answer,' he confesses, but that vacillation becomes part of the difficulty for writers who, unable to accommodate the chaotic, overemphasize the spiritual. After all, as MacNeice suggests in 'Whit Monday', '*The Lord's my shepherd*—familiar words of myth | Stand up better to bombs than a granite monolith, | Perhaps there is something in them.'[67] Yet that is a faith which MacNeice ultimately cannot share, and which even Stephen Spender, a poet who struggles with religious belief more than MacNeice, rejects as self-deceiving or egotistical. The overemphasis on the spiritual against the chaotic moves Spender's dead to warn him of an inappropriately religious understanding after they hear his 'shamelessly entreating prayer': ' "O God, tonight | Spare me from death that punishes my neighbour!" ' ('Rejoice in the Abyss').[68] Only by accepting emptiness, they tell him, will lives be spared from ' "feed[ing] upon the deaths of others" '.[69] This fierce rejection acknowledges, by negative example, the essential meaninglessness of the bombardment, where the destruction of particular individuals and houses constitutes nothing more than chance. Connecting with the Blitz requires not only the sense of its splendour and suffering, but a knowledge that metaphor, making sense of one thing in terms of another, risks becoming false to the random effects of the bombing.

Anecdotes of the bombardment often focus on amazing escapes. A fireman in William Golding's *Darkness Visible* varies a theme

---

[66] MacNeice, 'London Letter [5]: Reflections from the Dome of St. Paul's', 135.

[67] MacNeice, *Collected Poems*, 201.

[68] Spender, *Collected Poems 1928–1953*, 136.   [69] Ibid. 137.

common to Blitz narratives: watching 'a wall six storeys high fall on him all in one piece' and 'wondering why he was still alive', he discovers that 'the brick surround of a window on the fourth storey had fitted round him neatly'.[70] The human inclination to bestow meaning on such accidents is one which poetry, with its arrangement of disparate elements into a formal order, finds especially hard to refuse: the lyric poet is obliged to brood over that which the prose writer might mention only in passing. Partly for that reason, very few poets record the arbitrary nature of the Blitz without entering into wider metaphorical, theological, or mythical patterns. It is the willingness to preserve, and not interpret, the random which accounts for the unorthodoxy of N. K. Cruickshank's 'Enemy Action', as bombs fall on an Audenesque list of 'the young, the usual, the plain':

> And the one who simply went across the road
> To post a letter or to look around
> Holds his redeemed breath, struggles from a load
> Of smouldering dread. After, with what profound
>
> Wonder, what thankful, what extensive fears,
> Standing alone in the bright summer weather,
> Examines that mild choice, which now appears
> A least hinge swinging, lightly as it were a feather,
> The vast door, opening, of some forty years.[71]

Some of this—'smouldering dread', 'profound || Wonder'—may be inert; but as its title suggests, the poem outlasts these faults by playing on different kinds of 'action'. The deliberate and malign enemy bombardment contrasts with the lucky survivor's 'mild choice' which, exercised for the most fortuitous of reasons, has 'vast' consequences. On one side of the door is death, and on the other, many more years of life—and Cruickshank offers nothing from the spectrum of spirituality to help foretell which is which, or credit with design the choices unthinkingly made. Often those endangered by the Blitz feel

[70] William Golding, *Darkness Visible* (London: Faber, 1979), 11.
[71] N. K. Cruickshank, 'Enemy Action', in Reilly (ed.), *Chaos of the Night*, 35.

they lack even that level of influence over their destiny. 'What I say is, | If there's a bomb made for YOU, | You're going to get it': the fatalism of the 'dancing girl' in Desmond Hawkins's 'Night Raid' comforts itself by reinstating, and reconnecting with, a world of purposeful causes and inexorable effects. But by shattering the links between actions and their consequences more thoroughly than the dancing girl allows, the Blitz licenses a poetry akin to nonsense verse in its reliance on the incongruous and its renunciation of rational or allegorical exegesis. When Lois Clark in 'Picture from the Blitz' tries to make sense of an episode repeatedly experienced as a flashback, she matches that compulsion with repetitions in her retelling: linear narrative cannot free her from the image of a 'shock-frozen woman' sitting 'in her big armchair, | grotesque under an open sky, | framed by the jagged lines of her broken house'. Clark's own shock-frozen state is broken only by her running towards the woman and into further horror, as she treads on 'something soft' and fights her nausea to discover nothing more than 'a far-flung cushion, bleeding feathers'. The poem ends as it began, 'under the open sky', with the woman lifted tenderly out of her armchair, trailing khaki wool behind her.

Elizabeth Bowen's character insists that the Blitz cannot connect with life or literature because it is 'preposterous'. To make even a verbal architecture out of a bombardment seems inherently contradictory, but Clark shows that the preposterous, existing beyond the shaping blandishments of myth, can be preserved by poetic form. One of the strongest poems inspired by the Blitz, Margery Lea's 'Bomb Story (Manchester, 1942)', uses the preposterous to unify the stories of a neighbourhood hit by a bomb. Rather than trying to make sense out of the senseless, Lea tells the story of that one bomb by juxtaposing numerous stories of damaged furniture as well as damaged lives, of minor annoyance

[72] Desmond Hawkins, 'Night Raid', in Gardner (ed.), *Terrible Rain*, 57.

[73] Lois Clark, 'Picture from the Blitz', in Reilly (ed.), *Chaos of the Night*, 27.

[74] Quoted in Rawlinson, *British Writing of the Second World War*, 83.

as well as fatality. The bomb creates the poem by producing familial and neighbourly love among the ruins, as well as soggy breakfasts (when hoses are misdirected and 'errant spray' trespasses through broken windows) and tremendous new opportunities for the green-fingered:

> Our neighbour's garden had a crater that would hold two buses.
> He said the rich soil thrown up was most productive,
> And round the perimeter he grew excellent lettuces
> The next spring of the war.
> Meanwhile his wife's lace corselet and her mended red jumper
> Hung forty foot up in an elm
> Whose leaves were scorched off.[75]

This comic account of vernal regeneration, in which death (in the form of bombs) brings about the ideal circumstances for new life (the bathetic sustenance of 'excellent lettuces'), and a corselet and jumper replace the 'scorched off' leaves, is evidence enough that Manchester can take it. New rules apply during the Blitz: a lace corselet goes on permanent display, boundaries between public and private realms having been eradicated by bombs which tear open the interiors of houses. ('[S]ometimes, when a house has been cut in half,' MacNeice nonchalantly remarks, 'you get the pleasant effect of a doll's house'.[76]) Housewives sweep up the broken glass, and are overheard complaining of ruined carpets and dirty settees. Already, the morning after the attack, a commonplace cheerfulness has been restored:

> at seven sharp the milk was on the step,
> And at seven-thirty the newsboy came cycling,
> Zigzagging among the firemen;
> Whistling, surprisingly, an air from a Nocturne of Chopin—
> The most beautiful sound in the world.[77]

---

[75] Margery Lea, 'Bomb Story (Manchester, 1942)', in Reilly (ed.), *Chaos of the Night*, 75.
[76] MacNeice, 'London Letter [1]: Blackouts, Bureaucracy & Courage', 102.
[77] Lea, 'Bomb Story', 76.

Chopin's Nocturne may seem to bear little relation to the nocturnal discord previously described by Lea: the 'endless heavy roar | Of the bombers circling' and the 'booming racket of the ack-ack guns'.[78] But it is the bombing which, antiphonally, concentrates the beauty of the newsboy's whistling. Lea's achievement in 'Bomb Story' lies in her ability, undistracted by the reassurances of myth, to connect with the whole of the Blitz—its allure, its horror, its beauty, its comedy, its eerie music of love and death, and, most of all, its preposterousness.

[78] Ibid. 75.

8

The Vision of Keith Douglas

Shell-shocked at the Somme, Wilfred Owen spent the second half of 1917 recuperating in Craiglockhart War Hospital in Edinburgh. During that time he began taking lessons in German, first at the nearby Berlitz school, and then with the Librarian of Edinburgh University, Frank Nicholson. Jon Stallworthy relates:

There were three or four of these lessons and after the last of them . . . Owen spoke as he rarely did of the horrors of the Front. He told Nicholson of photographs of the dead and mutilated that he carried in his wallet and his hand moved towards his breast-pocket, only to stop short as he realized, with characteristic delicacy, that his friend had no need of that particular lesson in reality.[1]

But there is no external evidence that those photographs existed. Dominic Hibberd suggests that a subaltern could not have obtained such material without falling foul of the military censor and his fellow soldiers. Owen's wallet, Hibberd maintains, probably carried nothing more than a new war poem with which the poet hoped to 'assault the civilian conscience'.[2] The confusion may have arisen because of Owen's description of one of his poems, 'A Terre', as a 'photographic representation'.[3] Owen's 'characteristic delicacy' would not have been the only reason for his second thoughts. Whether visual or verbal, he often found the photographic

---

[1] Jon Stallworthy, *Wilfred Owen* (Oxford and London: Oxford University Press and Chatto, 1974), 222.

[2] Dominic Hibberd, *Owen the Poet* (London: Macmillan, 1986), 129.

[3] Wilfred Owen to Susan Owen, ? April 1918, in Owen, *Collected Letters*, ed. Harold Owen and John Bell (Oxford: Oxford University Press, 1967), 545.

style inadequate, as he told Siegfried Sassoon after one traumatic incident:

the boy by my side, shot through the head, lay on top of me, soaking my shoulder, for half an hour.

Catalogue? Photograph? Can you photograph the crimson-hot iron as it cools from the smelting? That is what Jones's blood looked like, and felt like. My senses are charred.[4]

Believing that 'every poem, and every figure of speech should be a *matter of experience*',[5] Owen on this occasion considers photography a betrayal of that experience, incapable of capturing what Jones's blood 'looked like'. It is characteristic of Owen that when he does find a metaphor to describe the indescribable—of 'crimson-hot iron as it cools from the smelting'—the visual becomes subservient to the tactile.

Owen's credo that experience must precede and shape poetic inspiration was partly a reaction against the sanitized propaganda with which the government and media controlled public opinion: photographs of dead Allied soldiers, for example, were prohibited as bad for morale. Other Great War poets shared Owen's anger. Almost three decades later, in 1943, Edmund Blunden would remember his bitterness at official disinformation when, as tutor at Merton College, Oxford, he reassured an ex-student that 'The fighting man in this as in other wars is . . . the only man whom Truth really cares to meet.'[6] His correspondent was a 23-year-old Alamein veteran called Keith Douglas. Douglas, by this stage, needed little encouragement, having told his friend and fellow poet J. C. Hall just six days before Blunden's letter that his self-appointed task was to 'write true things'.[7] Like the Great War poets before him, Douglas derived an authority from his experiences which led him to dismiss the work of poets back in

---

[4] Owen to Siegfried Sassoon, 10 Oct. 1918, ibid. 581.

[5] Owen to Leslie Gunston, 25 Nov. 1917, ibid. 510.

[6] Edmund Blunden to Keith Douglas, 16 Aug. 1943, in Keith Douglas, *A Prose Miscellany*, ed. Desmond Graham (Manchester: Carcanet, 1985), 129.

[7] Douglas to J. C. Hall, 10 Aug. 1943, in Douglas, *The Letters*, ed. Desmond Graham (Manchester: Carcanet, 2000), 295.

England. He informed Hall: '[Your poetry] is getting too involved and precious, chiefly because you now find yourself in a backwater and have nothing to write about that is relevant. The same applied to me in pre-Alamein days.'[8] Douglas repeated the charge in his essay 'Poets in This War', sardonically complaining that poets currently springing up 'among the horrors of War Time Oxford . . . are technically quite competent but have no experiences worth writing of'.[9] The 'important test' of Alamein having been passed,[10] Douglas had earned the right to his poetic vocation. His 'true things' may have been truer to the facts of the battlefield than those of his civilian contemporaries, but the difference between the horrors of the desert campaign and those of 'War Time Oxford' created artistic dilemmas similar to those with which Owen had wrestled: how might the poet bridge the gap to make his audience see what he had seen, understand what he had endured? That Douglas and Owen arrived at radically different solutions is illustrated by Douglas's more consistently positive attitude to photographs and photographic techniques—an attitude which cannot be attributed merely to the intervening decades of technological advance.

As a fully qualified camouflage officer, Douglas was one of the few soldiers entitled to a camera.[11] He did not always use the privilege for strictly military purposes. Writing to his publisher, M. J. Tambimuttu, in January 1944, he aired the idea for a book containing his 'prose, verse, photographs and drawings'; as for the photographs, he had lately rediscovered his negatives of some of them, 'though not as yet of the dead men'.[12] Amongst the subjects of his drawings were corpses, men being hit by an anti-personnel mine, and the face of a man burning to death. Sharing little of Owen's 'characteristic delicacy', Douglas confirmed to Tambimuttu that the

---

[8] Douglas to J. C. Hall, 10 June 1943, ibid. 287.
[9] Douglas, 'Poets in This War', ibid. 351.
[10] Douglas, *Alamein to Zem Zem*, ed. John Waller, G. S. Fraser, and J. C. Hall (London: Faber, 1966), 15.
[11] Douglas to Jean Turner, 4 Nov. 1942, in Douglas, *Letters*, 251: 'I have a camera and a permit to use it.'
[12] Douglas to M. J. Tambimuttu, 2 Jan. 1944, ibid. 313.

drawings gave 'an accurate idea of the appearance of things', with just one exception: 'In the case of the man burning to death I have had to retain all the features, to give the chap some expression, although of course they're expressionless, as their faces swell up like pumpkins.'[13] The one disruption to the photographic style merely aggravates the horror. Douglas's 'of course'—'of course they're expressionless'—is a disingenuous presumption of knowledge which stresses his own intimacy with the barbaric nature of war. He has witnessed so much atrocity that it has become commonplace, to be photographed, drawn, and described with throwaway nonchalance.

Douglas's poetry and prose are, like his drawings, photographic in their ambition to give 'an accurate idea of the appearance of things'. His stated intention is to provide 'a series of pretty simple pictures',[14] and he describes his style as 'extrospective'—defined by the *OED* as 'regarding external objects rather than one's own thoughts and feelings'. Douglas, in Owen's terms, aims to present what it 'looked like', not what it 'felt like'. 'Réportage and extrospective' poetry, he insists, is the sort 'that has to be written just now, even if it is not attractive.'[15] Answering Hall's complaints that he is writing 'too remotely, cleverly but not movingly',[16] Douglas counterattacks by proposing that his friend should develop 'a little more cynicism, or should I say indifference to emotion once felt'.[17] This dispute traces the fault line between Owen's pity and Douglas's dispassion: as Kevin Crossley-Holland states, 'Douglas deliberately distances himself from all that he sees in such a way that it is difficult to feel close to him.'[18] The poet becomes a camera, but only, his detractors argue, at the expense of his humanity.

When in his essay 'Poets in This War' Douglas begins a roll-call of Great War poets, Owen heads the list, but with a misattributed

[13] Douglas to M. J. Tambimuttu, 30 Jan. 1944, ibid. 316.
[14] Douglas to Edmund Blunden, 3 Sept. 1943, ibid. 297.
[15] Douglas to J. C. Hall, 10 June 1943, ibid. 287.
[16] J. C. Hall to Marie Douglas, 10 Oct. 1942, in Douglas, *A Prose Miscellany*, 121.
[17] Douglas to J. C. Hall, 26 June 1943, in Douglas, *Letters*, 288.
[18] Kevin Crossley-Holland, quoted in William Scammell, *Keith Douglas: A Study* (London: Faber, 1988), 205.

image which comes from Rosenberg: 'Instead, arose Owen, to the sound of wheels crunching the bones of a man scarcely dead.'[19] Douglas is recalling Rosenberg's 'Dead Man's Dump', in which a limber's wheels crunch bones and graze 'dead face[s]'.[20] But, whatever his admiration for Rosenberg, Douglas is not challenged by him to develop a conflicting aesthetic, as he is by Owen. The poet who, before active service, embellishes a photograph of himself in his army finery with the Horatian motto condemned by Owen as 'The old lie'[21] — 'Dulce et Decorum Est Pro Patria Mori' — is a poet driven to acts of aggression against much of what Owen's work stands for. 'My subject is War, and the pity of War,' proclaimed Owen.[22] 'To be sentimental or emotional now is dangerous to oneself and to others,'[23] Douglas affirmed, as if providing the perfect riposte.

The problem lies in judging whether Douglas's photographic detachment ever slipped into affectation or worse. Whereas Owen spoke 'rarely . . . of the horrors of the Front', Douglas related his own experiences of battle with what sounded sometimes like gratuitous enthusiasm, sometimes callousness. While training in England, he had examined the corpses of a German crew whose plane had come down near regimental headquarters in Gloucestershire: they 'stank', and one of them 'was hung in a tree some yards away from his own head'.[24] Active service did nothing to abate his descriptive zeal: having met Douglas in Cairo after the desert victory, the expatriate literati reported that 'He was delighted with his war',[25] and his talk

[19] Douglas, 'Poets in This War', 350.

[20] Isaac Rosenberg, 'Dead Man's Dump', in *The Poems and Plays*, ed. Vivien Noakes (Oxford: Oxford University Press, 2004), 142.

[21] Wilfred Owen, *The Complete Poems and Fragments*, i: *The Poems*, ed. Jon Stallworthy (London: Chatto & Windus, Hogarth Press, and Oxford University Press, 1983), 140.

[22] Wilfred Owen, *The Complete Poems and Fragments*, ii: *The Manuscripts and Fragments*, ed. Jon Stallworthy (London: Chatto & Windus, Hogarth Press, and Oxford University Press, 1983), 535.

[23] Douglas to J. C. Hall, 10 Aug. 1943, in Douglas, *Letters*, 295.

[24] Douglas to Jean Turner, 21 Mar. 1941, ibid. 170.

[25] Lawrence Durrell, 'Introduction', in Douglas, *Alamein to Zem Zem*, 12.

'was all of burning tanks and roasting bodies'.[26] The dead body is, overwhelmingly, the central image in Douglas's work, and each corpse poses new ethical challenges for the poet and the reader. 'Cairo Jag', from 1943, ends with a starkly photographic image: 'a man with no head | has a packet of chocolate and a souvenir of Tripoli'.[27] Yet the rhythms tell a more frivolous story, pairing nouns so that no-nonsense monosyllables—'man/head'—give way to 'packet/chocolate' and, trippingly, 'souvenir/Tripoli'. For all its *reportage*, the poem cannot take the scene too seriously, and offers at least the suspicion of a joke in the absurdity of the headless man's chocolate—how would he eat it? The trash of souvenirs invites parallels with the trash of corpses littering the landscape. And the poet's knowledge of the man's possessions comes, it is safe to assume, from the widespread though illegal practice of looting the dead. If Owen showed 'characteristic delicacy' in withholding the contents of his wallet, Douglas in poetry and conversation risked seeming characteristically indelicate, proudly flaunting his experiences to entertain his audience and demonstrate that he was—as Ian Hamilton disapprovingly declares—'a tough guy'.[28]

To appreciate Douglas's motivation, it is necessary to understand that what he saw, what he spoke and wrote about, and the extrospective style he developed, were inalienably connected; if he saw nothing new, he had nothing new to say. Douglas confessed to Hall in June 1943, 'I am not likely to produce anything but virtual repetitions of [my earlier work], until the war is cleared up now, because I doubt if I shall be confronted with any new horrors or any worse pain.'[29] G. S. Fraser recalled Douglas's belief in Cairo that 'he had seen everything that was necessary. Everything else would

---

[26] G. S. Fraser, quoted in Desmond Graham, *Keith Douglas 1920–1944: A Biography* (Oxford: Oxford University Press, 1974), 225.
[27] Douglas, *The Complete Poems*, ed. Desmond Graham (Oxford: Oxford University Press, 1987), 97.
[28] Ian Hamilton, 'Tough Guy', *London Review of Books*, 8 Feb. 2001.
[29] Douglas to J. C. Hall, 26 June 1943, in Douglas, *Letters*, 289.

be repetition, waste.'[30] The title of Douglas's prose memoir of the desert campaign, *Alamein to Zem Zem*, indicated that the A–Z of war had already been mapped; there were no further lessons to be learnt. Those lessons Douglas had already learnt, he had learnt by looking ('he had seen everything that was necessary'); and looking, his work establishes, need not be the morally neutral or morally reprehensible activity which several critics have alleged.

The prominence of the visual is singular and fundamental to Douglas's work: it constitutes nothing less than—in Charles Tomlinson's suggestive phrase—an 'ethic of sight'.[31] To betray such an ethic is to fail in a moral duty. This belief informs Douglas's mature war poetry, but it is already apparent in 'Death of a Horse', a short story probably dating from late 1940, two years before he saw active service. 'Death of a Horse' narrates a vet's shooting and dissection of the injured animal: ' "You're lucky to see this," ' he tells the spectators. The story's main character, Simon, does not merit the privilege, and responds inadequately to the occasion:

'The horse has a small stomach,' said the vet. 'Look!' And he flapped the stomach in front of him, like an apron. The stench was unbelievable. Simon began at last to feel sick . . . The horrible casualness of the vet's voice grew more and more apparent; the voice itself increased in volume; the faces merged and disintegrated, the wreck of the horse lay in a flurry of colours, the stench cemented them into one chaos. He knew it was useless. His one thought, as he felt himself falling, was that he had let the horse down.[32]

Significantly, Simon lets down neither himself nor the vet who allows him to spectate, but the dead horse. The story is a clandestine manifesto, outlining what Douglas's work expects of itself and its audience. The abasement of the dead is transformed through detailed visualization—at whatever cost to the spectator—into a new nobility. Simon reports how the horse became 'invested with the dignity due to a chosen victim': 'From this came the impression

[30] G. S. Fraser, quoted in Graham, *Keith Douglas 1920–1944*, 225.
[31] Charles Tomlinson, quoted in Scammell, *Keith Douglas*, 211.
[32] Douglas, 'Death of a Horse', in *Letters*, 354–5.

that the dead horse was taking a pride in its own dissection.' To look is to sympathize, in the Burkean sense defined by David Bromwich: 'To have the sense of the pain of another person, while one watches that person suffer.'[33] It does not palliate, but it may give meaning to suffering. Turning away or, in Simon's case, fainting, represents a final insult to the dead.

Less subtle than Douglas's war poetry, 'Death of a Horse' neverthe-less begins to articulate a rejoinder to Owen's emphasis on the pity of war. Owen objects to the photograph because it is unable to convey what Jones's blood looked like or felt like. This employs the verb 'to feel' predominantly according to its tactile but also according to its emotional meaning: 'My senses are charred,' Owen acknowledges. Albeit in far less horrific circumstances, Simon's senses are charred too. His queasiness blurs the focus, revealing a culpable self-regard. This negative example indicates one advantage of Douglas's extro-spective art: clear-sighted, it performs an autopsy (from the Greek for 'seeing with one's own eyes') on the dead by achieving a level of self-forgetfulness which more emotional responses cannot hope to attain. 'Extension to Francis Thompson', written around the same time as Douglas's short story, ends with the 'wise man' learning the art of 'analysis in worshipping'.[34] Shifting emphasis slightly, 'Death of a Horse' implies that analysis *is* worshipping.

'Death of a Horse' is inspired by Douglas's training in horse-manship as an officer cadet during the late summer of 1940. Unsurprisingly, however, the tone of his poetry has more in com-mon with the 'horrible casualness of the vet's voice' than with Simon's squeamishness. 'Look!', the vet commands, as he flaps the horse's stomach out in front of him. 'Look' also happens to be the most frequent imperative in Douglas's poetry, as the reader is pushed into the same predicament that Simon fails to withstand. The imperative is shared by two of Douglas's best-known poems,

---

[33] David Bromwich, 'How Moral Is Taste?', in *Skeptical Music: Essays on Modern Poetry* (Chicago: University of Chicago Press, 2001), 237.
[34] Douglas, 'Extension to Francis Thompson', in *Complete Poems*, 66.

'*Vergissmeinnicht*' and 'How to Kill', both dating from the summer of 1943. Revisiting the 'nightmare ground' of battle, and finding a three-week-dead German soldier 'sprawling in the sun', '*Vergissmeinnicht*' persists with a detailed examination of his personal effects: 'Look. Here in the gunpit spoil | the dishonoured picture of his girl'.[35] In 'How to Kill', the imperative again invites scrutiny of a dead enemy. The poem ensures that a sniper's 'sorcery', as he singles out his unsuspecting victim, will be properly appreciated: 'Death, like a familiar, hears ‖ and look, has made a man of dust | of a man of flesh.'[36] With an authority which need not raise its voice through exclamation marks, both poems compel a heightened visual awareness, and seem to linger over the bloodshed, at the moment when the instinct to turn away is most intense. The soldier fighting against Nazism fights for us, and what he is asked to do, he does in our name and for our benefit. Should we look, or turn away, when the poet invites us to stare down the sniper's rifle at the unsuspecting German or to examine the rotting corpse? Whatever we decide, Douglas forces us to acknowledge the moral cost of that decision.

The unwavering focus of '*Vergissmeinnicht*' and 'How to Kill' provokes a queasiness similar to that felt by Simon in 'Death of a Horse'; there is no respite from a bullet-like vision which, Edna Longley argues, 'does not so much look from alternative angles, as aim at progressive penetration'.[37] Douglas's imperatives are calculated affronts to the sensibilities of his audience. They constitute a poetic buttonholing, much as he buttonholed the Cairo literati; but they also achieve something more. Examining the use of imperatives in poetry, John Hollander has argued that 'Wise poets are usually careful about their commands, whereas foolish ones ... write as if they expected to be taken literally.'[38] 'Look', as a poetic command, can never

---

[35] Douglas, '*Vergissmeinnicht*', in *Complete Poems*, 111.

[36] Ibid. 112.

[37] Edna Longley, ' "Shit or Bust": The Importance of Keith Douglas', in *Poetry in the Wars* (Newcastle: Bloodaxe, 1986), 105.

[38] John Hollander, 'Poetic Imperatives', in *Melodious Guile: Fictive Pattern in Poetic Language* (New Haven: Yale University Press, 1988), 66.

hope to be literal, because it gestures towards a scene from which the audience is temporally and geographically displaced. Douglas's imperatives are a technique for translating the detached and verbal into the immediate and visual, implicating the audience, forcing us to see. However, they also act as internal prompts for the poem itself. Hollander goes on to describe the ability of great poetry to talk to itself 'in that double way of speech by which we *hear* it addressing a putative, if fictional, hearer, while its commanding of itself is only overheard'.[39] On its lyric scale, Douglas's 'Look' attempts nothing so grandiloquent as, for example, Milton's imperative, 'Sing, Heav'nly Muse',[40] but the need for self-inspiration and self-encouragement (especially when facing 'new horrors') remains the same. Just as *Paradise Lost* personifies itself with the injunction to begin singing, so Douglas's poems command themselves, as well as their audience, to keep looking. One psychological reason for this insistence is suggested by comparison with Akira Kurosawa's *Something Like an Autobiography*, in which Kurosawa remembers the aftermath of the Great Kantō Earthquake. As he surveys 'every kind of corpse imaginable', and looks away involuntarily from the horror, his older brother insists, 'Akira, look carefully now':

I failed to understand my brother's intentions and could only resent his forcing me to look at these awful sights . . . I felt my knees give way and I started to faint, but my brother grabbed me by the collar and propped me up again. He repeated, 'Look carefully, Akira.'[41]

Startled the following morning by his lack of nightmares, Kurosawa is reassured by his brother that 'If you shut your eyes to a frightening sight, you end up being frightened. If you look at everything straight on, there is nothing to be frightened of.'[42] Knowledge restrains the passions, and encourages an enlightened apatheia. But

[39] Ibid. 74.
[40] John Milton, *Paradise Lost*, ed. Alistair Fowler (London: Longman, 1971), i. 41, l. 6.
[41] Akira Kurosawa, *Something Like an Autobiography*, trans. Audie E. Bock (New York: Vintage, 1983), 52–3.
[42] Ibid. 54.

even if Douglas, like Kurosawa, endures 'an expedition to conquer fear', he also courts and dramatizes criticisms of what may seem like indifference to the bloodshed or even voyeuristic gloating. The sniper of 'How to Kill' represents the ultimate in detached observation, watching his victim 'move about in ways | his mother knows, habits of his',[43] before invoking death and metamorphosing flesh into dust; his only emotion, as he sees 'the centre of love diffused | and the waves of love travel into vacancy', is amusement. As David Wheatley has noted, the enjambment in 'I cry | NOW', as the sniper pulls the trigger, voices the expected pity, only to replace it immediately with a cold-blooded moment of killing.[44] The sniper's injunction to 'look', in these circumstances, is akin to the French '*Voilà*', requiring applause for a splendid trick. Looks can kill: the sniper never refers to his gun or to pulling the trigger, but destroys his target by studying his victim through a 'dial of glass'.

Although less murderous, '*Vergissmeinnicht*' seems to betray a similar indifference, and visually loots the decaying corpse. Steffi, the girl in the dead German's photograph,

> would weep to see today
> how on his skin the swart flies move;
> the dust upon the paper eye
> and the burst stomach like a cave.[45]

The strong iambics, disrupted only by the 'swart flies' and the gaping assonance of the 'burst stomach like a cave', conceal the curiousness and the curiosity of this stanza. Steffi becomes the channel for emotion, as the poem imagines her reaction to a scene which she will never witness; the impossible scenario is exploited as the motive for further and closer inspection. Discovering the dead soldier, Douglas's speaker had recognized that 'We see him almost with content'. But there is nothing complacent about the use of the first person plural, as Douglas wills his emotion on the reader and prevents any conniving

[43] Douglas, *Complete Poems*, 112.
[44] David Wheatley, 'Posturing for Peace', *The Guardian* (*Review*), 24 May 2003.
[45] Douglas, *Complete Poems*, 111.

in a response of shocked and pitying decency. That near-contentment invites comparison with the amusement felt by the sniper in 'How to Kill'; it is also easy to detect the more natural phrasing of the near-homonym, 'almost with *contempt*'.

'It may almost be said that before verse can be human again it must learn to be brutal,' wrote J. M. Synge in 1908.[46] This statement has been subsequently applied to Great War poetry,[47] but its most complete embodiment—even with the hesitations of Synge's 'almost'—comes in poems like '*Vergissmeinnicht*' and 'How to Kill'. Douglas's work is brutally human and brutally honest in its ambivalent response to the sight of a dead enemy who would himself have been a killer. His personae are survivors and destroyers who record their relief, their satisfaction, and their pride at a soldier's job well done. By avoiding pity, Douglas denies the consolatory gesture of inserting a human sensibility between the reader and the horror, and lays bare—perhaps more powerfully than any other poet of his century—the risks and the guilty pleasures of spectatorship. As Burke argued,

Whenever we are formed by nature to any active purpose, the passion which animates us to it, is attended with delight, or a pleasure of some kind, let the subject matter be what it will; and as our Creator has designed we should be united by the bond of sympathy, he has strengthened that bond by a proportionable delight; and there most where our sympathy is most wanted, in the distresses of others. If this passion was simply painful, we would shun with the greatest care all persons and places that could excite such a passion; as, some who are so far gone in indolence as not to endure any strong impression, actually do.[48]

Burke's exploration of the pleasures derived from the sufferings of others is pertinent because, as far as possible, Douglas's poetry dispenses with any disguise. The burden of emotion has shifted from

[46] J. M. Synge, 'Preface', in *Collected Works*, i, ed. Robin Skelton (Oxford: Oxford University Press, 1962), p. xxxvi.

[47] John H. Johnstone, *English Poetry of the First World War: A Study in the Evolution of Lyric and Narrative Form* (Princeton: Princeton University Press, 1964), p. x.

[48] Quoted in Bromwich, 'How Moral Is Taste?', 240.

the poet—as in Owen—on to the readers, who must therefore not merely approve the poet's response but acknowledge their own disturbing emotions. As a consequence, Douglas has been noisily misread by those who refuse the challenge. For John Carey, he 'coveted the immunity of the less sensitive, and formulated a *sang froid* of his own'; Ian Hamilton detects 'the tight-lipped insensitivity of the officers' mess'; Roy Fuller dismisses him as a 'snob' and incipient fascist.[49] Such readings boast their own sensitivity by attacking Douglas as insensitive; but the immunity which Carey accuses Douglas of coveting is exactly what those critics seek by turning away appalled from the scene of risk.

Douglas is not incapable of pity, but suspicious of its motivations. Like the Stoics as described by Montaigne, he holds pity to be a 'vicious passion', and would wish us to 'aid the afflicted, but not to faint, and co-suffer with them'.[50] In *Alamein to Zem Zem*, while observing the bloody minutiae of a dead man on the battlefield, Douglas finally considers that 'This picture, as they say, told a story. It filled me with useless pity.'[51] Reality is reduced to a 'picture', the same word that Douglas employs for the photograph of Steffi in '*Vergissmeinnicht*'; and 'pity', the keynote of Owen's response, becomes censured as a 'useless' and passive indulgence. The phrase raises two related questions: what are the uses of pity? and who might benefit from it? For Freud, pity constitutes a 'reaction-formation' against the sadistic drive, dressing in a more amenable form our pleasure at watching others suffer.[52] Douglas's persona, viewing dead enemies almost with content, refuses to sweeten his responses. His own relentless emphasis on the visual rejects the sanctuaries of brotherhood and consolation in which Owen's work, despite the poet's denials in his 'Preface', often seeks refuge. Writing a 'Homage

[49] Quoted in Scammell, *Keith Douglas*, 207, 200, 210.
[50] Michel de Montaigne, *The Essays of Montaigne*, trans. John Florio (London: Dent, 1910), i. 18.
[51] Douglas, *Alamein to Zem Zem*, 51.
[52] Freud, quoted in Jahan Ramazani, *Poetry of Mourning: The Modern Elegy from Hardy to Heaney* (Chicago: University of Chicago Press, 1994), 82.

to Keith Douglas', Geoffrey Hill has asked how far Owen's poetry, in thrall to 'a residual yet haunting echo of ... nineteenth-century rhetoric', 'applies a balm of generalized sorrow at a point where the particulars of experience should outsmart that kind of consolation'.[53] In the double meaning of Hill's 'outsmart' can be heard praise for the refusal of Douglas's work to succumb to consolation. Hill reverses the value judgements of Douglas's detractors, revealing how the same scrupulous dispassion which they deplore is the only means by which the full horror may be expressed. The swart flies, the eye coated in dust, the burst stomach—these particulars of experience smart with an agony (all the more burning for being mixed with pleasure) which renders aesthetic balm ineffective and irrelevant.

Douglas's true things find expression through the avoidance of sentimentality. If pity is a weakness, it follows that to shun it must be a strength. Douglas recommends to Hall in June 1943 that he should become less willing to show he is 'deeply affected': 'a little more of the traditional Englishman—however much you deplore him—would make your poetry stronger and more effective'.[54] And when a friend objects to unpleasant elements in *Alamein to Zem Zem*, Douglas replies: 'You want "selectivity" again—a suppression of something ugly but true ... I am afraid I refuse to cut it out to suit [your] connnoisseur sensibilities ... I'm not sure that the instinct for selectivity isn't based on sentimentality anyhow.'[55] The extrospective art records without judging or censoring. This should not imply that Douglas understands less than Owen about the sufferings of war, or about the 'feeling of comradeship with the men who kill [us] and whom [we] kill'.[56] Desmond Graham's biography recounts how on one occasion Douglas was ejected from the cinema after watching 'the usual newsreel in which an aerial dogfight was concluded with the German plane spinning to the ground in flames';

---

[53] Geoffrey Hill, ' "I in Another Place": Homage to Keith Douglas', *Stand*, 6/4 (1964/5), 7.
[54] Douglas to J. C. Hall, 26 June 1943, in Douglas, *Letters*, 288.
[55] Douglas to Jocelyn Baber, 28 Apr. 1944, ibid. 342.
[56] Douglas, *Alamein to Zem Zem*, 16.

reacting with rage to cheers from the audience, he climbed on to his seat to shout at them, 'You shits! You shits! You shits!'[57] And although sentimentality may be banished, *réportage* does not so much exclude emotion as find different ways of provoking it. 'It is hard to write coolly of something about which I feel so strongly,'[58] Douglas the rebellious 15-year-old explained to his headmaster, having catalogued the injustices endured at school. Emotion exerts a constant, if unarticulated, pressure, as Douglas struggles to write coolly about scenes which inspire strong emotion. '*Vergissmeinnicht*' and 'How to Kill', as the most rebarbative examples, provide the evidence: the references to mother and girlfriend situate the soldiers in a wider sphere, emphasizing the scale of the loss. Yet the natural movement towards compassion must coexist with the pleasurable empowerment of the survivor who has brought about that loss. Like 'Death of a Horse', '*Vergissmeinnicht*' starts with the degradations of death—the German is initially described as 'abased'—before adopting a dignified and even afflated tone as the victim becomes more than a mere soldier:

> For here the lover and killer are mingled
> who had one body and one heart.
> And death who had the soldier singled
> has done the lover mortal hurt.[59]

Douglas has it both ways. The high register, aided by inversion, form-alizes and ritualizes the scene, recognizing its gravity. But alternatively and simultaneously, the effect is mocking: this is no chivalrous romance, and the style is deliberately juxtaposed with the true squal-or of the decaying corpse. The balance of brutality and compassion is also accomplished by that imperative, 'Look'. What is probably the most famous usage in literature also draws attention to a corpse. With his dying words Lear imagines signs of life in Cordelia: 'Look on her. Look, her lips. | Look there, look there' (V. iii. 284–5). 'Look, | their

[57] Graham, *Keith Douglas 1920–1944*, 100.
[58] Douglas to H. L. O. Flecker, ? Dec. 1935, in Douglas, *Letters*, 46.
[59] Douglas, *Complete Poems*, 111.

gestures,'[60] Douglas's 'Fragment' says of the remembered dead. This
allusion rings less sonorously in the imperatives of '*Vergissmeinnicht*'
and 'How to Kill', but it distantly endures as a tacit 'Look there,
look there' amidst the inventories of decay.

Like Burke's criticism of the indolent who avert their gaze,
Douglas's ethic of sight proposes that to look is a moral act — an act
of self-recognition which also recognizes affinities between sufferer
and spectator. Awarding vision such authority, what Douglas finds
most appalling about the corpses he encounters on the battlefield are
their eyes — final proof of man's inhumanity to man. The 'swart flies'
and 'dust upon the paper eye', observed in '*Vergissmeinnicht*', parallel
the discovery in *Alamein to Zem Zem* of a dead Libyan soldier: 'As I
looked at him, a fly crawled up his cheek and across the dry pupil of his
unblinking right eye. I saw that a pocket of dust had collected in the
lower lid.'[61] Later, Douglas examines another corpse: 'The dust which
powdered his face like an actor's lay on his wide open eyes, whose
stare held my gaze like the Ancient Mariner's.'[62] Common to all three
descriptions, the 'dust' recalls not only the burial service and the way
of all flesh, but also Isaac Rosenberg's 'Break of Day in the Trenches',
where the poppy in the protagonist's ear is 'Just a little white with
the dust'.[63] Rosenberg's speaker hints that he may have begun to
decay even before his imminent and inevitable death; the soldiers in
the trenches are as good as dead already. The corpses that Douglas
describes are incontrovertibly dead, despite fleeting impressions.[64]
However, like Rosenberg's poem, or the sniper's instantaneous trans-
formation of flesh into dust in 'How to Kill', the strong possibility
remains that the dust is not something external, but a product of
decay: the eyes of the dead are rapidly and horribly mouldering.

War, *Alamein to Zem Zem* recurrently insists, destroys vision, not
only filling the eyes of corpses with dust, but also blinding the living.
Looking is a self-actuatingly moral, albeit not necessarily a benign,
act, and the cruel activity of war fosters oversights, confusions, and

---

[60] Ibid. 108.   [61] Douglas, *Alamein to Zem Zem*, 38.   [62] Ibid. 51.
[63] Rosenberg, *Poems and Plays*, 128.   [64] Douglas, *Alamein to Zem Zem*, 50.

misrecognitions. The narrative of *Alamein to Zem Zem* is driven by countless errors of vision. Early in Douglas's account, he reports that a friend had painted a 'huge eye' on the side of a Sherman tank. This represents the all-seeing eye of Horus, 'the nearest thing in Egypt to the God of battles'.[65] The choice of deity may at first seem appropriate: the desert war was considered one in which 'Nothing and nobody can be hidden'[66]—hence Douglas's frustration with his job as camouflage officer and his consequent desertion to the front line. Yet events in *Alamein to Zem Zem* prove otherwise. Tank squadrons lose each other in the desert, or are victims of friendly fire; sleeping soldiers risk being run over by their own side's heavy machinery; enemy tanks on the horizon are mistaken for a clump of trees; the dead look like they are alive, while the living appear dead; corpses or loot hide booby-traps. On two occasions Douglas's tank comes within yards of the enemy before the two sides even notice each other's presence. And Douglas himself is seriously injured after stumbling over a trip-wire attached to a group of mines: 'I realized that I had seen it and discounted it because of its newness, and because subconsciously I had come to expect such things to be cunningly hidden.'[67]

Looking in *Alamein to Zem Zem* possesses neither the ambition nor the necessary alchemical magic to transform analysis into worship. Despite the emphasis on *réportage* and extrospective poetry, Douglas never forgets that there are many different ways of looking, that the act is subjective and therefore often flawed. His persona not only describes what he sees, he describes himself seeing; and his way of seeing may be murderous like the sniper's in 'How to Kill'. Optical instruments, which might be expected to add a more scientific accuracy to observation, do not deliver a clearer vision: Simon in 'Death of a Horse' 'might have been watching ... through binoculars';[68] 'Simplify me when I'm dead' alludes

---

[65] Douglas, *Alamein to Zem Zem*, 31.

[66] Lieutenant Schorm, quoted in Scammell, *Keith Douglas*, 161.

[67] Douglas, *Alamein to Zem Zem*, 129.

[68] Douglas, 'Death of a Horse', in *Letters*, 354–5.

to 'Time's wrong-way telescope';[69] the sniper of 'How to Kill' looks through his 'dial of glass' (perhaps glimpsing his own reflection in the 'soldier who is going to die').[70] Douglas may not share Owen's reservations, but he still understands the responsibilities of the photographic art, and portrays it as pathological not only in his own pictures of dead men, but in his poetry: 'if I talk to you I might be a bird | with a message, a dead man, a photograph',[71] 'The Knife' concludes; Marcelle, the 'Parisienne' of 'Cairo Jag', has all the photographs and letters of her 'dull dead lover' 'tied in a bundle and stamped *Décedé* in mauve ink';[72] the connection between photography and death pervades '*Vergissmeinnicht*' as well, although this time it is not the subject of the photograph but her soldier lover who is dead. Douglas predicts Roland Barthes's argument that all photographs are of corpses, photography being 'a figuration of the motionless and made-up face beneath which we see the dead'.[73] No instrument can aid the human task of keeping the right distance, keeping everything literally in perspective. The courage of Douglas's extrospective art lies in its willingness to attempt dispassion without detachment, autopsy without intrusion. It must negotiate between the alternatives explored in 'Landscape with Figures I' as it switches unsettlingly from long-shot to close-up, from 'a pilot or angel looking down | on some eccentric chart', to the prying impertinence of 'you who like Thomas come | to poke fingers in the wounds'.[74]

These examples of the fallibility of sight acknowledge that war corrupts and erodes empirical techniques. It can be no coincidence that a poet whose biblical allusions are infrequent should refer in his work to three passages where vision merges into spiritual revelation: Christ's appearance to Thomas, Saul's conversion on the road to Damascus, and Christ's healing of the blind man at Bethsaida. Vision allows a redemptive knowledge: the pleasurable sympathy

[69] Douglas, *Complete Poems*, 74.   [70] Ibid. 112.   [71] Ibid. 91.
[72] Ibid. 97.
[73] Roland Barthes, *Camera Lucida*, trans. Richard Howard (London: Jonathan Cape, 1982), 32.
[74] Douglas, *Complete Poems*, 103.

in the suffering of others, Douglas hints several times in his work, may yet lead to compassion. To stress this unduly is to be guilty of the kind of sentimental reading which would defuse the moral danger of poems like '*Vergissmeinnicht*' and 'How to Kill' (both of which were written after Douglas's more allusively religious poems). Yet Douglas's religious references form part of the same enterprise: to consider the relationship between analysis and worshipping. He believed his locale was auspicious for such spiritual discoveries: in January 1943 he told Margaret Stanley-Wrench, 'I have an idea it's somewhere round here St Paul made one of his journeys.'[75] The following month he produced a version of 'Cairo Jag', which differs from the published form by virtue of its two extra sections. The poem's final section, which Douglas eventually dropped, describes a Pauline conversion:

> You do not gradually appreciate such qualities
> but your mind will extend new hands. In a moment
> will fall down like St. Paul in a blinding light
> the soul suffers a miraculous change
> you become a true inheritor of this altered planet.
>
> I know, I see these men return
> wandering like lost sounds in our dirty streets.[76]

The men in question, rendered ghostly by the comparison to 'lost sounds', are the 'noble dead' of the poem's previous section. His eyes having been spiritually opened, the poet inherits the earth, in its 'altered', war-ravaged form, along with the gift of seeing these wandering souls. However, with the exception of the last two lines, the poem asserts rather than reveals; Douglas's speaker 'know[s]' like a gnostic believer, but does not find a means of expressing that knowledge.

The final section of 'Cairo Jag' prepares for Douglas's embodiment, in 'Desert Flowers', of an almost religiously intense mode of

[75] Douglas to Margaret Stanley-Wrench, 8 Jan. 1943, in Douglas, *Letters*, 256.
[76] Douglas, *Complete Poems*, 137. See letter to Olga Meiersons, ? Feb. 1943, in Douglas, *Letters*, 264.

seeing—a mode which, he recognized, gave his work originality. Contemptuous of the wasteful repetition of war, Douglas had no desire to repeat the work of his predecessors: they had 'so accurately described' their experiences that 'Almost all that a modern poet on active service is inspired to write, would be tautological.'[77] In 'Desert Flowers', from the spring of 1943, it is Rosenberg, rather than Owen, whom Douglas seems to have difficulty avoiding: 'Living in a wide landscape are the flowers— | Rosenberg I only repeat what you were saying.'[78] As Fran Brearton has noted, 'All the Great War elements are here.'[79] But 'Desert Flowers' escapes repetition by describing a way of looking peculiar to Douglas. Breaking off from its descriptions of the 'wide landscape' with an abrupt dismissal—'But that is not new' (ironically quoting Blunden's 'But that's not new'[80])—the poem makes another, more conclusive, attempt at originality:

> Each time the night discards
>
> draperies on the eyes and leaves the mind awake
> I look each side of the door of sleep
> for the little coin it will take
> to buy the secret I shall not keep.
>
> I see men as trees suffering
> or confound the detail and the horizon.
> Lay the coin on my tongue and I will sing
> of what the others never set eyes on.

'Desert Flowers' is structured around the crossing of thresholds—sleep and wake, life and death. Douglas's speaker has seen a secret 'the others' did not see; he will sing of it in death, paid for by the coin laid on his tongue so that he may cross the Styx. This may be a promise of future revelation, but the process of enlightenment

---

[77] Douglas, 'Poets in This War', 352.   [78] Douglas, *Complete Poems*, 102.
[79] Fran Brearton, *The Great War in Irish Poetry: W. B. Yeats to Michael Longley* (Oxford: Oxford University Press, 2000), 269.
[80] Edmund Blunden, 'Darkness', in *Selected Poems*, ed. Robyn Marsack (Manchester: Carcanet, 1982), 103.

has already begun. Freely mixing Christian and classical references, Douglas alludes not only to Charon's fee but to Christ's healing of the blind man at Bethsaida: 'when [Jesus] had spit upon his eyes, and put his hands upon him, he asked him if he saw ought. And he looked up, and said, I see men as trees, walking' (Mark 8: 23–4).[81] Douglas's speaker exists in this interim state, still prone to errors of vision prior to the second part of the healing process: 'after that [Jesus] put *his* hands again upon his eyes, and made him look up: and he was restored, and saw every man clearly' (Mark 8: 25). To 'see men as trees suffering' therefore constitutes only a partial revelation, even though Douglas's speaker knows that eventually he will see more, and more clearly, than 'the others' who have 'never set eyes on' what he will sing about. Because the poem begins with an acknowledgement of poetic belatedness, those 'others' are less likely to be fellow soldiers than Douglas's Great War predecessors. This is the proudest boast of his poetry: through its brave and incessant acts of looking, it will attain a vision not just different from, but surpassing, even their achievement. In 'Desert Flowers' only death can provide this ultimate vision and allow the poet to sing the secret he has seen. Yet by the time he was killed in Normandy the following year, at the age of 24, Douglas had already seen and sung more than enough to fulfil those high claims for his work.

[81] Compare 'the trees like ominous old men are shaking', in 'Soissons', in Douglas, *Complete Poems*, 47.

9

Self-Elegy: Keith Douglas
and Sidney Keyes

1. KEITH DOUGLAS

'If I should die'.[1] Rupert Brooke's address to the reader at the
start of his best-known poem, 'The Soldier', weighs the possible
against the inevitable. Does the poet *expect* to die? Do we think he
will or *should* die? 'In a hypothetical clause relating to the future,'
the *OED* reports, '*should* takes the place of *shall* ... when the
supposition, though entertained as possible, is viewed as less likely
or less welcome than some alternative'. Death would certainly be
less welcome than life despite the posthumous colonization of 'some
corner of a foreign field' which would ensue. Death may also prove
'less likely'. Brooke's conditional clause, and the subjunctive form
'should', seem to safeguard the poet from any expectation that his
hypothesis will be fulfilled: *if it so happen that I die*; or even, *in
the unlikely event of my death.* Yet a second and less immediate
sense of 'should', as a statement of 'duty, obligation, or propriety',
brings death closer: if the poet should (*ought to*) die, then he has no
choice but to do so. This alternative may be forgotten as the reader
is invited to consider the poet's glorious afterlife; nevertheless, the
tonal ambivalence of 'If I should die' denotes a fleeting tension in
Brooke's attitude to his fate. 'The Soldier' postulates a destiny at
once unlikely and ineluctable.

---

[1] Rupert Brooke, 'The Soldier', in *The Poetical Works*, ed. Geoffrey Keynes (London:
Faber, 1960), 23.

Brooke is frequently dismissed as the naïve voice of 1914. Even
the defence that, had he lived to experience Gallipoli or the Western
Front, he would have 'written as realistically as Owen and Rosen-
berg',[2] concedes the case against him. A phrase such as 'If I should
die' reflects the complex uncertainties of its time in a way that soon
begins to annoy the retrospectively wise. Although briefly enam-
oured of Brooke's sonnets, for example, Ivor Gurney writes in 1917
a 'counterblast' sequence as the protest of 'informed opinion against
uninformed',[3] while Charles Sorley complains as early as April 1915
that Brooke was

> far too obsessed with his own sacrifice, regarding the going to war of himself
> (and others) as a highly intense, remarkable and sacrificial exploit, whereas
> it is merely the conduct demanded of him (and others) by the turn of
> circumstances, where non-compliance with this demand would have made
> life intolerable.[4]

However accurate a characterization of Brooke's war poetry as a
whole, Sorley's 'merely' misses the barb of Brooke's 'If I should
die', in which the sense of compulsion—of being obliged to
die—momentarily incriminates the poem's audience as compli-
cit in the potentially doomed speaker's fate. Brooke's poetic response
to war observes no incompatibility between what Sorley depicts as
the either/or of 'sacrificial exploit' and 'the conduct demanded of
him'. Something of Sorley's objection is replayed in 1939, when
John Jarmain begins his sonnet 'Thinking of War' with 'If I must
die'.[5] Brooke's play of freedom against fatalism has gone; the con-
ditional remains to broach the possibility of an alternative, but the
protection offered by the subjunctive, 'should', makes way for the
unambiguous necessity of 'must'. The twin pressures of obligation

[2] Jon Stallworthy, *Anthem for Doomed Youth: Twelve Soldier Poets of the First World War* (London: Constable, 2002), 15.
[3] Ivor Gurney to Marion Scott, 14 Feb. 1917, in *Collected Letters*, ed. R. K. R. Thornton (Ashington and Manchester: MidNag/Carcanet, 1991), 210.
[4] Charles Sorley, quoted in Jon Silkin, *Out of Battle: The Poetry of the Great War* (Oxford: Oxford University Press, 1972), 75–6.
[5] John Jarmain, 'Thinking of War', in *Poems* (London: Collins, 1945), 43.

and inevitability, balanced against hope for life in Brooke's poem, here leave little room for survival, or even for 'remarkable and sacrificial exploit'.

Writing to his tutor, Edmund Blunden, a week after the declaration of war in 1939, Keith Douglas finds comfort in small mercies: 'Thank heavens I can't see what is going to happen to us all as clearly as you must be able to.'[6] What sounds initially like an admission of ignorance ('I can't see what is going to happen to us all') turns into something potentially more knowing. Tutored in the sufferings of Blunden's generation, Douglas can see (albeit less clearly than the Great War survivor) his own destiny. But 'Thank heavens' his vision is not completely clear. Douglas understands that to foresee is to foresuffer, the cost of flawless vision being death: 'Lay the coin on my tongue and I will sing | of what the others never set eyes on.'[7] This belief that the poet must become his own corpse or ghost places Douglas in the great tradition of self-mourners—Keats, Dickinson, Hardy—whose poetic perspective has become posthumous.

Throughout the war Douglas repeated to friends his conviction that he would not survive. It was the foresight of what he called, in an undergraduate essay, 'The Happy Fatalist', whose impartiality makes him 'inhuman and superhuman', losing the pleasure of hope but gaining in 'immunity from despair'.[8] Fatalism shaped Douglas's poetic preparation for war. Desmond Graham remarks that, before embarking for Egypt in 1941, Douglas, like Brooke, exploited 'an important moment to make a poem which could provide his own elegy if he should not return'.[9] Although Graham slips into Brooke's vocabulary, the opening lines of 'Simplify me when I'm dead' dispense with ifs and shoulds altogether:

[6] Keith Douglas to Edmund Blunden, 11 Sept. 1939, in *The Letters*, ed. Desmond Graham (Manchester: Carcanet, 2000), 74–5.

[7] Douglas, 'Desert Flowers', in *The Complete Poems*, ed. Desmond Graham (Oxford: Oxford University Press, 1987), 102.

[8] Douglas, quoted in Desmond Graham, *Keith Douglas 1920–1944: A Biography* (Oxford: Oxford University Press, 1974), 97–8.

[9] Ibid. 125.

> Remember me when I am dead
> and simplify me when I'm dead.[10]

We all owe God a death, but this speaker does not expect to enjoy a full biblical span: 'Time's wrong-way telescope will show | a minute man ten years hence'. The distance between 'If I should die' and 'when I am dead' is not so much the distance between innocence and experience as between hope and its absence. As Douglas told J. C. Hall in 1943, 'It sounds silly to say work without hope, but it can be done.'[11]

Douglas may model his self-elegy in opposition to Brooke's 'The Soldier', but he also alludes to (and seems to merge) the opening lines of two poems by Christina Rossetti: 'When I am dead, my dearest' and 'Remember me when I am gone away'.[12] The comparison emphasizes the presence of a new vision unblinkered by sentiment: Douglas replaces Rossetti's euphemistic 'gone away' with the punishing and repeated stress on 'dead'; and the elision of 'when I'm dead' begins the simplification already, as the cadences of the previous line are shown to be little more than rhetorical afflatus. His poem goes on to consider the decomposition of the body and, relatedly, the simplifying deductions and reductions of posterity, before ending with a repetition of the opening lines; progress is impossible. Brooke consoles his audience in the event of his death by insisting on his magnificent permanence: 'there's some corner of a foreign field | That is for ever England'.[13] Douglas, by contrast, knows that death diminishes, and he refuses to allay the consciences of the readers for whose well-being he will kill and die. Responding in *Cherwell* a year earlier to criticisms of high-spirited undergraduates, Douglas had aggressively denounced the detractors:

[10] Douglas, *Complete Poems*, 74.
[11] Douglas to J. C. Hall, 10 Aug. 1943, in *Letters*, 295.
[12] Christina Rossetti, *The Complete Poems*, ed. R. W. Crump and Betty S. Flowers (Harmondsworth: Penguin, 2001), 52 and 31.
[13] Brooke, *Poetical Works*, 23.

for some time yet we shall continue to hear the slurs cast on us, until the chances of war have made us deaf to them. The thought that we shall fight to save these futile critics so that their futile criticism may outlive us is one of the greatest burdens and discouragements we have to bear.[14]

'Simplify me when I'm dead' assumes that the reader will outlive the poet, whose death is imminent and inevitable. 'We', the fighting men, will die, leaving Douglas's audience composed not necessarily of 'futile critics' with their 'futile criticism', but nevertheless of 'learned' men who should 'leisurely arrive at an opinion'. Leisure is an indulgence the speaker is unlikely to share. The poem's attitude to posterity, unlike Brooke's, is suspicious, and even antagonistic: refusing to make the consolatory gesture, Douglas ensures he gets his retaliation in first.

'Writing', W. H. Auden argues, 'begins from the sense of separateness in time, of "I'm here to-day, but I shall be dead to-morrow, and you will be active in my place, and how can I speak to you?"'[15] Construing all literature as self-elegy, Auden's comment happens to summarize the overt intentions of 'Simplify me when I'm dead', except that it lacks the disdain audible in Douglas's addressing of those 'active in [his] place'. Douglas's self-elegy exploits the genre's natural tendency towards temporal and spatial dislocations, mixed tenses and confused or complex chronologies: set in a present where its author is still alive, the poem projects a future after his death in which the audience will look back. 'Time's wrong-way telescope' will reduce the poet to 'a minute man ten years hence'; the same telescope pointing the right way must provide him with a close-up and detailed understanding of the future. The poet aims to render posterity redundant, its actions controlled or at least gainsaid by the insistent imperatives of his last will and testament.

Self-elegy crosses between life and death, as the lyric consciousness writes its own extinction in a near or distant future. Usually, the

---

[14] Douglas, quoted in Graham, *Keith Douglas 1920–1944*, 100.
[15] W. H. Auden, 'Writing', in *The English Auden: Poems, Essays and Dramatic Writings 1927–1939*, ed. Edward Mendelson (London: Faber, 1977), 305–6.

present provides an anchor to secure a safe return: 'Simplify me when I'm dead' implies, even in its title, that the poem's speaker is still alive. Douglas's *ars moriendi* has not yet reached the posthumous perspective of the kind achieved by Emily Dickinson: 'I heard a Fly buzz—when I died'.[16] Deferring the ultimate test of negative capability, Douglas does not try to imagine what it would be like to be dead except inasmuch as his corpse and his reputation will be 'stripped' by the living. He therefore avoids the paradox outlined by Freud: 'Our own death is indeed, unimaginable, and whenever we make the attempt to imagine it we can perceive that we really survive as spectators.'[17] Any act of imagination must necessarily involve spectating, but to imagine one's own death is to employ faculties which, Freud implies, death would extinguish. Douglas comes to the same realization in 'Dead Men':

> you would forget
> but that you see your own mind burning yet
> and till you stifle in the ground will go on
> burning the economical coal of your dreams.[18]

Freud's paradox constitutes more than a redundant reminder that, whatever authors like Dickinson may feign to the contrary, poems are written by the living; it also provides a reason for the ontological uncertainties of self-elegy, in which the bi-located poet must find ways of surviving and spectating in order to experience Death-in-Life and Life-in-Death.

Much of Douglas's best work is imbued with the sense that he is dead already, and survives only as a ghostly spectator. No poet since Hardy has been so haunted and self-haunted. His earliest ghost appears in 'Canoe', first published in May 1940, which describes an idyllic summer in terms inviting comparison with the legendary

---

[16] Emily Dickinson, *The Manuscript Books*, i, ed. R. W. Franklin (Cambridge, Mass.: Harvard University Press, 1981), 591.

[17] Freud, quoted in Paul Fussell, *The Great War and Modern Memory* (Oxford: Oxford University Press, 1975), 192.

[18] Douglas, 'Dead Men', in *Complete Poems*, 96.

innocence of 1914. This time the poet is aware of the 'doom' which 'hovers in the background', but he promises to come back next summer regardless of circumstances:

> What sudden fearful fate
> can deter my shade wandering next year
> from a return? Whistle and I will hear
> and come another evening, when this boat
> travels with you alone towards Iffley:
> as you lie looking up for thunder again,
> this cool touch does not betoken rain;
> it is my spirit that kisses your mouth lightly.[19]

Addressed to a lover, 'Canoe' lacks the aggression of 'Simplify me when I'm dead', and offers elegiac consolation instead. The shifting of tenses is typical of self-elegy. The poem opens by acknowledging that 'this may be my last | summer', but possibility soon becomes inevitability: within a year the poet will be dead. As future blends proleptically into present, the poet becomes his own revenant, a 'spirit' disembodied in the act of self-elegizing. 'Death is not an event in life,' argued Wittgenstein; 'we do not live to experience death.'[20] Douglas profoundly disagrees: to write a self-elegy is to experience death imaginatively, and this foresufferance translates poetic composition into a stripping of physical life, just as the skeleton of 'Simplify me when I'm dead' has been 'stripped'.

Douglas often records a congruence between the writing of poetry and the death of the poet. By necessity, the poet is a spectral figure speaking from beyond the grave: 'The Poets', from 1940, acknowledges that 'we ourselves are already phantoms',[21] with the choice of noun possibly influenced by Hardy's 'I Travel as a Phantom Now'. Like Hardy's poem, Douglas depicts poets as ghostly travellers, at one remove from a physical world which for Hardy is 'Strange'

---

[19] Douglas, 'Canoe', ibid. 40.
[20] Ludwig Wittgenstein, *Tractatus Logico-Philosophicus*, trans. D. F. Pears and B. F. McGuinness (London: Routledge & Kegan Paul, 1971), 6.4311, 147.
[21] Douglas, 'The Poets', in *Complete Poems*, 50.

and 'gloomy',[22] and for Douglas, 'squalid' and 'sad'. Increasingly, death is described not as an eventuality situated beyond the poem's end (as in 'Simplify me when I'm dead'), but as a moment endured and surpassed in the process of writing self-elegy (as in 'Canoe'). Self-elegy becomes suicide: the poet crosses into death, and is left bodiless and spectral. This is particularly evident in several of Douglas's later poems (most notably 'How to Kill' and '*Vergissmeinnicht*') which pretend to inhabit real time. Just as 'Canoe', in the space of sixteen lines, transforms a young man who may be enjoying his last summer into a 'spirit', so 'How to Kill' turns 'a man of flesh' into 'a man of dust',[23] performing his killing by typography in the capitalized 'NOW'. The hint of self-elegy in the lines 'Now in my dial of glass appears | the soldier who is going to die' is more fully articulated by the poem's drafts: 'I am gliding | towards the minute when shadow and self are one', and 'How easy it is to be a ghost'.[24] (The source is Sorley's 'It is easy to be dead'.[25]) For the poet who calls Death a familiar, being a ghost and making a ghost are easy tasks, their sorcery enabled by the spell of poetic composition.

To this it might be objected that, whatever events they describe, all poems consist of words; they are a fiction which can be enjoyed safely; no one *really* gets hurt. Douglas refuses to indulge such convenient excuses, and constantly strives to implicate the moral sense of the reader. Nor does he exonerate himself, but accepts the cost to be exacted in return for this power. The protagonist of 'How to Kill' considers himself 'damned', and the phantom poets of 'The Poets' are 'hated, known to be cursed'; Douglas's speaker in 'Saturday Evening in Jerusalem' feels 'alone and cursed

---

[22] Thomas Hardy, *The Complete Poems*, ed. James Gibson (Basingstoke: Palgrave, 2001), 458.

[23] Douglas, *Complete Poems*, 112.

[24] Quoted in Graham, *Keith Douglas 1920–1944*, 219; and Douglas, *Complete Poems*, 141.

[25] Charles Hamilton Sorley, 'When you see millions of the mouthless dead', in *The Poems and Selected Letters*, ed. Hilda D. Spear (Dundee: Blackness Press, 1978), 77.

by God'.²⁶ The poet's sinister powers render him a moral outcast; like the soldier, he is a condemned figure wielding the power of life and death even while he finds himself trapped between the two states. When Douglas expresses his overwhelming sense of alienation from his surroundings, he identifies with the wandering Jew, another figure caught between death and life (and punished for offending Christ). He portrays the phantoms in 'The Poets' as 'boneless, substanceless, wanderers'. 'The Hand' develops this image to describe the mind's solitude when it must 'navigate alone the wild | cosmos, as the Jew wanders the world'.²⁷ In 'Saturday Evening in Jerusalem', 'among these Jews I am the Jew | outcast, wandering down the steep road'²⁸—where the casting out and isolation of the poet are effected by a cruel enjambment. A late unfinished poem, 'Actors waiting in the wings of Europe', records the soldiers' 'excitement | in seeing our ghosts wandering'.²⁹ This both evokes and resists the consolations provided by the tradition of the revenant: the war-dead do not return home, but wander aimlessly. Douglas, as a soldier and a poet, is twice condemned, twice empowered, and twice removed. 'Syria' doubles (and seems to treble) the sense of alienation: 'Here I am a stranger clothed | in the separative glass cloak | of strangeness'.³⁰

This emphasis on 'strangeness' in Douglas's work implies a division not only of the self from its environment (hence the recurrent theatrical metaphors and the wandering rootlessness), but an internal division out of which self-elegy may be produced. 'There never was a war that was | not inward,'³¹ explains Marianne Moore. Answering to the war without, the self is the battleground within, where life and death struggle and coexist. In one of his strongest love poems, 'The Prisoner', Douglas makes this discovery after tenderly touching the face of his beloved Cheng:

²⁶ Douglas, *Complete Poems*, 112, 50, 105.
²⁷ Ibid. 80.   ²⁸ Ibid. 105.   ²⁹ Ibid. 117.   ³⁰ Ibid. 85.
³¹ Marianne Moore, 'In Distrust of Merits', in *Complete Poems* (London: Faber, 1984), 138.

today I touched a mask stretched on the stone-
hard face of death. There was the urge
to escape the bright flesh and emerge
of the ambitious cruel bone.[32]

The skeleton is bursting to escape the prison-house of flesh. As soldier and self-elegist, Douglas remains preternaturally aware that in the midst of life we are in death, that we carry our death with us, and that it is integral to us. This amounts to more than an acknowledgement of the skull beneath the skin, although it does incorporate that vision of mortality. 'The Prisoner' reveals the doubleness of identity, the Death-in-Life which is more subtly realized in 'How to Kill':

The weightless mosquito touches
her tiny shadow on the stone,
and with how like, how infinite
a lightness, man and shadow meet.
They fuse. A shadow is a man
when the mosquito death approaches.[33]

The forces of the previous stanza, also rhyming *abccba*, had acted centrifugally as the poet-sniper killed his victim: 'Being damned, I am amused | to see the centre of love diffused | and the waves of love travel into vacancy.' Yet in this concluding stanza, the rhymes and repetitions draw the eye back to the focal point of the middle couplet through a series of mirrorings: 'the mosquito death' reflects the 'weightless mosquito', and 'A shadow is a man' recalls 'her tiny shadow on the stone'. Within the couplet, 'like' chimes with 'lightness', 'how' with 'shadow'. Killing may be a dispersal of love, but the instant of death represents a self-reconciliation, as expressed in that delicate central near-rhyme 'infinite/meet' as death and life, man and shadow, fuse.

The recognition of a self-divided doubleness permeates Douglas's poetry. Assembling a book of his poetry, prose, drawings, and photographs in 1944, he proposes the title 'Bête Noire', which is

---

[32] Douglas, 'The Prisoner', in *Complete Poems*, 67.   [33] Ibid. 112.

'the name of a poem [he] can't write'.[34] The beast in question is 'indefinable', although Douglas notes that its tracks are clearly visible through some of his other poems. Fragments of the attempts to write 'Bête Noire' survive, and they show Douglas describing something more than a black dog of depression; the beast, it appears, is an aspect of the self very close to the haunting or deathly figure seen elsewhere in his poetry. In fragment A (i), the monster is 'curled in the belly', and its presence cannot be confessed 'to those who are happy, whose easy language | I speak well, though with a stranger's accent'.[35] Self-division necessitates performance and spectatorship, although distinctions between the real self and the beast become increasingly hard to maintain; in fragment A (ii) the beast 'walks about inside me: I'm his house | and his landlord', yet fragment B describes the beast as the 'jailer'. Fragments C and D declare that the poet has 'a beast on [his] back', but it proves impossible to locate him so precisely because, as Douglas has already admitted, the beast 'speaks out of [the poet's] mouth': he 'writes what I write, or edits it (censors it)'. Dangerous though it may be to define precisely what Douglas himself calls 'indefinable', this search for the black beast suggests clear parallels with the skeleton under the 'bright flesh' in 'The Prisoner' and with the shadow of 'How to Kill'. Douglas seems to be trying and failing to write a poem which can neatly separate death from life, even though he admits that his poetry is a work of dual authorship: the fragments are testament to the impossibility of escaping from one's shadow.

These poems dwell on Death-in-Life—the shadow, the Black Beast, the skeleton. Many of Douglas's living not only contain death inside themselves, but may even appear dead, like the sleepers in *Alamein to Zem Zem*, the unfortunates of 'Poor Mary' and 'Egypt', or the speaker of 'Mersa' who observes how the 'logical little fish | converge and nip the flesh | imagining I am one of the dead'.[36] As if reciprocally (and again, perhaps, remembering *King Lear's* final

---

[34] Douglas, 'Note on Drawing for the Jacket of *Bête Noire*', in *Complete Poems*, 120.
[35] Ibid. 118–19.   [36] Ibid. 95.

scene), in *Alamein to Zem Zem* the dead sometimes show signs of life: 'His expression of agony seemed so acute and urgent, his stare so wild and despairing, that for a moment I thought him alive.'[37] Douglas is intrigued by the blurred distinction, and in 'Landscape with Figures 2' he surveys the dead from an eschatological no-man's-land between the two states:

> The eye and mouth of each figure
> bear the cosmetic blood and hectic
> colours death has the only list of.
> A yard more, and my little finger
> could trace the maquillage of these stony actors
> I am the figure writhing on the backcloth.[38]

He who writes, writhes—giving the lie to repeated criticisms of Douglas's alleged aloofness. (Lewis Carroll's Mock Turtle, who learnt 'Reeling and Writhing' at school, may be the unlikely inspiration.) Writhing on the backcloth, the poet is distinct from, and yet integral to, this deathly landscape, separated by that crucial yard which would unite him with the horizontals in the theatre of war. The dead with their maquillage and cosmetic blood may be alive after all, and just as Douglas writhes, so they 'wriggle'. The difference between the poet and the dead is a matter of finesse: a yard, a consonantal quibble between writhing and wriggling.

Appreciating this intimacy, Douglas experiments with Life-in-Death as well as with Death-in-Life.[39] In 'Dead Men' he exhorts himself to 'leave the dead in the earth, an organism | not capable of resurrection'.[40] Yet the poet, a moral outcast cursed by God, does possess the power to usurp God's authority and resurrect the dead. The most convincing proof comes in 'The Sea Bird', Douglas's awed

[37] Douglas, *Alamein to Zem Zem*, ed. John Waller, G. S. Fraser, and J. C. Hall (London: Faber, 1966), 50.

[38] Douglas, *Complete Poems*, 103.

[39] See Ted Hughes, 'Keith Douglas', in *Winter Pollen: Occasional Prose*, ed. William Scammell (London: Faber, 1994), 218.

[40] Douglas, *Complete Poems*, 96.

demonstration of the power of his imagination, as he sees through a 'curtain of thought'

> a dead bird and a live bird
> the dead eyeless, but with a bright eye
>
> the live bird discovered me
> and stepped from a black rock into the air—
> I turn from the dead bird to watch him fly,
>
> electric, brilliant blue,
> beneath he is orange, like flame,
> colours I can't believe are so,
>
> as legendary flowers bloom
> incendiary in tint . . .[41]

This bringing the dead to life amazes even the sorcerer, whose syntax leaves room for more mundane explanations. Douglas may replenish the eyeless dead and send it on its glorious flight, or he may merely scare the living bird into the air, leaving the dead behind. However, the bird seems more than real, with its unbelievable colours and its comparison to 'legendary flowers'. The ontological ambiguity returns in the final stanza, where the bird 'escapes the eye, or is a ghost | and in a moment has come down | crept into the dead bird, ceased to exist'. The bird is real or imaginary, alive or dead, 'escapes the eye, or is a ghost'. One might assume it makes a difference which; but the voicing of these polarized alternatives allows their coexistence. The poem demonstrates much more than elegiac renewal. Like so many of Douglas's subjects, the sea bird fuses life and death, implying the resurrective power of the poet's imagination even while the syntax cannot quite bring itself to sanction such blasphemous authority.

Douglas's poetry explores the price of this power. In 'Adams', which is either an earlier draft or an extended revision of 'The Sea Bird', a dead officer is compared to the mysterious bird, and having been resurrected, his ghost troubles the poet: 'Till Rest, cries my

---

[41] Ibid. 83.

mind to Adams' ghost; | only go elsewhere, let me alone | creep into the dead bird, cease to exist.'[42] The living dead are a painful burden, so much so that Douglas portrays his mind as 'possessed': the 'idiot crew' of 'Devils' (1942) cry out 'against my sleep';[43] and in a reconfiguration of the miracle of the Gadarene swine, the angels and devils of 'Landscape with Figures 3' prosecute their 'dark strife | the arguments of hell with heaven', having been 'driven | into my mind like beasts'.[44] 'Dead Men' constitutes a careful meditation on the need to 'leave the dead in the earth', and concludes that the prudent response to the dead is that of either a lover—who gives them no thought—or a wild dog, a 'cynic' for whom they are no more than 'meat in a hole'.[45] (A fellow soldier recalled Douglas seeing, and later drawing, 'a German soldier being pulled out of his grave by wild dogs, pariahs, and sort of noshing him'.[46]) The poet, nevertheless, acknowledges that he belongs with the dead:

> Tonight the moon inveigles them
> to love: they infer from her gaze
> her tacit encouragement.
> Tonight the white dresses and the jasmin scent
> in the streets. I in another place
> see the white dresses glimmer like moths. Come
>
> to the west, out of that trance, my heart—
> here the same hours have illumined
> sleepers who are condemned or reprieved
> and those whom their ambitions have deceived;
> the dead men, whom the wind
> powders till they are like dolls . . .

The poet's 'heart' may be with the lovers, but *he* remains in 'another place', the west—traditionally a place of death, not least according to ancient Egyptian mythology which viewed the western desert as

---

[42] Douglas, *Complete Poems*, 82.   [43] Ibid. 88.   [44] Ibid. 104.
[45] Ibid. 96.
[46] John Stubbs, 'A Soldier's Story: Keith Douglas at El Ballah', *P.N. Review*, 47, 12/3 (1985), 27.

the realm of the dead. Douglas's typically bi-located self-division between life and death ensures that neither the lover's nor the dog's attitude can be embraced. In his most often-quoted letter, to J. C. Hall in 1943, he reports: 'I never tried to write about war . . . until I had experienced it. Now I will write of it, and perhaps one day cynic and lyric will meet and make me a balanced style.'[47] 'Dead Men' cannot emulate either the lover's lyricism or the dog's cynicism ('cynic' derives from the Greek *kuōn*—dog). Despite concluding that the dead are 'not capable of resurrection', Douglas's imprudent mind will not leave them at rest in the earth.

Appraising the psychology of self-elegy, Wallace Stevens finds redemptive potential in the poet's ability to convert impending destruction into 'a different, an explicable, an amenable circumstance'.[48] Whether experimenting with Death-in-Life or Life-in-Death, Douglas's self-elegies rarely offer such reassurance. Survival beyond death, on which posthumous art must be predicated, does admittedly provide rewards in 'Canoe'; but more often Douglas's ghosts are wandering and dishevelled, and the soldier-poet experiences so much hell on earth ('I am the figure burning in hell'[49]) that, like the wandering Jew, he perceives death as enticing only when it promises the sleep of oblivion. Douglas more commonly converts destruction into an 'amenable circumstance' when he describes the moment of death, which may be as sudden and painless as a mosquito bite, or may provide a revelatory instant as promised by world religions *passim*:

> The finale if it should come is
>
> the moment my love and I meet
> our hands move out across a room of strangers
> certain they hold the rose of love.[50]

[47] Douglas to J. C. Hall, 10 Aug. 1943, in *Letters*, 295.
[48] Wallace Stevens, quoted in Jahan Ramazani, *Poetry of Mourning: The Modern Elegy from Hardy to Heaney* (Chicago: University of Chicago Press, 1994), 121.
[49] Douglas, 'Landscape with Figures 3', in *Complete Poems*, 104.
[50] Ibid. 113.

This particular 'finale', from 'This is the Dream' (1943), surprisingly adopts a Brookean conditional—with an ambiguous 'should'—and the romantic union has an air of Hollywood schmaltz. Sending the poem to Edmund Blunden, Douglas admitted that it seemed 'just good enough not to scrap'.[51] Even this limited compliment may be undeserved, but by connecting death and romance 'This is the Dream' prepares for Douglas's last, great self-elegy, 'On a Return from Egypt', in which the poet explores and finally dismisses the possibility of translating imminent destruction into amenable circumstance.

His having survived the desert war and returned to England in preparation for D-Day failed to alleviate Douglas's premonitions of impending death, and seems rather to have intensified them.[52] 'To Kristin Yingcheng Olga Milena' (1944) is a valediction in which the poet 'give[s] back perforce | the sweet wine to the grape'.[53] The drafts of that poem rewrite Brooke's 'If I should die' with a fatal addition: 'If I should die tomorrow'.[54] Death in battle has become inescapable, leaving only the timing uncertain. Yet the drafts of 'On a Return from Egypt' tentatively express hope for survival, and are much less certain about the poet's fate than most of Douglas's poetry:

> Tomorrow I set out across Europe to find
> these islands, this land beyond the mountains
> these are the things which may happen to me
> to find them suddenly at the end of years
> to continue to death like the Jew
> to trip suddenly and fall in the earth, disintegrating.[55]

Douglas may have read and remembered Sidney Keyes's 'Advice for a Journey', in which the soldiers will 'find, maybe, the dream under the hill— | But never Canaan, nor any golden mountain'.[56]

[51] Douglas to Edmund Blunden, ? Oct. 1943, in *Letters*, 308.
[52] See Graham, *Keith Douglas 1920–1944*, 250–2.
[53] Douglas, *Complete Poems*, 121.
[54] Quoted in Graham, *Keith Douglas 1920–1944*, 249.   [55] Ibid. 253.
[56] Sidney Keyes, 'Advice for a Journey', in *Collected Poems*, ed. Michael Meyer (Manchester: Carcanet, 2002), 16.

Canaan was the land covenanted by God to Abraham and his people after violence had ceased, and the possible identification of Canaan with Douglas's 'land beyond the mountains' is strengthened by the subsequent reference to the wandering Jew. The three possible fates listed in the final three lines equate to life, Death-in-Life, and death.

'Well, fair stands the wind for . . . ?'[57] Douglas's allusion in the last line of his last letter outwits the censor. The title of his last poem, however, does not look forward to his next destination, but back to the war zone he has left. Like Brooke's 'The Soldier' and Douglas's own 'Simplify me when I'm dead', 'On a Return from Egypt' is a self-elegy written on the eve of departure for battle, but this time war lies behind as well as ahead. The poem's development reflects this Janus quality, as it moves from past, to present, to future—or from Egypt, to England, to Europe:

> And all my endeavours are unlucky explorers
> come back, abandoning the expedition;
> the specimens, the lilies of ambition
> still spring in their climate, still unpicked:
> but time, time is all I lacked
> to find them, as the great collectors before me.
>
> The next month, then, is a window
> and with a crash I'll split the glass.
> Behind it stands one I must kiss,
> person of love or death
> a person or a wraith,
> I fear what I shall find.[58]

As Edna Longley has noted, the incomplete rhyme 'window/find' stops the poet 'just this side of the glass'.[59] Douglas had encountered 'wraiths' once before, in 'Negative Information', where news of the war-dead had been casually received: 'You and I are careless

---

[57] Douglas to Jocelyn Baber, 28 Apr. 1944, in *Letters*, 343.

[58] Douglas, 'On a Return from Egypt', in *Complete Poems*, 122.

[59] Edna Longley, ' "Shit or Bust": The Importance of Keith Douglas', in *Poetry in the Wars* (Newcastle: Bloodaxe, 1986), 107.

of these millions of wraiths.'⁶⁰ When, in that poem, the poet and his companion meet in dreams their own 'dishevelled ghosts', 'the modest hosts | of our ambition stare them out'. Life and hope for the future keep death at bay. In 'On a Return from Egypt', however, Douglas mourns that 'the lilies of ambition' have been left behind unpicked, and the resourceless poet must kiss the 'wraith' which may be lurking behind the glass. This sense of an intractable destiny befits a poem in which the poet, facing the prospect of imminent death, writes posthumously. Douglas depicts himself as 'disheartened', 'depleted', 'colder'—this may refer to the relative climatic conditions of Egypt and England, but when Douglas announces that 'the heart is a coal', his metaphor remembers Shelley's fading coals and indicates a dwindling of poetic as well as personal strength. His expedition has failed; he lacked time; he has already been defeated. The result is a new kind of self-elegy: enervated, yet about to crash through the glass; fearing death, yet dead already.

Every self-elegy dares fate to intervene by making that poem the poet's last, and thus investing words with prophetic power. 'On a Return from Egypt' leaves the poet's destiny as an ellipsis for posterity to complete: the admission of fear betrays an explicit vulnerability very different from the aggressive challenges in 'Simplify me when I'm dead' or the acceptance of the happy fatalist. Nevertheless, as he stands fearfully in the wings of Europe, Douglas cannot entirely regret his destiny; on the contrary, his *amor fati* is expressed in the violent action of splitting the glass. War, as William James noted, 'is human nature at its uttermost. We are here to do our uttermost.'⁶¹ Douglas would readily have assented: the battlefield is, after all, 'the simple, central stage of the war: it is there that the interesting things happen'.⁶² Crashing through the window, Douglas successfully marries 'the conduct demanded of him' to 'remarkable and sacrificial exploit'. The poem dallies with the possibility of

⁶⁰ Douglas, 'Negative Information', in *Complete Poems*, 79.
⁶¹ William James, quoted in David Bromwich, 'How Moral Is Taste?', in *Skeptical Music: Essays on Modern Poetry* (Chicago: University of Chicago Press, 2001), 241.
⁶² Douglas, *Alamein to Zem Zem*, 15.

survival, yet ends with a line which dispels much of that Brookean uncertainty: 'I fear what I shall find'—'shall', not 'may'. Douglas foresees and foresuffers, but only by splitting the glass will he leap out of self-elegy and finally kiss the wraith tracked so insistently throughout his work.

2. SIDNEY KEYES

Douglas's essay 'Poets in This War' expresses little more than disdain for the work of contemporaries. John Heath-Stubbs is quickly dispatched for having 'published some of the decade's worst printed verse'; John Lehmann 'is encouraging the occupants of British barrack rooms to work off their repressions in his pages'; and there is not, Douglas announces magisterially, a single poet of the war who 'stands out as an individual'.[63] Nevertheless, one name does come through the bombardment relatively unscathed. When Douglas dismisses the poets of 'War Time Oxford' as having 'no experiences worth writing of', he concedes that some of them, 'notably Sidney Keyes', are 'technically quite competent'.[64] Nowhere in the essay does Douglas risk higher praise. Yet his information about Keyes's lack of experience is already out of date: Keyes had left Oxford in April 1942 to join the army, and was shipped out to Tunisia with his regiment in March the following year. Writing 'Poets in This War' in early May 1943, Douglas would almost certainly not have known that Keyes had been killed in action just days before, on 29 April, aged 20.

The poems which Keyes is believed to have been composing during his fortnight of active service were not recovered after his death, so all his work precedes experience of battle. That circumstance points to a fundamental distinction. Douglas not only has experiences worth writing of, but the opportunity to write of them; Keyes writes a war poetry of anticipation, coming to terms with the

---

[63] Douglas, 'Poets in This War', in *Letters*, 351.   [64] Ibid.

future by ranging over past conflicts. Whereas Douglas records extrospectively and retrospectively, Keyes wrestles with the fears of his imagination; and whereas Douglas speaks with the assurance of the first person empirical voice, Keyes makes use of multifarious voices from the battlefields of history. But in other ways, to read one is to be reminded of the other, and not merely because they stand above their contemporaries as the most gifted poets of the war.[65] It is suggestive to argue that their respective tastes in European poetry signal profound temperamental differences: Douglas translates Rimbaud, while Keyes finds Rilke 'the most important European poet since Goethe and Wordsworth'.[66] Yet such a simple division ignores underlying affinities. Douglas in Egypt reports having been given 'a book [he] wanted very much, the poems of Rainer Maria Rilke';[67] and Keyes, noting the number of his own poems 'relating to the French symbolists', considers 'making some translations of Rimbaud'.[68] Douglas 'work[s] without hope'; Keyes admits that it is 'entirely impossible to hope for the future',[69] and groups himself with those artists who 'have given up hope of gaining anything except our own extinction . . . from society and its expedients'.[70] And Keyes joins Douglas in the awkward squad when he confesses that he dislikes his army rank: 'It means nothing, but gives me power I do not want, and others power over me which they have no right to.'[71] Most of all, Douglas and Keyes share a vision of impending death. Douglas insists that he will not survive the war. 'Of all those friends who were about to go to war,' Milein Cosman remembers of Keyes, 'I don't recall anyone so constantly obsessed with death.'[72] That recollection is explicitly contradicted by Michael Meyer's argument

[65] For conflicting accounts of whether Douglas and Keyes ever met, see Graham, *Keith Douglas 1920–1944*, 99.
[66] Sidney Keyes, 'Notebook: 1942–43', in *Minos of Crete: Plays and Stories*, ed. Michael Meyer (London: Routledge, 1948), 164.
[67] Douglas to Marie J. Douglas, ? Sept. 1943, in *Letters*, 298.
[68] Keyes to John Heath-Stubbs, 8 Aug. 1941, in *Minos of Crete*, 170.
[69] Keyes to Milein Cosman, 21 June 1942, ibid. 176.
[70] Keyes, 'Notebook: 1942–43', 159.   [71] Ibid. 163.
[72] 'Memoir by Milein Cosman', in Keyes, *Collected Poems*, 115.

that Keyes 'was [no more obsessed] than most of our generation in those years, or our predecessors in 1914–18'.[73] But Meyer is defending Keyes against an unreal foe. Although barely a poem goes by without some mention of death, the fact of that fixation does not impose restrictions on his achievement. Keyes belongs with Douglas among the greatest self-elegists in English poetry.

'Meditation of Phlebas the Phoenician', written in January 1939 when Keyes was 16, is spoken by a 'corpse long-drowned, | Tricked out in foamy lace':[74] his imaginative excursion from *The Waste Land* already allows Keyes to adopt the posthumous voice so often heard in his mature work. Death having been present from the start, war only sharpens the focus. Four years and all Keyes's best poetry later, evidence for a continuity of preoccupations is provided by a notebook entry: 'I can still realize the power of the Drowned Man, pressed between sea and sky like a dead flower in a book.'[75] Earlier in the notebook, Keyes reports a memory of a river entering 'a deserted mill through a kind of portcullis, which I sometimes thought was for catching the corpses of the drowned'.[76] The drowned resurface sporadically throughout Keyes's poetry. 'Nocturne for Four Voices' includes the repeated imperative 'Drown yourself', and imagines that the stars 'Are drowned men's eyes, tangled in floating spars | Of trees. The moon's a swollen corpse.'[77] Given this predilection, it comes as no surprise that Keyes should find the suicide of Virginia Woolf amenable to poetry, or that his poem on the subject holds her body in its watery grave. Elsewhere, children's drifting corpses are mauled by 'grumbling seals';[78] a foreign corpse is thrown up by the tide, its limbs 'Drawn limp and racked between the jigging waves';[79] and drowning men are imagined 'coughing out their lungs', pulled down 'on the tide's whim, their bare feet scraping sand'.[80] A letter to a girlfriend comparing love with 'the moment of drowning when one

---

[73] Michael Meyer, 'Preface to the 1988 Edition', ibid. p. xvi.
[74] Keyes, *Collected Poems*, 104.   [75] Keyes, 'Notebook: 1942–43', 163.
[76] Ibid. 153.   [77] Keyes, *Collected Poems*, 4.
[78] Keyes, 'The Glass Tower in Galway', ibid. 31.
[79] 'Seascape', ibid. 80.   [80] 'Moonlight Night on the Port', ibid. 93.

is said to *want* to go under'[81] reveals the cause of Keyes's fascination. Even as it fights for life, his poetry is always tempted by that desire to 'go under'.

Keyes defines literary periods according to their portrayals of death: death as the Leveller up to the Elizabethans, as a metaphysical problem in the seventeenth century, and in the eighteenth as the end of life. The difficulty begins with the Romantics, who 'raised a spectre' by using sensual imagery to make death 'a part of life'.[82] Keyes explains that his love of Rilke is a consequence of this problematic legacy:

By the later C.19, and up to our own time, it had resulted in a clearly apparent *Death Wish*, as the only solution to the problem—since the solution must come in sensual terms. It was left to necrophilious Germany, to Rilke in fact, to provide the best solution short of actually dying.[83]

Rilke is the 'Poet of Death', who embodies in its highest form the 'persistent death wish in German poetry'.[84] Germany has now 'gone crazy with this passion'; what Keyes admires in poetry, he must resist in war. That complication exacerbates (and exasperates) his ambivalence. Whereas he writes straightforwardly after joining the army that 'I am not yet reduced to the (literally) dead level and hope not to be',[85] his poetry tantalizes itself with the attractive fate of those who succumb to the death wish: Woolf can now 'sleep well, safe from the rabid winds | Of war and argument';[86] Schiller conquers fear of death, and is 'ready to set out' into the freedom it promises;[87] and an assortment of maidens, ladies, and lovers are successfully courted by Death ('Four Postures of Death'). Keyes argues that 'It remains for someone to make an art of love',[88] but his own love poetry rarely amounts to more than a temporary respite from the

[81] Keyes, quoted in *Collected Poems*, 134.   [82] 'Notebook: 1942–43', 163–4.
[83] Ibid. 164.
[84] Keyes, quoted in 'Memoir by Michael Meyer', in *Collected Poems*, 122.
[85] Keyes to Milein Cosman, 25–6 May 1942, in *Minos of Crete*, 174.
[86] Keyes, 'Elegy for Mrs Virginia Woolf', in *Collected Poems*, 18.
[87] Keyes, 'Schiller Dying', ibid. 50.
[88] Keyes, quoted in 'Memoir by Michael Meyer', 123.

serious business of dying and thinking about death. 'I am in love with the wildness of the living,' he claims promisingly enough in 'Two Offices of a Sentry'; but immediately he must temper that love of life with a more fully and memorably expressed love: 'I am in love with the rhythms of dead limbs. | I am in love with all those who have entered | The night that smells of petals and of dust.'[89] Love is like drowning because death swallows love, its sensual solution amounting to a near-sexual dissolution. Attempting to catch a celebratory mood, 'Epithalamium' only marvels at the mistaken optimism of the betrothed couple:

> O live and love to see your happy children
> Deny the sorrow of a burning world.
>
> Though you will have no bells and the winter is coming
> I sing your courage, who expect the spring.[90]

This is a false happiness, attained by ignoring the evidence. Whether the poet or the couple is expecting the spring, in fact 'winter is coming', and the world burns. In a letter to John Heath-Stubbs, Keyes quotes from the *Pervigilium Veneris*: 'cras amet qui nunquam amavit, quique amavit cras amet' ('tomorrow let the loveless and the lover love'). This is 'as pleasant a thought as could occur to anyone',[91] but Keyes never treats it as anything more than wishful thinking. 'Epithalamium' performs dutifully while knowing that the courage involved in making an art of love is deluded; only after the many tomorrows of winter have been endured might a shift of focus be possible.

Keyes identifies with the decrepit and recently dead. His dramatic monologues are for Prospero, Schiller dying, William Byrd as an old man, Gilles de Retz awaiting divine judgement, or Yeats in Limbo. Not the most obvious of Keyes's precursors, Alexander Pope appears as the subject of 'Sour Land', but only at the stage in his life when

---

[89] Keyes, 'Two Offices of a Sentry', in *Collected Poems*, 76.
[90] Keyes, 'Epithalamium', ibid. 87.
[91] Keyes to John Heath-Stubbs, 24 May 1942, in *Minos of Crete*, 173.

'illness and disillusionment were beginning to oppress him'.[92] Set in Stanton Harcourt, where (an authorial note helpfully states) Pope completed the fifth book of his *Iliad*, the poem finds 'No peace for the wanderer waiting only death'. That is as sufficient a description of Keyes as of Pope, and it soon becomes hard to tell them apart. Descriptions of the vicinity situate Pope less in an Oxfordshire landscape than a Keyesian mindscape: 'ponds', as the reader of Keyes might have come to expect, 'are cloudy, filled with eyeshot corpses'. This moment of rhetorical excess is matched by the presence of a 'running demon' which jogs along the fallow all night long, the houses 'blind as leprosy', and the 'acrid-tasting air'. Keyes urges the reader to remain 'unseduced' by the overtly gothic 'country', and not to look 'overmuch | Nor listen by the churchyard wall'. But he himself is intimate with its deathly ways, speaking as the condemned man warning off the innocent. And when Keyes describes Pope as having been driven by sorrow 'to Troy and other men's despair', he paints a self-portrait: disillusioned like Pope, inhabited by the sorrow of a burning world, and with his own death imminent, Keyes increasingly turns to other men's Troys for his subject-matter.

Keyes is the poet of apprehension. 'My tongue is schooled in every word of fear,'[93] he writes, and that proud confession is borne out by the explicit naming of 'fear' several dozen times in his work. (Douglas's final line of his final poem, 'I fear what I shall find', also happens to be his most Keyesian.) Resisting the fate to which it is drawn, Keyes's poetry struggles—as one of his titles puts it—'to keep off fears'. 'Fear was Donne's peace,' another poem observes, but for Keyes, every 'good day' only increases the fear that 'all my life must change and fall away'.[94] And again, at 'the twelfth hour of unrelenting summer', Keyes can think only of those 'whose ready mouths are stopped', and weep for 'those whose eyes are full of sand';[95] summer may seem unrelenting, but everything after the

[92] Keyes, *Collected Poems*, 13.   [93] Keyes, 'Not Chosen', ibid. 76.
[94] Keyes, 'Time will not Grant', ibid. 38.
[95] Keyes, 'Two Offices of a Sentry', ibid. 76.

zenith of the twelfth hour is a decline towards death. The only thing that fear cannot do is 'Subdue the writing hand'.[96] Each poem therefore seeks to constitute a rebuttal of the pervasive fear embodied in it. 'Fear of jammed windows and of rising footsteps', 'Fear of the moonlight shifting against the door', and fear 'of tripwire and garotte', lead to urgent self-encouragement: 'Then let me never crouch against the wall | But meet my fears and fight them till I fall.' The real conflict is not between rival armies, even though that will inevitably result in the poet's death. Keyes is concerned only with his inner conflict—his fear of fear—and his poetry is an attempt to meet fears and master them. Action in battle would be one way of escaping fear altogether: as 'Advice for a Journey' exhorts, 'go on, go out | Into the bad lands of battle, into the cloud-wall | Of the future, my friends, and leave your fear'.[97] Thought is a curse because it breeds fear—the thoughtful 'leave their bones', Keyes declares, 'In windy foodless meadows of despair'. And the demon who jogs 'Black under moonlit cloud' every night in 'Sour Land' is eventually identified:

> This is the country Ulysses and Hermod
> Entered afraid; by ageing poets sought
> Where lives no love nor any kind of flower—
> Only the running demon, thought.[98]

Although his circumstances count him among the 'ageing poets', Keyes is an unwilling citizen of that country, regretting the thoughts which prompt his torturing fears.

Not having experienced it for himself, Keyes exercises understandable restraint in his descriptions of battle. All the same, the ability to foresuffer helps him to overcome fear. Keyes achieves that foresufferance by looking back to previous wars, just as he looks back to the example of previous artists beset by fears. Stationed at Dunbar in the early summer of 1942, he writes a poem haunted by the war-dead of three centuries earlier. Its title, 'Dunbar, 1650',

---

[96] Keyes, 'Extracts from "A Journey through Limbo"', ibid. 28.
[97] Ibid. 16.   [98] Ibid. 14.

refers to one of the most catastrophic battles in Scottish history, when an English army led by Cromwell—hungry, cornered, and exhausted—took advantage of the Scots' inept military tactics to inflict a crushing defeat on a much stronger enemy. Historically informed, the poem refers to the Scots' willing sacrifice of the high ground, the Covenanters who disastrously overruled their general's strategy, and Cromwell's ruthless pursuit of the retreating army:

> Crossing the little river
> Their pikes jostled and rang.
> The ditches were full of dead.
> A blackbird sang.
>
> The southern terrible squire
> Rode them down in the marsh.
> The preachers scattered like crows—
> The name of the day was WRATH.[99]

This offers evidence for Jeffrey Wainwright's claim that 'Often [Keyes's] best effects come in poems where he shortens the line'.[100] The dimetric simplicity of 'A blackbird sang' captures the insouciant celebration of the natural world, and (by implicit contrast) the unnaturalness of war and the crow-like preachers. But the poem's most salient characteristic is its concern with the experiences of the Scots. Only when mentioning 'the southern terrible squire' in the final stanza does Keyes reveal the enemy as English; otherwise, he is entirely interested in defeat and death. The possibility of identifying with the victorious survivors is one which Keyes, even with the added encouragement of national affiliation, cannot countenance.

'Dunbar, 1650' may be the work of a poet expecting the worst, but at least its specific incidents and temporal remoteness prevent an obvious equivalence to Keyes's own situation. His imaginative encounters with death can often be more direct. In August 1942 he reports having seen Robert Helpmann's *Hamlet* ballet twice in

---

[99] Keyes, 'Dunbar, 1650', *Collected Poems*, 74.
[100] Jeffrey Wainwright, 'Introduction', ibid. p. xii.

Edinburgh, and asserts that 'its total effect is one of great horror and pain—all the more so, because one can well imagine that the moment of death will take such a form—though I certainly pray that it will not!'[101] His anxiety proves the immediate relevance of the question of dying, and the formality of 'one can well imagine' points to much more fevered imaginings. When Death approaches the lady in 'Four Postures of Death', she welcomes his arrival: 'In a dream | Or perhaps a picture, quite without surprise | I turn to meet the question in his eyes.'[102] But that implies a degree of volition denied to those who die in battle. Keyes's masterpiece, 'The Foreign Gate', unflinchingly represents their pain—and his own pain seen in prediction; it knows that 'A soldier's death is hard; | There's no prescribed or easy word | For dissolution in the Army books.'[103]

Consensus insists that 'The Foreign Gate' is uneven. Jeffrey Wainwright grants the poem an 'intermittent brilliance', but concludes that it 'cannot be said to succeed as a whole'.[104] In this he follows Vernon Scannell's view that 'while as a whole it must be accounted a failure, it is an interesting one with a number of incidental felicities'.[105] Prompted by an editorial note stating that Keyes began writing the poem 'at great pressure after he had already prepared the rest of *The Iron Laurel* for publication', Scannell finds 'many of the marks of over-hasty writing'.[106] Although often just in its particulars, such criticism—coupled with the double-edged praise of 'intermittent brilliance' and 'incidental felicities'—does not satisfactorily account for the scale of Keyes's ambition. A fairer judgement might point out the indebtedness of a poet like Geoffrey Hill, whose agonizing over his obligation to speak for the war-dead can be traced directly back to 'The Foreign Gate'. When Hill writes a sequence attempting 'a florid grim music' broken by the 'grunts and shrieks' of

[101] Keyes to John Heath-Stubbs, 25 Aug. 1942, in *Minos of Crete*, 179.
[102] Keyes, *Collected Poems*, 90.   [103] Ibid. 63.
[104] Wainwright, 'Introduction', p. xi.
[105] Vernon Scannell, *Not Without Glory: Poets of the Second World War* (London: Woburn Press, 1976), 87–8.
[106] Ibid. 88.

the dying at Towton,[107] he learns from Keyes's post-battle battlefield which (in a horribly discordant rewriting of *The Tempest*'s sounds and sweet airs) is 'full | Of noises and dead voices'.[108] And Hill's pained failure to bring solace to the dead is shared and effectively articulated by Keyes: 'The probing mind | Of poet cannot reach to comfort them.'

Keyes wrote 'The Foreign Gate' during February and March 1942. The published letters and notebooks provide little specific insight into the making of the poem; but a letter from May of that year, in which Keyes announces that 'I am not a man but a voice',[109] hints at his understanding of the poet's role. 'The Foreign Gate' encourages the war-dead to inhabit the poet's mind, and speak through him:

> fill the solitary
> Tower of my mind with your high singing; seek
> My ruined house, you bird-shaped passengers,
> Cheated and eager far-sent messengers
> Pass through the lovelocked gate to my bright lure.

The poet acts as a medium, having made a 'bridge' for the 'voiceless speakers' and given them the opportunity to 'Cry through the trumpet of my fear and rage'. He therefore becomes not a man but the voice—or rather, the voices—of the dead, who 'call continually' from their curious afterlives of iced woods and fiery forests, foliage of bone, marble trees, gates with pillars of mist, ruins, and cold rocks. Illuminated by 'starshine', they tell snatches of their stories, or cry out to lovers without expecting answers. Keyes's historical perspective is geographically and temporally panoramic, so that the dead of Naseby and Tannenberg press no less urgently than the voice recalling that ' "At Dunkirk I | Rolled in the shallows" '. Nor is anyone spared death's agony: the idealist 'fighting for a dream' in the Spanish Civil War ends up on a 'black Spanish hillside',

---

[107] Geoffrey Hill, 'Funeral Music: An Essay', in *Collected Poems* (Harmondsworth: Penguin, 1985), 200 and 199.

[108] Keyes, *Collected Poems*, 62.

[109] Keyes to Milein Cosman, 25–6 May 1942, in *Minos of Crete*, 174.

vomiting his 'faith and courage out among the stones'. 'Their pain cries down the noise of poetry,' Keyes affirms of the dead, but he has already put his poetry at the disposal of their pain; his is an attempt not so much to 'conquer chaos'—the poem later admits that it cannot—but to accommodate it, give it voice, and be true to it without superimposing the anaesthetic language of commemoration.

In its dislocations, interruptions, and multiple voices, 'The Foreign Gate' is never an easy poem. As if suddenly unsure of its ground, it becomes even more tentative when Keyes searches for restitution or makes a consolatory gesture. He invokes Rilke ('A pale unlearned poet out of Europe's | Erratic heart') as an example of a man who 'cried and the great Orders heard him', but by unostentatiously translating the opening of the *Duino Elegies*, Keyes rules out such supernatural authority for himself: 'Were I to cry, who in that proud hierarchy | Of the illustrious would pity me?' Despite his reluctance to reveal the 'great Orders' and the 'illustrious' as angelic (the 'Engel Ordnungen' in Rilke), Keyes finds that their presence in a 'high-pillared house' beyond the human souls offers 'a scroll of peace | Unrolled before the shattered face | Of the dead soldier and the straying lover'. 'Death', the poem loftily proclaims, 'is conquered', 'and the great' (that is, the angels) 'have come home, whom all the clamour of history | Will never deafen or decrease their glory'. But Keyes's metaphysical appeal to a salvation outside history cannot be sustained. The final section returns to the spirits which 'call and cower' among the ruins, and finds the human problems as intractable as before:

> The great have come home and the troubled spirits have spoken:
> But help or hope is none till the circle is broken
> Of wishing death and living time's compulsion,
> Of wishing love and living love's destruction.

Even the angels, and even a voice for the dead, can only do so much. Keyes's poetry is itself caught in that 'circle', compelled by time and yet tempted by death, seeking love and yet destroying what it seeks. 'The Foreign Gate' ends with the poet telling himself that 'It is well to remember the stone faces | Among these ruins'; but although those 'stone faces' represent angels, the 'ruins' have (or literally, are) the last word. 'I do pray, or would if I prayed at all except "the bone's prayer to Death its god", that there will be a time when our lives are not strung on a succession of wretched train journeys,'[110] Keyes writes in December 1942. His allusion is to T. S. Eliot's 'The Dry Salvages', published the previous year. But whereas Eliot's poem refutes its own belief that 'There is no end of it, the voiceless wailing' with the Christian hope provided by 'the hardly, barely prayable | Prayer of the one Annunciation',[111] for Keyes the voiceless wailing will continue along with the wretched train journeys, and the bone's prayer to Death will remain the only prayer likely to be answered.

---

[110] Keyes to Renée-Jane Scott, 21 Dec. 1942, ibid. 180.
[111] T. S. Eliot, *The Complete Poems and Plays* (London: Faber, 1969), 186.

10

Fighting Back Over the Same Ground: Ted Hughes and War

'When I first started writing,' Ted Hughes acknowledged, 'I wrote again and again and again about the First World War.'[1] He ascribed that compulsion to three factors: the stories told by his father, who had survived his regiment's massacre at Gallipoli; a love of Wilfred Owen's poetry; and the West Yorkshire landscape where he grew up believing that 'the whole region is in mourning for the first world war'.[2] Despite his best efforts, Hughes never managed to free himself from his subject. In *Wodwo* (1967) he was already writing poetry designed to 'get rid of the entire body of preoccupation': 'I finally decided that really [the First World War] had nothing to do with me.'[3] The exorcism failed: a series of poems in *Wolfwatching* (1989) returned Hughes to his first inspiration in the wartime experiences of his father and uncle. Those poems are among the most visible signs of a pressure which shapes his writing career.

War is the abiding concern of Hughes's poetry. As a teenager beginning to write in the early 1940s, he viewed contemporary conflict through the lens of the past, and the fear that his elder brother's war would prove as terrible as their father's became his

---

[1] From a transcript of Ted Hughes reading at the Adelaide Festival, Mar. 1987, accessed at <http://www.zeta.org.au/~annskea/Adelaide.htm> on 15 May 2003.

[2] Ted Hughes, 'The Rock', in Geoffrey Summerfield (ed.), *Worlds: Seven Modern Poets* (Harmondsworth: Penguin, 1974), 126.

[3] Ted Hughes at the Adelaide Festival, Mar. 1987.

'permanent preoccupation'.[4] His post-war poetic maturity continued to perceive experience through that lens: Hughes characterizes his poems as 'battleground[s]' where his imagination, excited by 'the war between vitality and death', celebrates 'the exploits of the warriors of either side'.[5] Writing about the natural world, he therefore appears less a war poet *manqué* than a war poet by other means. This position requires some defending because, notwithstanding his own prompts and observations, the bulk of critical writing on Hughes remains silent about war.[6] Primitivism, shamanism, Trickster myth, pastoral, post-pastoral, ecology, parapsychology—it sometimes seems that there is no context so esoteric that it has not been used to explain Hughes's work. War is considered only in passing, if at all, and is typically assumed to be representative of something larger: 'war itself is the occasion rather than the subject of the best "war poems" in *The Hawk in the Rain*. Their subject is death and grief.'[7] The inverted commas in this example from Terry Gifford and Neil Roberts insinuate that Hughes's 'war poems' are not really war poems at all. Wilfred Owen, to whom Hughes professes a fundamental indebtedness, rates barely a mention in most critical studies.

Whatever insights the various approaches to Hughes have afforded, their blindness to his belief that experience cannot be disentangled from the influence of war guarantees that they miss the forming impulse of his poetry. That impulse, Hughes recognized, originates in a war fought on the home front as well as internationally: 'Owen, when I came to know his poems, grew to represent my father's experience, and later on [Keith] Douglas my brother's (who was in North Africa through the same period). So that pattern of antithetical succession was prefigured, for me, and quite highly

[4] Ted Hughes, 'Postscript 1: Douglas and Owen', in *Winter Pollen: Occasional Prose*, ed. William Scammell (London: Faber, 1994), 215.

[5] Hughes, 'The Rock', 126.

[6] The closest to an exception is Dennis Walder, whose *Ted Hughes* (Milton Keynes: Open University Press, 1987) spends 14 pages considering Hughes and war.

[7] Terry Gifford and Neil Roberts, *Ted Hughes: A Critical Study* (London: Faber, 1981), 84.

charged.'[8] Casting Owen as poetic father and Douglas as older brother, Hughes positions himself squarely within a tradition of war poetry, transforming it into a family drama where he as latecomer must negotiate between two rival males who struggle for supremacy. Owen or Douglas? It is the question which, Hughes implies in an introduction to Douglas's work, challenges and categorizes the most important of their English poetic successors. Hughes maintains that Owen's style was 'duly taken over, with only a few modifications, by, for instance, Philip Larkin'.[9] In the final sentence of his essay, he pays a similar compliment to Douglas:

And like Owen, after producing a few examples of what could be done with [his style], he died and left it to others.

TED HUGHES
[1987][10]

This is as much a signing up as a signing off. Having already situated Larkin in the Owen tradition, Hughes adds his own name as first in the list of Douglas's successors. The antithesis which critics routinely detect in the rival achievements of Larkin and Hughes is predetermined and 'prefigured' by the 'polar opposition of Owen and Douglas'.[11] Hughes credits those two poets with begetting the dominant traditions of post-war English poetry.

Hughes's account of modern literary history (perhaps itself a product of the First World War's *versus* habit'[12]), and his own self-portrayal as a belated war poet, endorse Francis Hope's judgement that 'In a not altogether rhetorical sense, all poetry written since 1918 is war poetry.'[13] Finding that inheritance riven by a power struggle, Hughes displays a loyalty to Douglas in his prose that does not

---

[8] Hughes, 'Postscript 1: Douglas and Owen', 215.

[9] Hughes, 'Introduction', in Keith Douglas, *The Complete Poems*, ed. Desmond Graham (Oxford: Oxford University Press, 1987), p. xxvi.

[10] Ibid, p. xxvii.   [11] Ibid, p. xxi.

[12] Paul Fussell, *The Great War and Modern Memory* (Oxford: Oxford University Press, 1975), 79–82.

[13] Francis Hope, quoted in Jon Silkin, *Out of Battle: The Poetry of the Great War* (Oxford: Oxford University Press, 1972), 347–8.

accurately represent the imaginative sympathies of his early poetry. His preoccupation with the First World War pre-dates his discovery in the late 1950s of Douglas's work, and, accordingly, Owen rather than Douglas is the presiding spirit of *The Hawk in the Rain* (1957). The first poem of a first collection provides significant clues as to how the poet views himself, and how he wishes to be viewed by others. The title poem which opens *The Hawk in the Rain* projects Hughes as a nature poet, but one who experiences nature in terms of First World War combat:

> I drown in the drumming ploughland, I drag up
> Heel after heel from the swallowing of the earth's mouth,
> From clay that clutches my each step to the ankle
> With the habit of the dogged grave . . .[14]

'[T]he ground was not mud, not sloppy mud, but an octopus of sucking clay . . . relieved only by craters full of water,' Wilfred Owen told his mother. 'Men have been known to drown in them.'[15] The ploughland, the sucking mud, the reference to drowning, the constant proximity of death, the struggle against the carnivorous earth—Hughes might be describing a battlefield landscape from the First World War. However, the only enemy is the environment: 'banging wind kills these stubborn hedges, ‖ Thumbs my eyes, throws my breath, tackles my heart, | And rain hacks my head to the bone'. This illustrates a problem which besets much of Hughes's work: shearing wartime atrocity from its specific historical contexts, his poetry risks sounding absurdly overwritten. As a result, the collection's group of poems explicitly about the First World War loses its force. 'Bayonet Charge' describes a soldier 'Stumbling across a field of clods towards a green hedge | That dazzled with rifle fire',[16] but despite a similar landscape, the poem's language fails to match the intensity of 'The Hawk in the Rain'. Hughes's

---

[14] Hughes, *Collected Poems*, ed. Paul Keegan (London: Faber, 2003), 19.
[15] Wilfred Owen to Susan Owen, 16 Jan. 1917, in *Collected Letters*, ed. Harold Owen and John Bell (Oxford: Oxford University Press, 1967), 427.
[16] Hughes, *Collected Poems*, 43.

portrayals of violence rarely concern themselves with the necessary calibrations, so that getting caught in a bad storm sounds at least as dangerous as a bayonet charge into gunfire. Hughes's language fights the First World War, going over the top even when his subjects do not.

When Hughes speaks, almost a decade later, of 'the terrible, suffocating, maternal octopus of English poetic tradition',[17] his ungainly borrowing of Owen's octopus metaphor proves that one unspoken battle in 'The Hawk in the Rain' is between the ephebe and an inescapable precursor. Thinking of his poetic predecessors, Hughes cannot see past Owen, who has become both father and mother. In 'Bayonet Charge', Hughes's unnamed protagonist 'plunged past with his bayonet toward the green hedge', as the luxuries of 'King, honour, human dignity, etcetera' were discarded: the sentiment is Owen, *passim*, and the plunging might have been taken from either 'Dulce et Decorum Est' ('He plunges at me, guttering, choking, drowning')[18] or Owen's only poetic description of a bayonet charge, 'Spring Offensive' ('plunged and fell away past this world's verge').[19] 'Bayonet Charge' is something less than Hughes's best work, but it allows the son to relive his biological father's experience in the same vicarious way that he rewrites the poetry of his poetic father. Similarly, in 'My Uncle's Wound' Hughes takes his uncle back to the battlefield where a bullet had 'picked him up by the hip-bone | And laid him in a shell-hole';[20] the poet's ambition to appropriate the experience for himself—'I wanted the exact spot'—springs from a desire to understand (and, perhaps, to be wounded in war) which is also a profound jealousy that he can never achieve the authority of the combatant poet. In Hughes's early poetry the need to re-create wartime experiences proves stronger than the need for originality, whatever the aesthetic cost: his stage-managed performances rely on familiar props, as telegrams open more terribly than bombs

---

[17] Hughes, 'Keith Douglas', in *Winter Pollen*, 213.
[18] Wilfred Owen, *The Complete Poems and Fragments*, i: *The Poems*, ed. Jon Stallworthy (London: Chatto & Windus, Hogarth Press, and Oxford University Press, 1983), 140.
[19] Ibid. 193.   [20] Hughes, *Collected Poems*, 101.

('Griefs for Dead Soldiers'), photographed young men never age ('Six Young Men'), and death's spectators stand helpless as ghosts ('The Casualty').

Over a decade after writing the war poems of *The Hawk in the Rain*, Hughes may have provided one reason for his failure:

Perhaps the more sure of itself a truth is, the more doubtful it is of the adequacy of words. This struck me forcibly once when I was collecting material for what I hoped would be a long poem about the campaign on Gallipoli during the First World War. I read memoirs and histories, eloquent and detailed. But however eloquent and detailed such writings are, one always half dismisses them, because they are inevitably false. The actuality must always have been different—in every way that really matters. ... The same principle works in all sorts of situations. At every point, a man's deeper sufferings and experiences are almost impossible for him to express by deliberate means.[21]

Hughes moves characteristically from the First World War to other 'situations': the lens of war again colours experience 'at every point'. His positing of an antagonistic relationship between truth and language befits a First World War mentality in which language has become corrupted by propaganda. Yet this distrust fails to distinguish what Owen calls the truthfulness of true poets from the lies, distortions, and euphemisms engendered by war. Hughes's preoccupation with the First World War provokes a near-fatal conviction that for the true poet (and, for that matter, the true historian) to be truthful, he must renounce language. Unsurprisingly, his long poem about Gallipoli was never written.

Hughes's account does not give a date to this crisis, but his second collection, *Lupercal* (1960), betrays what may be consequent ruptures: whereas *The Hawk in the Rain* contains six poems directly about war, *Lupercal* has none. The omission ought to make redundant Hughes's attempt in *Wodwo* to persuade himself that the First World War has nothing to do with him. Whereof the poet cannot

21 Hughes, 'Orghast: Talking without Words', in *Winter Pollen*, 122–3.

speak, thereof he must remain silent: unable to write the truth about war, Hughes stops writing about war altogether. Only once, at the end of 'Mayday on Holderness', does the old preoccupation resurface, albeit in circumstances suggesting that the poet is operating under duress:

> The North Sea lies soundless. Beneath it
> Smoulder the wars: to heart-beats, bomb, bayonet.
> 'Mother, Mother!' cries the pierced helmet.
> Cordite oozings of Gallipoli,
>
> Curded to beastings, broached my palate,
> The expressionless gaze of the leopard,
> The coils of the sleeping anaconda,
> The nightlong frenzy of shrews.[22]

Hughes's long poem about Gallipoli has shrunk to these convulsing fragments. No longer does he try to write representational war poetry; instead, the images constitute the horrific return of what has been repressed, broaching (both meanings: initiating and piercing) the poet's palate. Hughes depicts Gallipoli as his 'beastings'—the colostrum which provided his earliest nutrition. That formative influence, no doubt aided by a pun on 'beast', invades the animal kingdom as well. Hughes's sustained fascination with predators is flavoured by the 'Cordite oozings' of war.

'Mayday on Holderness' admits that war is the prior condition which nourishes Hughes's work. But after the mixed results of *The Hawk in the Rain*, *Lupercal* understands that poetic re-enactments of battle cannot seem other than mannered exercises. Hughes's breakthrough comes in realizing—to reverse the opinion of Gifford and Roberts—that war, the subject of his poetry, need not also be its occasion. So, while the title of 'Wilfred Owen's Photographs' may seem to promise a war poem in the old style, it delivers an account of a parliamentary debate in which Parnell called for the abolition

---

[22] Hughes, *Collected Poems*, 60–1.

of the British Navy's cat-o'-nine-tails. Hughes reports elsewhere the source for his otherwise mystifying title:

Owen carried about, in his pocket, photographs of trench horrors which he would evidently have liked to see magnified and put on public display in London, his idea being to shock his non-participant fellow citizens into an awareness of the new day dawning in the trenches.[23]

Hughes bypasses the debate about whether those photographs existed, and his 'evidently' shows the strains of disguising guesswork as fact. Naturally enthusiastic about the validity of photographs which are not dependent on corrupted language, he applauds Owen's role as the purveyor of truth to a society which seeks to deny its own nature. It is a role for which Hughes is the willing successor as he pushes beyond the gentility principle to betray the animal passions in the parlour or the death-skull hidden behind the complacent smirks of acquaintances. Hughes finds in Owen's motives the template for all such revelations, and by seeming to cite the photographs as anterior to Parnell's parliamentary performance, he ensures that the First World War remains the point of origin to which the meaning of all other experiences should be referred. There is, nevertheless, a complication. Not content with embellishing the story of Owen's photographs, Hughes distorts Owen's temperament in the process. Far from pushing the truth of war into the shocked faces of his 'non-participant fellow citizens', Owen spoke only once about his photographs, and never showed them—a withholding which Jon Stallworthy attributes to his 'characteristic delicacy'.[24] In Hughes's misreading comes a sign that some new external force has disrupted his dependence on the First World War which fashioned his imagination. Hughes remakes Owen in another's image: the poet who photographed war's horrors, and who made plans to have his photographs published, was Keith Douglas.

---

[23] Hughes, 'Introduction', in Douglas, *The Complete Poems*, p. xxxi.
[24] Jon Stallworthy, *Wilfred Owen* (Oxford and London: Oxford University Press and Chatto, 1974), 222.

Like Owen, Douglas goes underreported in discussions of the influences on Hughes's work; as Edna Longley notes, 'studies of Hughes—far more abundant than of Douglas—make little room for an obvious ancestor and inspiration'.[25] Again, Hughes's prose writings make the case explicitly, and again they have been taken at less than their word. 'Speaking of Keith Douglas in 1964,' Seamus Heaney observes, 'Hughes could have been speaking of himself';[26] 'Hughes's comments on Keith Douglas's language shed light on his own practice,' Paul Bentley maintains;[27] Gifford and Roberts use terminology from Hughes's account of Douglas to demonstrate 'his own most characteristic style';[28] Ekbert Faas finds in *Wodwo* a strategy reminiscent of something Hughes had defined 'in the later poetry of Keith Douglas'.[29] These are throw-away remarks which give the impression of a happy coincidence: not one of the critics stops to wonder why Hughes should sound like he is discussing his own poetry when he discusses Douglas's. Hughes himself, in his introduction to Douglas's poetry, is explicit about his obligation, praising 'an achievement for which we who come after can be grateful': 'His poetry in general seems to be of some special value. It is still very much alive, and even providing life.'[30] As Sylvia Plath reported to her mother in June 1962, she and Hughes felt Douglas's loss with keen immediacy: 'Both of us mourn this poet immensely and feel he would have been like a lovely big brother to us. His death is really a terrible blow and we are trying to resurrect his image and poems'.[31] Evidence for that admiration comes not least from

[25] Edna Longley, ' "Shit or Bust": The Importance of Keith Douglas', in *Poetry in the Wars* (Newcastle: Bloodaxe, 1986), 94.

[26] Seamus Heaney, 'Englands of the Mind', in *Preoccupations: Selected Prose 1968–1978* (London: Faber, 1980), 157.

[27] Paul Bentley, *The Poetry of Ted Hughes: Language, Illusion & Beyond* (Harlow: Longman, 1998), 27.

[28] Gifford and Roberts, *Ted Hughes*, 27.

[29] Ekbert Faas, *Ted Hughes: The Unaccommodated Universe* (Santa Barbara, Calif.: Black Sparrow Press, 1980), 18.

[30] Hughes, 'Keith Douglas', 215, 212.

[31] Sylvia Plath, quoted in Cornelia Pearsall, 'Complicate Me When I'm Dead: The War Remains of Douglas and Hughes', a paper given at the MLA, San Diego, 27 Dec. 2003.

Lupercal, where Douglas's influence is among the most significant factors to distinguish the collection from its predecessor, *The Hawk in the Rain*, especially in its attitudes to violence.

Drowning in the mud of his battlefield landscape, the poet of 'The Hawk in the Rain' had noticed the hawk hanging effortlessly above him, 'Steady as a hallucination in the streaming air'.[32] This is a hubris punished by the hawk's imagined death at the poem's end, as the 'ponderous shires crash on him'. By contrast, Hughes's persona remains earthbound and embattled, a passive sufferer without hope of reprieve. In *Lupercal*'s 'Hawk Roosting', poetry has taken wing and become predatory, giving voice to the hawk which proudly asserts its right to kill where it pleases. Hughes himself provides the best assessment of this psychology, discovering

one of those characters of supreme, heartless professionalism but supreme 'essence', such as Gourdjieff describes, gazing a whole day over the sights of a rifle, waiting for the traveller. What is distinctive about it is just that 'essence', that individualized temper superior to all circumstances, the diamond quality that has already survived the ultimate ordeals, a salamander quality that can act, and can remain intact and effective—and even feel at home—in the fires of the end.[33]

Hughes happens to be talking about Douglas's 'How to Kill', yet his commentary perfectly captures the essence of his own killer, a hawk undistracted by 'falsifying dream[s]': 'My manners are tearing off heads'.[34] The hawk's 'supreme, heartless professionalism' flies 'Through the bones of the living', and it asserts ownership of Creation without concerning itself with finicking debates about its entitlement to behave in this way: 'No arguments assert my right'. The hawk's is a temper 'superior to all circumstances'; 'The sun is behind me', it boasts, turning the life-giving force of the universe into a supporter and a hunting aid.

Hughes's selective interpretation of Douglas's poem applies more satisfactorily to the narrower tonal range of his own. 'Hawk Roosting'

---

[32] Hughes, *Collected Poems*, 19.   [33] Hughes, 'Introduction', p. xxv.
[34] Hughes, *Collected Poems*, 69.

is 'How to Kill' rewritten for the natural world, although Hughes neglects both Douglas's metaphysical dimension and his nimble transactions between the brutal and the delicate. Roy Fuller's misguided criticism of Douglas as an 'incipient fascist'[35] isolates and recoils from the single aspect of Douglas's work which most influences Hughes: the belief that killing and being killed, as Hughes argues in relation to Douglas's poetry, are the touchstone epiphanies of 'the cruelty—or indifference—of a purely material Creation'.[36] This is the same upper-case 'Creation' to which the hawk refers: 'It took the whole of Creation | To produce my foot, my each feather: | Now I hold Creation in my foot || Or fly up, and revolve it all slowly'. Might is right, and there is no higher court of appeal. However, the open invitation of 'Hawk Roosting' to extrapolate back to the human realm incurs serious difficulties. Hughes has stated that he wrote the poem with the idea that 'in this hawk Nature is thinking';[37] but a nature which thinks is no longer nature. The literary and historical sources have not been fully subsumed: in the same interview Hughes goes on to admit that the hawk sounds like 'Hitler's familiar spirit'. Turning nature into a Nazi, he makes Nazism seem natural.

The evident dangers of this interchange between human society and the natural world lead Hughes to agitate on behalf of his portrayals of violence. His riposte to those critics who condemn such portrayals as glorifying militarism follows a line of defence—or, more accurately, counterattack—inspired by the war poets' insistence that a society which requires its young men to kill strangers and die on its behalf is obliged not to turn away from truthful reports of wartime experience, no matter how horrific and morally discomfiting they may be. Hughes's modern-day equivalent of this hypocritical desire to evade is the 'vigorous human carnivore' who leaves the

---

[35] Roy Fuller, quoted in William Scammell, *Keith Douglas: A Study* (London: Faber, 1988), 210.

[36] Hughes, 'Introduction', p. xxiii.

[37] 'Ted Hughes and *Crow*', interviewed by Ekbert Faas, *London Magazine*, 10/10 (Jan. 1971), 10.

room sickened by 'the behaviour of predators killing and eating' on television:

For all who are horrified by this predation on the screen, our own internal involvement in the killing and eating of animals can only exist as an equally horrifying crime. And beneath it, but inseparable from it, moves our extraordinary readiness to exploit, oppress, torture and kill our own kind, refining on the way all the varieties of the lie and all the pleasures of watching others suffer.[38]

The Nazism of 'Hawk Roosting'—if it can be called Nazism— becomes justified by Hughes's belief that most of us are, in effect, Nazis: given the opportunity, he continues, 'most people will dutifully, zealously, zestfully inflict ultimate pain on others'. Like his story of Owen's photographs, Hughes aims to depict a violence which shocks society with this truth about itself and its actions. However, the ambition differs from that of Owen and other First World War poets in one critical respect: whereas Owen mourns soldiers who 'die as cattle',[39] Hughes dwells on active violation rather than passive suffering. Talking of the spectacle of 'lions killing and eating a zebra' on our television screens, he allows no doubt that we as humans should identify with the predators and not their prey.[40] As the relationship between 'How to Kill' and 'Hawk Roosting' already suggests, it is Douglas who informs this predator's vision and the moral questions which accrue. The central drama of Douglas's poetry, in which the survivor or killer surveys the dead, provides Hughes with a tableau for considering what he calls 'this strange tacit criminality of ours'.[41]

Lupercal interrogates this criminality through its abundance of corpses. Everywhere the poet stumbles across death and what remains after death, whether it be the last wolf killed in Britain, the woman sinking into the hospital pillow, the stoat nailed to a door, the pig spread across a barrow, the shore's flotsam of indigestible bones (one of which becomes a 'cenotaph'—again shadowed by memory

---

[38] Hughes, 'Poetry and Violence', in *Winter Pollen*, 256.
[39] Owen, 'Anthem for Doomed Youth', in *Complete Poems and Fragments*, i. 99.
[40] Hughes, 'Poetry and Violence', 257.   [41] Ibid.

of war[42]), the two pike high and dry in the willow-herb, or the ragged dog-fox hanging from a beam. One source for this morbid fascination is Edward Thomas's 'The Gallows', described by David Bromwich as the 'ur-Hughes poem',[43] in which the keeper shoots and hangs up weasels, crows, and magpies. Its influence is most conspicuous in Hughes's 'November' which ends, like Thomas's poem, by confronting a row of carcasses on an oak:

> And many other beasts
> And birds, skin, bone and feather,
> Have been taken from their feasts
> And hung up there together,
> To swing and have endless leisure
> In the sun and in the snow,
> Without pain, without pleasure,
> On the dead oak tree bough.
>
>   (Thomas, 'The Gallows')[44]

> The keeper's gibbet had owls and hawks
> By the neck, weasels, a gang of cats, crows:
> Some, stiff, weightless, twirled like dry bark bits
>
> In the drilling rain. Some still had their shape,
> Had their pride with it; hung, chins on chests,
> Patient to outwait these worst days that beat
> Their crowns bare and dripped from their feet.
>
>   (Hughes, 'November')[45]

The poems arrive at similar destinations by significantly different routes. Thomas, writing during the First World War, never flinches from the victims' fate. Each stanza tells the same story and ends with the inevitable deathly refrain. Having been seen alive in the sun with their families, thieving and murdering, talking and acting,

---

[42] Hughes, 'Relic', in *Collected Poems*, 78.

[43] David Bromwich, 'Ted Hughes's *River*', in *Skeptical Music: Essays on Modern Poetry* (Chicago: University of Chicago Press, 2001), 164.

[44] Edward Thomas, 'The Gallows', in *Collected Poems*, ed. R. George Thomas (Oxford: Oxford University Press, 1981), 115–16.

[45] Hughes, 'November', in *Collected Poems*, 81–2.

the animals are 'taken from their feasts': the poem presents an idyllic before and a dismal after, paralleling the outbreak of the First World War, to engage the reader's sympathy. However, Hughes's 'November' claims no prior knowledge of the animals' existence, and generates no pathos for their deaths. The poem starts with another corpse—'The month of the drowned dog'—and takes a detour to gaze at a tramp surprisingly alive: 'I took him for dead, || But his stillness separated from the death | Of the rotting grass and the ground.' The blurred distinction between living and dead is learnt from Douglas, but so is the poem's technique of steering between external facts and internal psychology. Whereas Thomas effaces himself in 'The Gallows', Hughes not only looks, but looks at himself looking: 'I stayed on under the welding cold || Watching the tramp's face glisten'. It is a way of implicating the self in the scene, so that the act of looking enters the moral realm, and judgement can be passed on the living as well as the dead. That judgement is damning, because the vision of the keeper's gibbet uncovers a transferred hostility. 'November' embodies a powerful refinement of, in Hughes's terms, 'the pleasures of watching others suffer'. The tramp has no more 'shape' or 'pride' than the recently slain animals which, like him and with equal futility, outwait the weather. Having mistakenly assumed the tramp dead, the poem makes every effort to restore that first impression.

Hughes considers the highest human inspiration to be predatory, and compares Mozart's brain with the thrush's 'bullet and automatic | Purpose' as it eats worms or the shark hungrily attacking its own blood-wound ('Thrushes').[46] The corpses in *Lupercal* therefore constitute victims of artistic violence; as Bromwich has argued, Hughes's 'tender intimacy with dead things, or with things void of all impulse, is the repose of a spent aggression'.[47] The equanimity with which the gamekeeper's gibbet is seen in 'November' suggests a passion satisfied after the subliminally angry encounter with the tramp. It

---

[46] Hughes, 'November', in *Collected Poems*, 82.
[47] Bromwich, 'Ted Hughes's *River*', 166.

is less Thomas's 'The Gallows' than Douglas's '*Vergissmeinnicht*', complimented by Hughes for being 'as final and universal an image of one of the ultimate battle experiences as exists on any page',[48] which provides the model for such poetry. Inspecting the dead enemy three weeks after the fury of battle, Douglas admits to feeling almost contented. Hughes's version of this confrontation between living and dead, transferred into the animal realm, is 'View of a Pig', the title of which explains why Hughes should write about the carcass at all: the ethics and psychology of viewing, as much as the object on view, excite the poem. 'View of a Pig' is not a sustained gaze, as Hughes and others have claimed.[49] Rather, it consists of a disappointment constantly reiterated: the pig is 'less than lifeless', 'too dead', 'Too deadly factual'.[50] The poet wants his emotions provoked, but thumps the carcass 'without feeling remorse', and finds it 'Too dead now to pity'. Owen's characteristic response, of pity, is not possible. Nor is Douglas's: Douglas had felt 'amused' (in another important poem for Hughes, 'How to Kill') at the sight of a dead German, but Hughes glumly observes that his pig 'was not a figure of fun'. Hughes considers bringing the dead to life by remembering the 'earthly pleasure' the pig once enjoyed, but quickly dismisses it as 'off the point'. Nevertheless, he temporarily circumvents his own objection and breaks out of the scene's inertia:

> Once I ran at a fair in the noise
> To catch a greased piglet
> That was faster and nimbler than a cat,
> Its squeal was the rending of metal.
>
> Pigs must have hot blood, they feel like ovens.
> Their bite is worse than a horse's—
> They chop a half-moon clean out.
> They eat cinders, dead cats.

48 Hughes, 'Introduction', p. xxv.
49 See Ted Hughes, *Poetry in the Making* (London: Faber, 1969), 58–61.
50 Hughes, *Collected Poems*, 76.

Douglas recalls in '*Vergissmeinnicht*' how the German had once tried to kill him. Hughes's attempt to turn the object of his gaze into a dangerous antagonist is inevitably less successful (as illustrated by the comic descent into the eating of cinders and dead cats), despite assigning to the pig a predator's bite and a vicious squeal. The poem fails to generate and spend its aggression, and ends with the resigned acknowledgement that the dead pig had 'long finished with' the porcine distinctions of its living brethren. 'I stared at it a long time,' the poet insists, but the pig resolutely refuses to meet his challenge. The poem is an exercise in frustration: no matter how long he stares and how hard he thumps, the war poem that Hughes wants to write cannot be written about a pig.

'View of a Pig' communicates a telling discontent with its own accomplishment: like *Lupercal* as a whole, it fails for reasons which Hughes, later determining to 'get rid of the entire body of pre-occupation', fully appreciates. Whether re-creating trench warfare or transposing the dramas of war on to the natural world, his first two books lack the immediacy and ethical danger evidenced by the poetry of his older family members, Owen and Douglas. Hughes is never able to disown their influence: for example, *Crow*'s 'black beast' is Douglas's 'bête noire';[51] the serpent's 'dark intestine' to which 'Theology' assigns humankind is the 'volatile huge intestine' which swallows everything in Douglas's 'Time Eating';[52] and the trench horrors of *Wolfwatching* (in the Owen-titled 'Anthem for Doomed Youth', for example) resurrect an early ambition to enact the father's experience and the father-poet's style. Yet, from *Wodwo* onwards, Hughes endeavours to break out of the gloomy, ghost-ridden repose of what he describes in 'Anthem for Doomed Youth' as 'war's drizzling afterdawn'.[53] *Wodwo* is the work of a poet no longer satisfied with his own belatedness. Its opening poem,

[51] Hughes, *Collected Poems*, 223; Douglas, *Complete Poems*, 118.
[52] Hughes, *Collected Poems*, 161; Douglas, *Complete Poems*, 71.
[53] Hughes, *Collected Poems*, 762.

'Thistles', signposts a new attitude to the war poets' legacy. Each of the thistles is

> a revengeful burst
> Of resurrection, a grasped fistful
> Of splintered weapons and Icelandic frost thrust up

> From the underground stain of a decayed Viking.
> They are like pale hair and the gutturals of dialects.
> Every one manages a plume of blood.

> Then they grow grey, like men.
> Mown down, it is a feud. Their sons appear,
> Stiff with weapons, fighting back over the same ground.[54]

The poem refers to the First World War legend that poppies draw their colour from the blood of the dead men buried amongst their roots. In doing so, it owes a debt to Blunden's 'I must go over the ground again' via Douglas's 'Returning over the nightmare ground'.[55] 'Thistles' therefore 'fight[s] back over the same ground', except that Hughes for the first time finds a prior myth which denies the war its privileged place as prime mover. Challenging his indebtedness even as he confesses it, Hughes portrays history as cyclical: violence becomes resurrected into each new generation, reducing the First World War to merely a local instance of some archetypal and organic pattern. Hughes clears imaginative space for himself not by disavowing the inevitability of fighting the wars of the fathers, but by stressing that the fathers were themselves bound to this repetitive inheritance. There can be no escape from the battleground in which Hughes's poetry finds itself obliged to operate.

Hughes's new approach to war has been initiated by his need to establish a less subordinate relationship with his war-poet predecessors. The thistles are his befitting emblems of adversity, the products of a panoramic vision which refuses to be confined within the narrower prospects apparent in *The Hawk in the Rain*

---

[54] Ibid. 147.
[55] See Scammell, *Keith Douglas*, 105. I am indebted to Dawn Bellamy for extending the connection between Blunden and Douglas to include Hughes.

and *Lupercal*. A new, historically unspecific figure crosses the poetic terrain of *Wodwo*, spotted first when a fern dances 'like the plume | Of a warrior returning' ('Fern').[56] His kin reappear in 'The Warriors of the North', which indulges in some dubious genealogy to discover the blood of marauding Vikings in 'the iron arteries of Calvin'.[57] The 'blood-crossed Knight' or 'Holy Warrior' finally reveals his true identity in 'Gog' as he rides across the womb of stone and 'Out under the blood-dark archway'.[58] This is no Sir Gawain slaying wolves and wodwos while honourably pursuing his pilgrimage. The warrior is identified as man—*vir* perhaps more than *homo*—whose weapons of lance or gun may be historically determined, but whose bellicose nature confirms that war is an unavoidable part of the human (or at least, human male's) condition. Similarly, in 'Karma', Hughes insists that violence ordains evolutionary design: 'a hundred and fifty million years of hunger | Killing gratefully as breathing | Moulded the heart and the mouth ‖ That cry for milk'. To distinguish between the many wars and atrocities of history misses the point of their karmic repetitiveness:

> When the world-quaking tears were dropped
> At Dresden at Buchenwald
> Earth spewed up the bones of the Irish.
>
> Queen Victoria refused the blame
> For the Emperors of Chou herding their rubbish
> Into battle roped together.
>
> The seven lamented millions of Zion
> Rose musically through the frozen mouths
> Of Russia's snowed-under millions.[59]

And so on, potentially *ad infinitum*: 'Karma', like 'Hawk Roosting', is sustained by Hughes's belief that we are most of us willing to inflict ultimate pain on others. Queen Victoria may have refused the blame, but we, presented with what is in effect another of Wilfred Owen's photographs, are encouraged to admit our criminal humanity.

[56] Hughes, *Collected Poems*, 153.   [57] Ibid. 167.   [58] Ibid. 163–4.
[59] Ibid. 167–8.

Hughes is recorded as saying in 1962 that 'you can't deal directly with Vietnam horror, it's much more effective to set it in the time-scale of history'.[60] (That generalized 'you' does not seem to accommodate the war's combatants.) Acknowledging the civilian's inability to forge a poetry of witness, Hughes insists on a perspective wide enough to begin transforming history into myth. Recent wars become more manageably proportioned when they can be interpreted as the consequences of an unalterable law, in which soldiers are haunted by dead predecessors and doomed successors, all 'concentrating | Toward a repeat performance'.[61] Yet, despite his determination to distance himself from the wars of Owen and Douglas, Hughes cannot give them up. 'Bowled Over' and 'Scapegoats and Rabies' (the latter published only in the American edition of *Wodwo*) revisit the battlefield of modern warfare, while 'The Wound' is an unperformable and virtually unreadable psychodrama of a shell-shocked survivor. And 'Out', the poem which Hughes wrote to coax himself away from the First World War, resists its author's palpable designs with a success which accentuates the impossibility of his task.

The tripartite structure of 'Out' attempts to map the poet's progress towards freedom. The title refers to being armed on the battlefield, but also gestures to Hughes's desire to rid himself of the damned spot of war. The poem's first section, ironically titled 'The Dream Time', observes the 4-year-old child as his father's 'luckless double' trapped by war's remnants and unable to 'move from shelter'. However, the following section finds release even for the war-dead: rewriting Christian resurrection ('the dead man in the cave'), Hughes shows the 'reassembled infantryman' reborn as 'just another baby'; and for once he resists the temptation to pursue the cycle to the next instalment of destruction.[62] The prospect of new beginnings leaves the third section to denounce the poppy and all that it represents as responsible

[60] Hughes, quoted by Rand Brandes, 'Hughes, History and the World in Which We Live', in Keith Sagar (ed.), *The Challenge of Ted Hughes* (Basingstoke: Macmillan, 1994), 142.

[61] Hughes, 'Scapegoats and Rabies', *Collected Poems*, 187.

[62] Hughes, *Collected Poems*, 165–6.

for weighing down the poet's 'juvenile neck'. As if finally shaking off that yoke, Hughes ends by rejecting the rites of remembrance, including the 'cenotaphs' which nourished him for so long:

> So goodbye to that bloody-minded flower.
>
> You dead bury your dead.
>
> Goodbye to the cenotaphs on my mother's breasts.
>
> Goodbye to all the remaindered charms of my father's survival.
>
> Let England close. Let the green sea-anemone close.[63]

Goodbye to all that: but it is an equivocal kind of renunciation which must still express itself in the language of the thing it renounces. Nor does a poet capable of describing his mother's nipples as cenotaphs seem a likely candidate for successful rehabilitation. Hughes's recidivistic mind, moulded by war and the literature of war, cannot deny its own identity, whether by outright abdications or by attempting to escape into the natural world. A poem he writes two decades later, about narcissi swaying in the wind, suddenly and unexpectedly evokes

> a rustling, silent film
> Of speeded-up dancing
> And laughing children
> From the 1918 Armistice.[64]

But for Hughes's poetry, the Armistice is never signed.

---

[63] Hughes, *Collected Poems*, 166.   [64] Hughes, 'Narcissi', ibid. 709.

11

Geoffrey Hill's Debts

King Log (1968), Geoffrey Hill's second full-length collection, comes accompanied by a prose essay which provides context for his sequence of eight unrhymed sonnets titled 'Funeral Music'. Those sonnets, set in the period 'popularly but inexactly known as the Wars of the Roses', attempt what Hill calls 'a florid grim music broken by grunts and shrieks',[1] as the 'distant fury of battle'—more particularly, the Battle of Towton (1461)—impinges on the world of ceremony and custom. Persuaded by contemporary chroniclers whose accounts describe 'a holocaust', Hill announces that 'imaginatively, the Battle of Towton commands one's belated witness'. The point is not dwelt on: his essay moves immediately to an assessment of the casualty figures at Towton, before sharing a report of how blood from the battlefield flowed along furrows and ditches for two or three miles when the snow melted. Yet the assertion that Towton 'commands one's belated witness', so precise and peculiar in its phrasing, raises questions vital to Hill's engagement with war and war poetry. How can one witness something one has not seen? Is Hill's assertion merely rhetorical that a battle fought half a millennium ago should have the authority to 'command ... witness', or does that battle continue to place an onus on the behaviour of the living? And what if responsibility to the past is simply ignored? Those questions recur in different guises throughout Hill's work. Three decades later in *The Triumph of Love* (1999), one of the poet's idiot accusers

---

[1] Geoffrey Hill, 'Funeral Music: An Essay', in *Collected Poems* (Harmondsworth: Penguin, 1985), 200 and 199.

(named after Keats's antagonist, Croker) insists that, despite Hill's marshalling of historical events, he '*wasn't there*'.[2] The objection is partially answered several pages on, when Hill finds himself in the 'dark wood' of the Great War ('Trônes, Montauban, | High Wood, Delville, Mametz'). 'We have been there,' he states, 'and are there still, in a manner of speaking.'[3] Nevertheless, the poem's next section cannot allow such a potentially outrageous appropriation to stand unmodified: 'But only in a manner of speaking. | I was not there, nor were you.'[4] Worrying at and about linguistic manners and mannerisms, Hill takes his reader to sites of conflict while acknowledging the ethical difficulties associated with the retrieval and artistic exploitation of history.

Hill's is a poetry of witness which, in all but a manner of speaking, '*wasn't there*'. That crucial fact of absence is never disguised. He observes earlier in *The Triumph of Love*, 'If | witness meant witness, all could be martyrs':[5] his awareness of etymological kinship discovers in the past a point of convergence for his correlated explorations of the poetry of war and the psychology of religious martyrdom. That witness no longer means witness (except in a manner of speaking often voiced by Hill) is a circumstance that he might be expected to deplore, having stated in 1981 that 'The history of the creation and the debasement of words is a paradigm of the loss of the kingdom of innocence and original justice'.[6] Some of Hill's admirers have been too credulous of the linguistic and religious claims made by such a self-consciously post-lapsarian vision, having never thought to enquire when and where this 'kingdom of innocence and original justice' existed. Whether the meaning of words is debased or evolves over time is a debate which never touches the poet's confidence that 'sematology is a theological dimension'.[7] Yet Hill's myth of origins,

---

    [2] Hill, *The Triumph of Love* (Harmondsworth: Penguin, 1999), 66.
    [3] Ibid. 73.   [4] Ibid. 74.   [5] Ibid. 51.
    [6] 'Geoffrey Hill', interviewed by John Haffenden in John Haffenden (ed.), *Viewpoints: Poets in Conversation* (London: Faber, 1981), 88.
    [7] Hill, 'Common Weal, Common Woe', in *Style and Faith* (New York: Counterpoint, 2003), 20.

itself originating in Ezra Pound's sentimental belief that 'The poet's job is to *define* and yet again define till the detail of surface is in accord with the root in justice',[8] enables him to sustain his role as a poet of war. Answering the call for witness may not require martyrdom, but it does at least interpret the word according to a fifteenth-century milieu contemporary with the Wars of the Roses. The *OED* offers as its first definition of *witness*, 'Knowledge, understanding, wisdom'; noting that the usage is now obsolete, it gives the latest example as 1482. Hill's witness is therefore 'belated' not only because it occurs more than 500 years after the event, but because it invokes an equally distant meaning. By witness Hill means understanding, and in case that should cause difficulties of its own ('*define* and yet again define'), he announces in *The Triumph of Love* that

> By understanding I understand diligence
> and attention, appropriately understood
> as actuated self-knowledge, a daily acknowledgement
> of what is owed the dead.[9]

All who have sacrificed themselves for a principled cause—especially soldiers and martyrs—are included among Hill's creditors, to be continually acknowledged in his elegiac witness poetry even though the debt is 'impossible to repay'.[10] Only by bearing witness to the dead of the Battle of Towton, and of wars and holocausts before and since, does the kind of self-knowledge valued by Hill become attainable.

Critics have remained notably reluctant to situate Hill's work in a tradition of war poetry. His reception has paralleled that of Ted Hughes, both poets having recorded many times their obligation to predecessors whom critical studies continue to ignore. This has less to do with Michael Longley's scruple that 'You have to be a war poet to write war poems'[11]—where definitions rather than

---

[8] Ezra Pound, quoted in Geoffrey Hill, 'Poetry as "Menace" and "Atonement" ', in *The Lords of Limit: Essays on Literature and Ideas* (London: André Deutsch, 1984), 3.

[9] Hill, *Triumph of Love*, 63.   [10] Ibid. 65.

[11] Michael Longley, quoted at <http://www.enitharmon.co.uk/books/viewBook. asp?BID=74>, accessed 13 Feb. 2005.

debts are at stake—than with an implicit value judgement which, regardless of the available evidence, would rather promote Eliot than Rosenberg as an important precursor. Yet Hill, author of an early uncollected poem 'For Isaac Rosenberg' as well as a major prose essay examining Rosenberg's achievement, has not been shy about naming the dead to whom he makes his daily acknowledgements. Rosenberg, Hill tells one interviewer, was a poet he 'read avidly' at a formative stage, singling out 'A worm fed on the heart of Corinth' as having 'gripped [him] in a deep and abiding way'.[12] Some passing observations in Hill's *Speech! Speech!* (2000) provide clues to Rosenberg's significance:

> His last efforts
> to survive—like THROUGH THESE PALE COLD DAYS—
> appear belated and timely acts
> of atonement.[13]

It is no coincidence that the word 'belated' should reappear. In Rosenberg's poem, atonement is enacted between the living poet and the 3,000-year dead, who 'see with living eyes' once more.[14] 'Through these pale cold days' may even have informed Hill's account of poetic atonement as 'an act of at-one-ment, a setting at one, a bringing into concord, a reconciling, a uniting in harmony'.[15] Hill's prose passage discusses atonement as a perfecting of a poem's technique, but the ambition to bring the past into concord with the present, and the dead into concord with the living, is the instinctive desire of his work. Witness, for Hill as for Hill's account of Rosenberg, involves an understanding of the past which, in its perfect (and therefore unattainable) form, would offer both reconciliation and expiation. 'Are you serious?', an unidentified voice interrupts in *Speech! Speech!* to challenge Hill's commentary. The reply, 'Well I'm ⎮ not joking

---

[12] 'Geoffrey Hill', interviewed by Haffenden, in *Viewpoints*, 79.
[13] Hill, *Speech! Speech!* (Washington: Counterpoint, 2000), 14.
[14] Isaac Rosenberg, *The Poems and Plays*, ed. Vivien Noakes (Oxford: Oxford University Press, 2004), 148.
[15] Hill, 'Poetry as "Menace" and "Atonement" ', 2.

exactly', places its doubt on 'joking', not 'exactly': his seriousness could not be more exact or exacting.

Ivor Gurney and Sidney Keyes, as well as Rosenberg, have been the beneficiaries of appreciative prose essays by Hill and several name-checks in his poetry. In addition, a 'Homage to Keith Douglas', in which Hill reviews Hughes's Faber *Selected* of that poet's work, calls Douglas 'one of the finest British poets of the last forty years', and groups him with Rosenberg as writers who deserve 'our constant gratitude'.[16] (Compare Hughes's praise of Douglas's work as 'an achievement for which we who come after can be grateful'.[17]) Those earlier poets' wars—the World Wars and attendant atrocities of 'Shock-Horror's century'[18]—inculcate the aesthetic and ethical bearings of Hill's work. Jon Silkin's estimation that twenty-one of *King Log's* forty-one poems are 'preoccupied with war and violence' fairly reflects the extent of that preoccupation throughout Hill's writing career.[19] Notwithstanding the statistics, Silkin shares a wider unwillingess to portray Hill as 'a "war" poet': Hill's poems, he declares, 'are at once "platonic" and palpable; the ideal (real) act stands behind the one actually committed'. The reservation might be justifiable, were it not that Silkin had already demonstrated, throughout his career as editor and critic, that the best war poets qualify as such because there is more to their work than war.

'I write for the dead,' Hill plainly states in *The Triumph of Love*, thereby setting up his derisive jibe at two Nobel Prize-winning rivals who write—with a killing enjambment—'for the living | dead'.[20] (This, too, may owe something to 'Through these pale cold days': 'They see with living eyes | How long they have been dead.'[21]) It should be understood that writing for the dead involves witnessing

---

[16] Hill, ' "I in Another Place': Homage to Keith Douglas', *Stand*, 6/4 (1964/5), 6 and 13.

[17] Ted Hughes, 'Keith Douglas', in *Winter Pollen: Occasional Prose*, ed. William Scammell (London: Faber, 1994), 215.

[18] Hill, *The Orchards of Syon* (Washington: Counterpoint, 2002), 63.

[19] Silkin, 'War and the Pity', in Peter Robinson (ed.), *Geoffrey Hill: Essays on his Work* (Milton Keynes: Open University Press, 1985), 118.

[20] Hill, *The Triumph of Love*, 54.   [21] Rosenberg, *Poems and Plays*, 148.

their lives and their sacrifices; but Hill also seems to advise, in another example of belatedness, that the dead are his audience (the opposite of writing for posterity), and that he writes on their behalf and for their benefit. The procedure shares nothing of the palatable hospitality suggested by Auden's well-digested maxim that art is a breaking bread with the dead. As Hill disgustedly (and self-disgustedly) puts it in 'History as Poetry',

> Poetry as salutation; taste
> Of Pentecost's ashen feast. Blue wounds.
> The tongue's atrocities. Poetry
> Unearths from among the speechless dead
>
> Lazarus mystified, common man
> Of death.[22]

Witness is again belated: the Pentecostal tongues of flame bringing revelation have now been extinguished, to leave only an 'ashen feast'. Saluting the dead, poetry risks desecrating their graves. Lazarus is dragged up into life, but rather than telling all, he remains throughout silent and 'mystified': the word suggests both his perplexity and the extent to which he has become distorted by modern perception. What poetry brings back from the dead is never the same as what was once alive. Hill's deep-seated suspicion of prosopopeia (belittled as glossolalia—'the knack of tongues'—in the poem's final line) disallows the possibility of free communication between the living and the dead, even while he most urgently desires it.

'To bring the dead to life,' writes Robert Graves, 'Is no great magic.' And yet Graves sounds a warning: he who would resurrect the dead by letting their 'forgotten griefs be now' and who copies their handwriting, their clothing, even their limp, may find that their grave is not empty: 'You in his spotted garments | Shall yourself lie wrapped.'[23] Bringing the dead to life is also a way of taking the living to death. 'History as Poetry' shows that Hill

[22] Hill, *Collected Poems*, 84.
[23] Robert Graves, 'To Bring the Dead to Life', in *Complete Poems*, ii, ed. Beryl Graves and Dunstan Ward (Manchester: Carcanet, 1997), 96.

recognizes the confines of his poetry's magic, and in 'Of Commerce and Society' he mocks those who overstate their powers: 'Artistic men prod dead men from their stone: | Some of us have heard the dead speak: | The dead are my obsession this week'.[24] But the dead do not always remain 'speechless' in Hill's poetry. 'Funeral Music' overhears and preserves the dying groans of those whose consummation subsumes the *petit mort* into the larger: 'the most delicate souls | Tup in their marriage-blood, gasping "Jesus".'[25] The linguistic choices of the sonnet sequence, Hill has reported, were influenced by his reading of Shakespeare's *Henry VI* plays.[26] *The Orchards of Syon* continues that homage with the recognition that 'Shakespeare | clearly heard many voices', and that 'voicing means hearing, at a price a gift, | affliction chiefly'.[27] Hill goes on to note that despair 'clamps and is speechless'—that word again—but his sense of Shakespeare's 'gift' for hearing the sufferings of others, like a particularly persuasive medium, touches on his own self-appointed duty. 'What we call the writer's "distinctive voice" is a registering of different voices,'[28] Hill affirms in a prose essay on Dryden. In one sense he is ill equipped for that task of registration. 'Can't do dialogue,' he confesses in *Speech! Speech!*, and has to muddle through with something more abrupt and impoverished: 'Snatched asides | pass for exchange'.[29] Yet this may be an appropriate mode for a poetry of interruptions and occlusions, of hesitations and self-questionings, of witness glimpsed but never fully achieved. *The Triumph of Love* and *Speech! Speech!*, in particular, explore the comic mishearings and misunderstandings which are symptoms of the failed communication not only between the living, but also between the living and the dead, as history strikes the poet—'(*splat!*)'[30]—forcefully but fragmentarily.

---

[24] Hill, *Collected Poems*, 49.   [25] Ibid. 72.

[26] 'Geoffrey Hill', interviewed by Haffenden, in *Viewpoints*, 81.

[27] Hill, *The Orchards of Syon*, 2.

[28] Hill, 'Dryden's Prize-Song', in *The Enemy's Country: Words, Contexture, and Other Circumstances of Language* (Oxford: Oxford University Press, 1991), 80.

[29] Hill, *Speech! Speech!*, 34.   [30] Hill, *Triumph of Love*, 71.

In his book-length poem, *The Mystery of the Charity of Charles Péguy*, Hill quotes Péguy—'"why do I write of war?"'—and straightaway provides Péguy's answer: '"Simply because | I have not been there. In time I shall cease | to invoke it." '[31] Hill's line-break illustrates the fatal proximity of ceasing to invoke war and simply ceasing. Péguy frees himself from war by sacrificing himself to it, discharging his obligation on the first day of the first Battle of the Marne; but Hill, having 'not been there', must ceaselessly invoke war in an imperfect act of witness. Unlike Péguy, he finds the debt unpayable, stating in an interview that if the previous generations 'died that we might live, then from time to time one thinks that we're not worth the sacrifice'.[32] That sacrifice, Hill goes on, must be 'remembered with gratitude', but Hill's is a gratitude always aware of its own limitations and oversights. His feelings of inadequacy plead guilty as charged to Wilfred Owen's accusation that 'These men are worth | Your tears. You are not worth their merriment.'[33] They also explain Hill's scathing rage against the fatuity of (much of) contemporary language and culture. That rage is self-incriminating: the American edition of *The Triumph of Love* comes with a cover blurb which carries the poet's imprimatur in its bald statement that Hill 'judges us for our failings [among which has been listed our "inability to acknowledge what is properly owed the dead"], but he judges himself more fiercely'.[34] Flagging the lines in *The Triumph of Love* about understanding being 'a daily acknowledgement | of what is owed the dead', this suggests that the poet himself fails as a witness to their lives. 'Memory', Hill notes defeatedly in *The Orchards of Syon*, 'proves forgetting'[35]—its own forgetting as well

---

[31] Hill, *Collected Poems*, 192.

[32] Hill, quoted in Andrew Michael Roberts, *Geoffrey Hill* (Tavistock: Northcote House, 2004), 67.

[33] Wilfred Owen, 'Apologia pro Poemate Meo', in *The Complete Poems and Fragments*, i: *The Poems*, ed. Jon Stallworthy (London: Chatto & Windus, Hogarth Press, and Oxford University Press, 1983), 125.

[34] Quoted by John Lyon, ' "Pardon?": Our Problem with Difficulty (and Geoffrey Hill)', *Thumbscrew*, 13 (Spring/Summer 1999), 13.

[35] Hill, *Orchards of Syon*, 15.

as society's. Even as it acknowledges what is owed, his poetry of war must acknowledge what it cannot and will not pay. Gratitude consorts curiously with ingratitude, so that when Hill wonders, in a poem which otherwise describes its working method as a 'trawl of gratitude', 'what's one left with if you fail to stint | on gratitude?',[36] there is no need to suspect an error of expression. Hill knows that gratitude must necessarily be stinted, and witness remain incomplete. It is a source of his greatest shame that, as *The Triumph of Love* admits, 'Late praise costs nothing',[37] pays no debts: Hill's poetry must constitute, at once, an acknowledgement and a withholding.

Hill makes short work of today's 'strange children | pitiless in their ignorance and contempt',[38] with their 'coarse efflorescence' (not, in this context, a natural flowering but a morbid discoloration) 'over the dead | proprieties'; and short work, also, of an England which, literally and figuratively, sells its dead cheaply. ('To the High Court of Parliament', the opening poem of *Canaan*, alludes to the selling of a Westminster graveyard for £1.) The nation is a debtor which keeps on taking: 'You owe me, Albion, I should have added | in Ivor's name not mine,' Hill writes on Gurney's behalf in *The Orchards of Syon*, and later describes England's 'quiet ways of betrayal'.[39] There is a national show of mourning and commemoration, but it is merely that. Hill remembers how England during the 1930s was 'at once too weepy and too cold'[40]—a complaint about more than the weather—and little has changed in the meantime: we are now, he finds with an epigrammatic disdain, 'a nation | with so many memorials but no memory'.[41] Memorials are depicted in Hill's work as less an acknowledgement or an attempt to understand than a licence to forget, a complacent belief that all debts can be paid in stone. (Auschwitz is diminished, in the

---

[36] Hill, 'A Treatise of Civil Power', in *A Treatise of Civil Power* (Thame: Clutag Press, 2005), n.p.

[37] Hill, *Triumph of Love*, 78.   [38] Ibid. 40.

[39] Hill, *Orchards of Syon*, 8 and 71.   [40] Hill, *Triumph of Love*, 74.

[41] Ibid. 40.

earlier 'Of Commerce and Society', to 'a fable | Unbelievable in fatted marble'[42]—'fatted' as if for sacrifice but therefore a horribly inappropriate memorial for starved victims of the death camps.) And if not stone, then outdated trinkets: 'Here's your Lost Empire | Medal for a life spent giving blood.'[43] 'Ingratitude | still gets to me,'[44] Hill seethes, his double meaning judging society with at least as much ferocity as he judges himself. And when he admits in 'ON READING *Milton and the English Revolution*' that his ordaining of 'a *dishonoured and discredited nation*' smacks of 'moral presumption', Hill nevertheless takes heart from the fact that 'Milton or Clarendon might well approve'.[45] Writing against the living, he writes for the dead.

Nor is modern Europe, with its political schemes for closer integration, spared Hill's censure. The pompous public spaces of the European project as portrayed in the fractured sonnet sequence 'De Jure Belli ac Pacis'—the 'elaborate barren fountains', the aqueducts projected 'where water is no longer found'[46]—symbolize the 'haughty degradations' which travesty the noble political visions of Grotius, Comenius, and the Kreisau conspirators who were executed for plotting against Hitler. When Hill states that those conspirators' 'martyred resistance serves | to consecrate the liberties of Maastricht', the bitterness of his irony returns to the theme that the present is undeserving of the past. Not only that, but the present exploits the past for its own ends, deriving a false authority from the bathetic implication that the conspirators died so that the Maastricht Treaty might live. (*The Triumph of Love* views such transactions even more brutally, as it imagines the remains of the dead 'accepted | as civic concrete, reinforceable | base cinderblocks'.[47]) Yet, as Hill makes clear when he directly addresses one of the conspirators, the sequence's dedicatee Hans-Bernd von Haeften,

[42] Hill, *Collected Poems*, 49.   [43] Hill, *Triumph of Love*, 46.
[44] Ibid. 40.   [45] Hill, *Treatise of Civil Power*, n.p.
[46] Hill, *Canaan* (Harmondsworth: Penguin, 1996), 30.
[47] Hill, *Triumph of Love*, 6.

> To the high-minded
> base-metal forgers of this common Europe,
> community of parody, you stand ec-
> centric as a prophet.[48]

The conspicuously awkward enjambment ensures that Hill's poetry centres von Haeften even as others push him to the margins, in the same way that his legacy is simultaneously used and distorted by those 'forgers' who, their description suggests, both make and fake. What society finds eccentric becomes central for Hill. The sequence often works through such double meanings, pointing up the coexistence of the noble with the debased and the ability of words, like political leaders, to dress one as the other.

Hill levels at modern European governance the charge not of forgetting to acknowledge what is owed the dead, but of misappropriating their sacrifice for purposes of self-justification: the politicians seek a return on their expressions of gratitude. That is an accusation in which war poetry, itself occupied with the task of making monuments from ashes, has good reason to feel implicated. 'Savage indignations | plighted with self-disgust become one flesh,'[49] Hill confesses in *The Triumph of Love*. Yet his acknowledged failures to bear proper witness and to repay his debts are as nothing to the contempt he reserves for certain other artistic portrayals of war. 'De Jure Belli ac Pacis' finds proof of Europa's decadence when she is depicted 'in her brief modish rags—| *Schindler! Schindler!*'[50] The search for exemplary figures of resistance to Nazism finds the story of Oskar Schindler (as told through Thomas Keneally's prose and Steven Spielberg's film) more fashionable and titillating than that of the Kreisau conspirators who, Hill tacitly suggests, make greater claims on our sympathetic witness. Hill's criticism becomes more strident in *The Triumph of Love*, as he takes issue with Spielberg ('Self-styled czar of ultimate | disaster movies'[51]) by mimicking his metonymic concentration on one victim of Auschwitz—sentimentally,

---

[48] Hill, *Canaan*, 33.   [49] Hill, *Triumph of Love*, 53.
[50] Hill, *Canaan*, 36.   [51] Hill, *Triumph of Love*, 41.

in *Schindler's List*, a little girl whose bright red coat stands out against the otherwise black and white film. Hill's seems to be a male victim, leaping aflame from a housetop in a burning ghetto, but the poem's directorial instructions expose how film choreographs atrocity: 'refocus that Jew—yes there, | that one'; 'caught at this instant | of world-exposure'; 'In close-up he maintains appearance'; 'Run it through again'.[52] In their pursuit of naturalistic entertainment, such techniques appear sadistic and obscene, making almost impossible, and treating as irrelevant, any distinction between a man dying and an actor performing. The fake replaces the authentic by stealing its authority. (American students ejected from a cinema for laughing at the murder of a Jewish prisoner in *Schindler's List* subsequently argued that it was 'not unusual for them to laugh at screen violence because they know it's not real'[53]—raising complex questions of blame.) 'Change insightfully caring to pruriently intrusive,'[54] Hill's editorial persona suggests later in *The Triumph of Love*. His witness poetry is painfully aware of how small that change would be.

'Great art', Christopher Ricks has written in a generous assessment of Hill's work, 'is often about the limits of what we should hope for even from the greatest of art, and among the many things which the imagination can realize on our behalf, one such is the limits of the sympathetic imagination.'[55] If this helps to explain Hill's stinting on gratitude, it also accounts for his mistrust of politics and art which fail to express self-mistrust in their dealings with the past. Like (he argues) Yeats's 'Easter, 1916', Hill's poetry of the Holocaust 'mistrust[s] its own mistrust'.[56] The celebrated lyric 'September Song', from *King Log*, starts by elegizing an unnamed

[52] Hill, *Triumph of Love*, 10–11. See Lyon, ' "Pardon?", 16–18.

[53] Quoted in Antony Rowland, *Holocaust Poetry: Awkward Poetics in the Work of Sylvia Plath, Geoffrey Hill, Tony Harrison and Ted Hughes* (Edinburgh: Edinburgh University Press, 2005), 70.

[54] Hill, *Triumph of Love*, 21.

[55] Christopher Ricks, 'Geoffrey Hill 1: "The Tongue's Atrocities" ', in *The Force of Poetry* (Oxford: Clarendon Press, 1984), 285.

[56] Hill, quoted by Ricks, ibid.

child victim of the extermination camps before intervening with a stanza in parentheses: '(I have made | an elegy for myself it | is true)'.[57] But *what* is true? The fact of the pogroms is not doubted, although that issue remains importantly different from any questions over the justice of the poem's self-proclamation to be 'true'. The claim of veracity may be limited to the poem's status as self-elegy (supported by the title which, borrowed from Anderson and Weill's song of that name, refers to the autumn of life), as the poet hears in the death camps the bell tolling for his own mortality. Or, relatedly, it may be an owning up to the fact that 'September Song' is a *selfish* elegy ('an elegy for myself'), using the deaths of innocents for the artist's personal gain and satisfaction. Voicing these excoriating self-doubts, Hill nevertheless writes and publishes the poem from his world of seasonal abundance:

> September fattens on vines. Roses
> flake from the wall. The smoke
> of harmless fires drifts to my eyes.
>
> This is plenty. This is more than enough.

The verb 'fattens' calls to mind the 'fatted marble' in 'Of Commerce and Society', and again offers a silent contrast with the emaciated victims of the death camps. Similarly, Hill's fires are 'harmless' to point up a contrast: he remembers, from the safe vantage-point of his own September, the fires of September 1942, when the open-pit burning of bodies began at Auschwitz. As many commentators have noticed, the poem's final line is therefore an acknowledgement both of natural plenitude and of poetic excess: 'more than enough' proves to be too much. Yet even in these final lines, Hill reinstates a moment of self-elegizing among the admissions of contrast. 'Roses | flake from the wall': the source, as Antony Rowland notices,[58] is Hardy's line

---

[57] Hill, *Collected Poems*, 67.
[58] Antony Rowland, *Tony Harrison and the Holocaust* (Liverpool: Liverpool University Press, 2001), 26.

'the rotten rose is ript from the wall',[59] an image expressing the transience of life and the vanity of human wishes, in 'During Wind and Rain'. (Rowland's argument that Hardy provides an 'elegiac lament for a dying aristocratic tradition' mistakenly elevates the subjects of his poem—Emma Hardy's family—well beyond their means.[60]) While recognizing his own privileged circumstances, Hill dares to propose that, in a manner of speaking, his destiny, and that of the anonymous child, are identical.

Primo Levi has commented that 'we, the survivors, are not the true witnesses'.[61] As the event which most 'commands our belated witness', and which (for the same reasons) denies the possibility of that witness, the Holocaust provokes in Hill a self-tortured and, inevitably, self-indulgent art. A poet's vocation, he has written, is of 'necessarily bearing his peculiar unnecessary shame in a world growing ever more shameless'.[62] The shame is unnecessary because the rest of the world seems to prosper without it. But while seeming to separate the poet from his 'world', this formulation also works to taint him with the same empirical guilt (or, as Hill over-elaborates, 'irredeemable error in the very substance and texture of his craft and pride'). The difference lies not in the guilty verdict but the reaction to it. Hill, like Hollywood, makes art out of atrocity—'makes flourish young | Roots in ashes'[63]—but his shame at the enterprise weighs against the shamelessness of its undertaking. That shame is also an ethical sensitivity, bound up in the act of witness: 'I think that it is a tragedy,' Hill has argued, 'for a nation or people to lose the sense of history, not because I think that the people is thereby losing some mystical private possession, but because I think that it is losing some vital dimension of intelligence.'[64] A poet who bears that sense of

---

[59] Thomas Hardy, *The Complete Poems*, ed. James Gibson (Basingstoke: Palgrave, 2001), 495.

[60] Rowland, *Tony Harrison and the Holocaust*, 26.

[61] Primo Levi, *The Drowned and the Saved*, trans. R. Rosenthal (London: Abacus Books, 1986), 63.

[62] Hill, 'Poetry as "Menace" and "Atonement"', 17–18.

[63] Hill, 'Two Formal Elegies', in *Collected Poems*, 30.

[64] Hill, quoted in Roberts, *Geoffrey Hill*, 54.

history must also bear the shame which is a product of it; when Hill speaks of a world growing more 'shameless', he is judging a world grown increasingly forgetful and morally unintelligent.

Accepting the reciprocity of judging and being judged, Hill's war poetry need not refrain from passing authoritative verdicts on politicians and fellow artists. Partly because of the shame he inherits from the past, he also feels himself entitled to judge those responsible for bringing about that inheritance: the past is a matter in which none of us can, or should want to, deny our obligations. In *The Triumph of Love*, for example, Hill speaks of

> the slow haul to forgive them:
> Chamberlain's compliant vanity, his pawn ticket saved
> from the antepenultimate ultimatum; their strict
> pudency, but not to national honour; callous
> discretion . . .[65]

'Those who regard Hill as habitually arrogating to himself an inflated role as prophet and judge would no doubt see this as further proof of hubris,' Andrew Michael Roberts states.[66] And Hill entertains that criticism (in the earlier-quoted 'ON READING *Milton and the English Revolution*') when he concedes that his complaints against England smack of moral presumption. After all, by what right, and fulfilling what need, does Hill strive (not, it would seem, with much prospect of success) to forgive Chamberlain and his kind? Roberts answers that perhaps 'Hill simply feels so intensely about the events of the twentieth-century that the need to try to forgive is, for him, a psychological necessity'. For 'simply' read complicatedly, and for 'psychological' read theological; and although Roberts is otherwise right, he does not explore sufficiently the underlying causes of this intense feeling. Hill's gratitude for the decency and sacrifice of those who died on our behalf would be merely gestural without a corresponding anger at all who misled them. (*The Triumph of Love* attaches itself explicitly to a tradition of *laus et vituperatio* in which,

---

[65] Hill, *Triumph of Love*, 4.   [66] Roberts, *Geoffrey Hill*, 70.

Peter McDonald notes, 'curse and blessing are implicate, one in the other'.[67]) The issue, accordingly, is not why he should engage so urgently (and at times, judgementally) with the past, but why others—more shameless and amnesiac—should not feel the same obligation. Hill is witness to a living history, the consequences of which continue to shape us and our society. He knows 'places where grief has stood mute- | howling for half a century',[68] or still longer:

> Grief—now, after sixty years—exacerbated
> through its very absurdity; anger stalled again
> for nations twice betrayed by our appeasements'
> false equities of common ash; the moral
> imagination an eccentric failure.[69]

The consensual reasonableness which renders such grief absurd is the same coercive force which (like modern Europe's marginalizing of the 'ec- | centric' von Haeften) decrees 'the moral | imagination an eccentric failure'. Hill's syntax intimates an identification of that modern attitude with past appeasement, as he blames our double betrayal of Czechoslovakia (to Hitler in 1938 and Stalin in 1948) on 'false equities of common ash'—a sense of humanity's equivalence which lacks the courage of moral convictions. Hill judges and condemns the appeasers for their cowardly refusal to judge and condemn.

'[T]he whole body of English war poetry of this war,' Keith Douglas wrote in 1943, 'will be created after war is over.'[70] Douglas meant the important poetry, rather than the poetasting of 'poetic pioneers and land girls ... desperately intelligent conscientious objectors, R. A. M. C. Orderlies, students'.[71] That the most gifted poet of the Second World War should not have survived has ensured the continuing difficulty of his prophecy's fulfilment. But it is *The Triumph of Love*, with its panoramic perspectives—the

---

[67] Peter McDonald, 'The Pitch of Dissent: Geoffrey Hill', in *Serious Poetry: Form and Authority from Yeats to Hill* (Oxford: Oxford University Press, 2002), 213.

[68] Hill, *Triumph of Love*, 40.   [69] Ibid. 14.

[70] Keith Douglas, 'Poets in This War', in *The Letters*, ed. Desmond Graham (Manchester: Carcanet, 2000), 353.

[71] Ibid. 352.

international politics, the private tragedies, the weapons of war, the poet's witnessing (in the modern sense) of Coventry being blitzed, the death camps, Dunkirk and Leipzig, the 'Bletchley magi',[72] Gracie Fields, and popular wartime culture—which most nearly approaches a post-war poetry worthy of Douglas's vision. Nevertheless, passing references to Arras and Haig and the Chums and Pals serve as proof that the dominance of one World War does not preclude memory of the other. The interplay of the wars is embodied in a 'canzone' to the Virgin Mary:

> Nor is language, now, what it once was
> even in—wait a tick—nineteen hundred and forty-
> five of the common era, when your blast-scarred face
> appeared staring, seemingly in disbelief,
> shocked beyond recollection, unable to recognize
> the mighty and the tender salutations
> that slowly, with innumerable false starts, the ages
> had put together for your glory
> in words and in the harmonies of stone.[73]

The most helpful way of approaching Hill's complex rhythms here and elsewhere in *The Triumph of Love* is to consider his own description, using some of Ivor Gurney's phrases, of that poet's 'verbal power':

While metre and rhythm in such poems as 'Tewkesbury' and 'It is Near Toussaints' seem to hover between standard pentameter and alexandrine, with abrupt stress-clusters making each line a law to itself, the 'slow spirit' of the sense goes straight on, taking enjambement in its stride, taking the measure of the 'passive unrhythmical mind and music', the 'trying not to resist Things', those massive determinisms which he sensed in the energies, inertias and attritions of the war and the post-war years.[74]

Gurney is the important model for Hill's metrics in *The Triumph of Love*. In each poet's case, the 'alexandrines' are usually only

---

[72] Hill, *Triumph of Love*, 15.   [73] Ibid. 28.
[74] Hill, 'Gurney's Hobby', F. W. Bateson Memorial Lecture, *Essays in Criticism*, 34/2 (Apr. 1984), 118.

approximate, and lines can keep going for fifteen syllables or more. Hill also has in common with Gurney the occasional 'standard pentameter' ('in words and in the harmonies of stone'), the 'abrupt stress-clusters' ('blast-scarred face'), the unhurried progress (matching the salutations which have been 'slowly . . . put together'), and the untroubled enjambing stride from line to line. Gurney's openness to the 'energies, inertias and attritions' of the Great War and its aftermath provides a precedent for Hill's treatment of the Second World War. And just as Gurney recalled his war as a rebuke to post-war society, so Hill finds that, linguistically, things were better 'even in—wait a tick—nineteen hundred and forty- | five of the common era'. That comic imperative pretends to buy time to assess the various options before alighting on a date. But 'wait a tick' also stresses that the Second World War and the present day are near neighbours, the Virgin needing only a brief pause to be transported by the poet from one to the other. Hill, like Gurney, witnesses war as a continuing reproach to contemporary peacetime society: although the architectural ruins of 1945 may have been cleared, he insists that decline (and not just linguistic decline) has continued under the rule of those 'vassal- | lord-puppet-strutters'—presumably, media celebrities—who are 'closely attended in their performance | of sacral baseness, like kings at stool'.[75] T. S. Eliot had brought the increasing inadequacy of language together with the vocabulary of war in 'East Coker', where the poet's each new venture is 'a raid on the inarticulate | With shabby equipment always deteriorating | In the general mess of imprecision of feeling, | Undisciplined squads of emotion'.[76] But Hill refuses to make such distinctions: his raids on the 'inarticulate' include among their principal targets the 'shabby equipment' itself.

Was it for this, Hill seems everywhere to ask as he surveys the cultural depravity of the present, that the Kreisau conspirators sacrificed themselves, or that on D-Day men 'drowned by the gross, in

---

[75] Hill, *Triumph of Love*, 27.
[76] T. S. Eliot, *The Complete Poems and Plays* (London: Faber, 1969), 182.

surf-dreck, still harnessed | to their lethal impedimenta'?[77] Dwelling on war's atrocities, he also finds manifested within it a courage and an honour which he looks for in vain among the 'undeniable powers'[78] of today's world. It is no coincidence, then, that twice in *The Triumph of Love* Hill should invoke the example of Abdiel, the only angel in Book V of *Paradise Lost* to remain 'unseduced' by Satan's beguiling rhetoric.[79] Abdiel may also help explain the book's title. Its direct allusion is to the first of Petrarch's six *trionfi*—the 'Triumph of Love': Hill's manner of speaking guarantees that he, like Petrarch, recalls the earliest meaning of *triumph*, as an army's solemn civic procession with the spoils of its victory. But why should love be associated with either spoils or a victorious army? A clue to the title's mystery comes from *Paradise Lost*, in which Milton reports of Abdiel that he was 'faithful found | Among the faithless', and that 'His loyalty he kept, his love, his zeal':[80] the story of Abdiel's resistance, which provides an exemplum for the courageous self-sacrifice of the Kreisau circle and for Hill's much less costly (and, therefore, often comically portrayed) confrontations with his own era's 'oligarchy of fraud',[81] constitutes the triumph of love over expediency.

In other ways, the title of *The Triumph of Love* is a misnomer for a book more concerned with defeats and hatreds. Looking back across the years, Hill comments caustically that 'What we arrived at without fail, | national débâcle, was sometimes called victory'.[82] Later he finds 'Stunned words of victory less memorable | than those urged from defeat',[83] but Hill's career-long emphasis on the hearing of—specifically—past affliction ensures that his poetry is itself urged from defeat. It is a defeat which, Hill believes, might easily have been ours: he refuses to credit Britannia with having brought about its own 'narrow | miracle of survival', which was

---

[77] Hill, *Triumph of Love*, 61.   [78] Ibid. 27.

[79] John Milton, *Paradise Lost*, ed. Alistair Fowler (London: Longman, 1971), v. 311, l. 899. See Hill, *Triumph of Love*, 12 and 43.

[80] Milton, *Paradise Lost*, v. 311, ll. 896–7 and 900.

[81] Hill, 'A Matter of Timing', *The Guardian*, 21 Sept. 2002, accessed at <http://books.guardian.co.uk/review/story/0,12084,795686,00.html.> on 3 Mar. 2005.

[82] Hill, *Triumph of Love*, 34.   [83] Ibid. 46.

'gifted' to us not so much by our own battlefield bravery as by 'crypytanalysts, | unpredictable Polish | virtuosi'[84] (who, Hill does not elaborate, shared their techniques for breaking the Enigma code with the British and French in July 1939). Britannia may survive, but it cannot be said to triumph. Even its weapons are failures. No spitfires dogfight bravely in English summer skies; instead, Hill's aircraft of choice is the 'much-vaunted' Fairey Battle, which his 7-year-old self was already capable of judging 'a dud'. A nation which requires its young men to fight might at least give them a fighting chance, but the detumescent Fairey Battle, obsolete and ridiculously vulnerable to attack, only swells Hill's angry gratitude: 'Honour the young men | whose eager fate was to steer that droopy *coque* | against the Meuse bridgeheads.'[85] Like the sacrifice of the Polish Ulany cavalry against German Panzers, such courage is presented as admirable, but unavailing. *The Triumph of Love* frequents the ruined places of defeat and suffering as it follows the war's destructive fires from Coventry to the burning ghetto to 'the sevenfold | fiery furnace' of Leipzig.[86] No miracle here, despite the allusion to the fiery furnace of the Book of Daniel. The fires of Leipzig do consume, leaving the 'things that stood' standing 'in unlikeness'. Hill is left as the connoisseur of ash, reporting the 'unmistakable sour tang | of paper-rubble' carried on the wind.

'There are triumphs that entrap and defeats that liberate,'[87] Hill has declared in his prose. *The Triumph of Love* speaks of a nation which, assuming itself victorious, becomes entrapped by its failure to understand what it has lost. A source of the poem's angry grief is that in victory Hill's beloved England has become (to borrow and redirect one of his book titles) the enemy's country, and the ill-disposed voices accommodated by the poem represent the poet's practising of some advice he once quoted from Plutarch: 'Where our wellwishers will

---

[84] Hill, *Triumph of Love*, 7.   [85] Ibid. 39.   [86] Ibid. 5.
[87] Hill, ' "Perplexed Persistence": The Exemplary Failure of T. H. Green', in *Lords of Limit*, 120.

give us no Councell, wee must make use of our Enemies words, and by a discreet application advantage our selves.'[88] While those enemies ask 'why is he still so angry?',[89] and trivially dismiss him as a 'Rancorous, narcissistic old sod',[90] Hill offers the knowledge that the war-dead are always with us, always dying into our present and future: 'Tomorrow he died, became war-dead, picked | off the sky's face. Fifty years back, the dead | will hear and be broken.'[91] The more society may forget, the more Hill finds the civic duty of his witnessing urgent and timely. Before long only that imaginative witness, based on an incomplete and insufficient memory of others' witness, will be left. As Hill observes in *The Orchards of Syon*, with a suitable acknowledgement of what must and yet cannot be paid to those who sacrificed everything for us, 'the veterans are dying. And I cannot say | what they care to remember.'[92]

[88] Trans. Henry Vaughan, quoted by Hill in 'Caveats Enough in their Own Walks', in *Enemy's Country*, 57.
[89] Hill, *Triumph of Love*, 2.   [90] Ibid. 20.   [91] Ibid. 41.
[92] Hill, *Orchards of Syon*, 44.

12

The Few to Profit: Poets Against War

> Here lies fierce Strephon, whose poetic rage
> Lashed out on Vietnam from page and stage;
> Whereby from basements of Bohemia he
> Rose to the lofts of sweet celebrity,
> Being by Fortune, (our Eternal Whore)
> One of the few to profit by that war,
> A fate he shared—it bears much thinking on—
> With certain persons at the Pentagon.[1]

Anthony Hecht's denunciation of Stateside poets who made a
healthy living out of Vietnam is not blind to the atrocities of war. As
a 20-year-old soldier serving in the 97th Infantry Division, Hecht had
participated in the liberation of Flossenbürg concentration camp, and
what he witnessed there became the source of continuing nightmares
in later life. His Holocaust poems are therefore, as Wilfred Owen
claimed every war poem should be, 'a *matter of experience*'.[2] The
same cannot be said for the 'poetic rage' of Hecht's 'fierce Strephon'.
If truth is the first casualty of war, then the job of the war poet since
Owen has been to keep truth alive. But when Hecht begins 'Here
lies', he refers as much to Strephon's mendacity as his mortality. At
some profound level, Strephon is found to be akin to the politicians

[1] Anthony Hecht, quoted in *Anthony Hecht in Conversation with Philip Hoy*, ed.
Philip Hoy (London: Between the Lines, 2001), 76. I am grateful to Jon Stallworthy for
telling me about this poem.
[2] Wilfred Owen to Leslie Gunston, 25 Nov. 1917, in *Collected Letters*, ed. Harold
Owen and John Bell (Oxford: Oxford University Press, 1967), 510.

he noisily condemns—a lying war-profiteer who works the sufferings of others to his personal advantage.

There may be urgent reasons for wanting to consider Hecht's poem unjust, or to limit its applicability to the poets of a particular nation (the United States) and a particular war (Vietnam). At subsequent conflicts, the onset of hostilities has coincided with an outbreak of anti-war poems and anthologies competing in their outraged disapproval. Timing is all: Todd Swift's *100 poets against the war*, which first appeared online the day Hans Blix delivered his weapons report on Iraq to the United Nations, claims to hold the record for 'the fastest poetry anthology ever published and disseminated'.[3] Not to be outdone, the following month Faber trumped Swift's title with the rush-publishing of *101 Poems Against War*. War sells poetry so effectively that very few, if any, of the new poems represented in these and other anti-war anthologies would under different circumstances have reached a comparable audience. It is no longer quite so newsworthy that poets should speak out against war: the hordes of fierce Strephons and the political uniformity of their response bring about diminishing returns, so that the 'lofts of sweet celebrity' are now open only for the briefest of visits. Nevertheless, poets enjoy seizing the moment to skirmish against the famous truism of their irrelevance. Confident in the knowledge of what anti-war poetry is against, Todd Swift gives a glimpse of what he thinks it might be *for*:

There is a tendency in some quarters to believe that poetry (in the ironic words of Auden) 'makes nothing happen.' *100 poets against the war* is proof that well-written (political) poetry does happen, and matters: it reveals powerfully (and poignantly) how many people oppose imperialist wars of aggression, or want peace, rather than full spectrum domination.[4]

---

[3] Cover blurb for Todd Swift (ed.), *100 poets against the war* (Cambridge: Salt Publishing, 2003).

[4] Swift, 'Editor's Introduction', *100 Poets Against the War*, ed. Todd Swift, p. i, accessed at <http://www.nthposition.com/100poets0.pdf> on 17 Aug. 2005.

The phrase from Auden is especially dangerous for Swift's enterprise, because, if true, it exposes his haste as a vulgar opportunism of the kind described by Hecht. Here it is defused, without evidence or discussion, as 'ironic': Auden appears not to have meant what he wrote, and perhaps meant something like the opposite. (Swift does not mention Auden's belief that 'the political history of the world would have been the same if not a poem had been written',[5] or that 'No words men write can stop the war'.[6]) Does a book titled *100 poets against the war* reveal, whether powerfully or poignantly or in any other way, the opinions of anyone other than its poets? If public opinion is strongly against a war, it hardly requires a poetry anthology to announce the fact. The rhetoric of fierce Strephons can sometimes reveal kinship with their political enemies. Who would not support a 'war on terror'? And who would not resist 'imperialist wars of aggression'?

'Opposed as I was to every aspect of the [Vietnam] war,' Hecht has said, 'I was also determined not to rant and rave in public poetry readings on the subject, which was only a kind of self-promotion.'[7] To read anti-war poetry as purely opportunistic is to risk seeming ungenerous. Even were the mixed motives of such poets conceded, among them would still be the desire of the individual conscience to challenge the actions of government by speaking out. Anti-war poets, it is difficult not to conclude, are honourable men and women. Yet poetry fails to serve democracy, as well as its own well-being, if it adopts democracy's failings by stooping to the linguistic crudity of the political realm. This is not a criticism of a political point of view: the execrable pro-war poetry published during the war in Iraq has near-invisibility as its sole virtue. But the problems which afflict it—the sanctimony, the opinionated doggerel, the fundamentalist

[5] W. H. Auden, 'The Prolific and the Devourer', in *The English Auden: Poems, Essays and Dramatic Writings 1927–1939*, ed. Edward Mendelson (London: Faber, 1977), 406.
[6] Auden, 'New Year Letter', in *Collected Poems*, ed. Edward Mendelson (London: Faber, 1976), 206.
[7] Hecht, *Anthony Hecht in Conversation with Philip Hoy*, 75.

assaults on other positions, the refusal to countenance complica-
tion—make pro-war poetry the mirror-image of its more celebrated
rival. A BBC news report on the founding of a pro-war poetry website
took understandable delight in quoting some of the more inept and
prejudicial contents: 'As men march off to war | so bravely for our
freedom | the students smoke their dope | and liberals whine like
women.'[8] But sexism reconciles political opposites: Tony Harrison's
'Iraquatrains' feels entitled to jeer at 'the broad Brum bum and bos-
oms' of a British cabinet minister.[9] The BBC report went on to prove
consanguinity deeper than any political division, by quoting the dis-
missive reaction of 'anti-war poet Adrian Mitchell' to the pro-war
website and concluding with a sample of Mitchell's own musings:
'Men, women, children, animals | slash them to pieces all alike | pre-
cision bombing, smart missiles | you are Jack the Ripper on a surgical
strike.' If the reading of poetry promises more than a lazy pleasure in
having pub talk rhymed, there is no reason to praise Mitchell above
the pro-war poets. War poetry which advertises its opinions with a
prefix is likely to be more interested in those opinions than in poetry.

Keith Douglas saw (and foresaw) in 1943 what must be 'got
rid of' from war poetry: 'the mass of irrelevancies, of "attitudes",
"approaches", propaganda, ivory towers, etc.'[10] Failing to heed
his advice, Andrew Motion has unconcernedly stated that 'We
can guess what attitude poets will take to a conflict before we
read a line they have written about it.'[11] So much the worse for
poetry, that it should have been reduced to a matter of predictable
attitudinizing. What Paul Fussell wrote of Vietnam applies (give or
take the changing formal fashions) to any subsequent conflict: 'no
one expects interesting poetry to emerge from that sad war. All we

---

[8] 'Pro-war poetry website launched', 5 Mar. 2003, accessed at <http://news.bbc.co.
uk/1/hi/entertainment/arts/2821455.stm> on 11 Aug. 2005.

[9] *The Guardian*, 1 Apr. 2003, accessed at <http://books.guardian.co.uk/
writersoniraq/story/0,12975,928753,00.html> on 16 Aug. 2005.

[10] Keith Douglas to J. C. Hall, 10 Aug. 1943, in Douglas, *The Letters*, ed. Desmond
Graham (Manchester: Carcanet, 2000), 294.

[11] Andrew Motion, 'Afterword', in Matthew Hollis and Paul Keegan (eds.), *101
Poems Against War*, (London: Faber, 2003), 136.

can expect is more of what we have, a few structureless free-verse dribbles of easy irony or easy sentiment or easy political anger.'[12] Fussell's emphasis on the ease of writing an anti-war poetry implies the difficulty of doing it well. 'Academic knowledge', Auden argues in a similar context, 'is not enough.'[13] But while Auden admits that 'the supreme masters' may be able to produce a war poetry not based on experience, his self-exclusion from that category should act as a warning to the brave or foolish who try. Careful not to overstate their sense of entitlement, the best poems in Swift's anthology seek equivalents of Edward Thomas's gift for writing about war by way of unpicked flowers or a fallen tree—tiny effects which the poets can see for themselves. Others are less restrained. It is partly the failure to notice difficulties in the artistic exploitation of violence which makes the bulk of contemporary anti-war poetry seem sentimental and morally dubious.

'Today, I am a poet | writing bad verse,'[14] a contributor to Swift's anthology endearingly confesses. Bad poetry about war is not a new phenomenon. The Boer War inspired a national outpouring of no less dutiful and incompetent verse, albeit overwhelmingly in favour of the war. But in recent times poetry written against war has sometimes chosen to camouflage itself as an anti-poetry which finds, as Keith Douglas found during the North African campaign, 'no reason to be either musical or sonorous about things at present'.[15] The most flagrant example has been Harold Pinter's verse, the language of which—'We blew the shit right back up their own ass', 'We blew them into fucking shit', 'We blew their balls into shards of dust'[16]—sets a simple trap for readers coaxed into disapproval:

[12] Paul Fussell, quoted by Jon Stallworthy, 'Foreword', in Subarno Chattarji, *Memories of a Lost War: American Poetic Responses to the Vietnam War* (Oxford: Oxford University Press, 2001), p. vii.

[13] Auden, quoted in Humphrey Carpenter, *W. H. Auden: A Biography* (London: HarperCollins, 1981), 207.

[14] Eileen Tabios, 'Why I want to be a Baconaut', in Swift (ed.), *100 Poets Against the War*, 11, accessed at <http://www.nthposition.com/100poets0.pdf> on 17 Aug. 2005.

[15] Douglas to J. C. Hall, 10 Aug. 1943, in *Letters*, 295.

[16] Harold Pinter, 'American Football (A Reflection upon the Gulf War)', in Hollis and Keegan (eds.), *101 Poems Against War*, 80.

the obscenities, the poem pre-emptively retaliates, are as nothing to the obscenities they describe. In its repetitive insistence, Pinter's vocabulary remains too monotonous to disconcert: thinking it has more urgent things to worry about than aesthetics, anti-war poetry risks denigrating both message and medium. Take, for example, the protest of Andrew Motion's quatrain-poem 'Causa Belli', which opens: 'They read good books, and quote, but never learn | a language other than the scream of rocket-burn.'[17] Either Motion means *casus belli*, or the Latinizing of his title is pompous (and misleading: despite the erroneous gloss accompanying the poem's first publication, 'causa' is singular). The body of the poem, similarly, veers between blunder and self-importance, as if the poet wants to be seen to say something but has nothing to say. Confident in his division of them and us, Motion goes on to refer to 'Our straighter talk', but his phrases refute that contrast: the line 'a language other than the scream of rocket-burn' seems chiefly motivated by the need to find a rhyme with 'learn'; and when he calls that 'talk' 'drowned but ironclad', he confusedly evokes an outmoded and sunken warship. (Why, and with what benefit, drowned *but* ironclad?) The final line, with its familiar anti-war list of the hidden causes of the Iraq War ('elections, money, empire, oil and Dad'), is equally revealing of the poem's *raison d'être*. Meaning, coherence, and value are of no consequence, so long as the poet should have signalled to like-minded readers his opposition to the war and his fluency in the accompanying patois.

Thanking his poets for freely donating their poems to his anti-war anthology, Todd Swift writes that 'it is brave and good of them'.[18] Bravery may come from unexpected quarters during war, but an individual whose sole act is to contribute fashionable views to a poetry anthology does not seem to offer a prima facie case. Emptying the word of signification, Swift cheapens the bravery of those who

[17] Motion, *The Guardian*, 9 Jan. 2003, accessed at <http://www.guardian.co.uk/uk_news/story/0,3604,871226,00.html> on 16 Aug. 2005.

[18] Swift, 'Editor's Introduction', p. i, accessed at <http://www.nthposition.com/100poets1.pdf> on 17 Aug. 2005.

have more at stake than their poetic reputations. Nor is this an isolated lapse. In the printed version of *100 poets against the war*, Swift notes that because more than 100 poets have now been included, 'our name is a charming anachronism that we have kept, in the spirit of that modest, yet brave, determination which typified the people of Britain' in 1941.[19] A nation blitzed but defiant in the face of Nazism is allowed the same 'spirit' as Swift's editorial decision to retain his anthology's title. Swift's weakness for inflationary language, mixed with self-congratulation, frustrates the linguistic accuracy which is never more urgently required than in time of war. At such times, poetry is valuable only in so far as it differs from less honest uses of language, and bears an exacting witness to truth rather than opinion and misinformation. Jon Stallworthy's 'A poem about Poems About Vietnam'—a title which already, in its play of upper- and lower-case letters, opens the assault on overweening contemporaries—identifies the precariousness of poetry's power if misused:

> Lord George Byron cared for Greece,
> Auden and Cornford cared for Spain,
> confronted bullets and disease
> to make their poems' meaning plain;
> but you—by what right did you wear
> suffering like a service medal,
> numbing the nerve that they laid bare,
> when you were at the Albert Hall?[20]

Stallworthy's poem reproves the unearned parading of sensitivity, expecting more than poetry from poets who profess to care so much. Byron, Auden, and Cornford are invoked as men who showed real and not merely rhetorical bravery in justifying their language with their actions—Auden's presence confirming that there are many ways for poets to serve without becoming combatants. But while it shares Hecht's sentiments, 'A poem about Poems About Vietnam'

---

[19] 'Editor's Introduction', *100 Poets Against the War*, p. xviii.
[20] Jon Stallworthy, *The Anzac Sonata: New and Selected Poems* (London: Chatto & Windus, 1986), 38–9.

adds a new accusation: that the more ostentatious of the anti-war poets undo the work of their more gifted predecessors, 'numbing the nerve that they laid bare'. Stallworthy implies that for all their well-rehearsed outrage, the anti-war poets are dangerously harmless, the predictability of their response acting as a narcotic for a society which, having become accustomed to their performance, no longer finds itself vulnerable to poetry's uncomfortable truths. Long gone are the days when, Keith Douglas argued, poets preferred to fall silent rather than repeat themselves and each other. 'Where there's war, there's an anti-war | of writers writing',[21] begins a villanelle in Swift's anthology, cheered at the thought. But the anti-war of writers writing usually occurs thousands of miles away from war, comfortably accommodated, and rewarded, by a society which wages war while entertained by their response.

Rejecting Sean O'Casey's *The Silver Tassie* for the Abbey Theatre in 1928, Yeats told the playwright, 'you are not interested in the great war; you never stood on its battlefields or walked its hospitals, and so write out of your own opinions'.[22] Yeats lived his own strictures, as 'A Reason for Keeping Silent' testifies: 'I think it better that in times like these | We poets keep our mouths shut, for in truth | We have no gift to set a statesman right.'[23] Whether, by turning down the chance to wear suffering like a service medal, Yeats was braver or more cowardly than his fellow contributors to Edith Wharton's *The Book of the Homeless* (an impeccable charity venture for Belgian refugees) is a question worth considering. Acting honestly, if not acceptably, Yeats alone laid himself open to criticism, his American patron John Quinn chiding him for a poem that was 'quite unworthy of [him] and the occasion'. Like Yeats, Stallworthy is dismissive of writers who replace experience with opinion, declaring that the poet-witnesses

[21] Ken Waldman, 'Where There's War', in Swift (ed.), *100 Poets Against the War*, 160.
[22] W. B. Yeats to Sean O'Casey, 20 Apr. 1928, in Yeats, *The Letters*, ed. Allan Wade (London: Rupert Hart-Davis, 1954), 741.
[23] Yeats, 'A Reason for Keeping Silent', in Edith Wharton (ed.), *The Book of the Homeless* (New York: Scribner's, 1916), 45.

are believed because 'they were there, | when you were at the Albert Hall'. This is not to insist that only poets in the war zone can write a poetry of war. Whitman, Kipling, and Auden ensured that 'they were there' even if not as combatants, but others such as Mew, Thomas, and MacNeice write out of experience by observing the effects of war on the environment in which they live. In later work Stallworthy has made a strong case for the poetry of the American conscientious objector John Balaban, who went to Vietnam (in Balaban's words) 'not to bear arms but to bear witness',[24] working first at a university in the Mekong Delta and then as a field representative for the Committee of Responsibility to Save War-Injured Children. Beside such an exemplary figure, the soon-forgotten indignation expressed by Stateside poets seems only to add to the welter of opinion and propaganda. Their poetry, lacking the authority of experience, is less a means of discovery and revelation than (at best) a redundant exercise in stating the obvious. As Keith Douglas remarks in *Alamein to Zem Zem*,

We talk in the evening, after fighting, about the great and rich men who cause and conduct wars. They have so many reasons of their own that they can afford to lend us some of them. There is nothing odd about their attitude. They are out for something they want, or their Governments want, and they are using us to get it for them. Anyone can understand that: there is nothing unusual or humanly exciting at that end of the war. I mean there may be things to excite financiers and parliamentarians—but not to excite a poet or a painter or a doctor.[25]

Douglas repudiates in a few sentences the subject which relentlessly distresses the anti-war poets—the exploitation of war by power-brokers. 'Anyone can understand that': a poetry which, nevertheless, pursues the theme so determinedly will not unsettle its audience. Even if Douglas seems to be mistaken in believing that there is nothing 'at that end of the war' to excite poets, he tells a truth

---

[24] John Balaban, quoted by Stallworthy, 'Foreword', p. viii.
[25] Keith Douglas, *Alamein to Zem Zem*, ed. John Waller, G. S. Fraser, and J. C. Hall (London: Faber, 1966), 15–16.

about war and excitement that anti-war poetry cannot countenance. Douglas keeps unusual company: that a poet or a painter might find war exciting is controversial enough; that a doctor might, too, shows the extent to which Douglas celebrates the quest for knowledge and experience. 'I never lost the certainty that the experience of battle was something I must have,'[26] he states, reporting how he abandoned his post as a camouflage officer to join up with his regiment at Alamein. His primary motivation is the understanding that war provides not just personal challenges but imaginative opportunities beyond the reach of peacetime. Douglas confronts with a perturbing honesty what most anti-war poetry cannot acknowledge even to itself: that war poets of all persuasions engage in the unholy alchemy of making art from violence, finding it a blessing to live in interesting times. War is material at its most raw, and anti-war poetry deludes itself if it denies its own contradictions when using that material. Terrible though it may seem to admit, poetry about war must be on the side of experience, its imagination liberated by an inspiring violence.

In their transactions between war and art, many anti-war writers exonerate themselves by placing special value on one redeeming emotion: pity. Arguing that on the Western Front 'something fundamental changed' in the way poets write about war, Andrew Motion has maintained that for the poetry of subsequent wars 'Pity' and 'truthfulness' remain the 'crucial ingredients'.[27] This promotes Owen as the only begetter of modern war poetry: 'My subject is War, and the pity of War. The Poetry is in the pity.'[28] But the unfortunate legacy of Owen's pity has been an acceptance or rejection of war poetry according to the extent to which it is seen to exhibit the requisite sentiment. Motion's reading of literary history neglects important precursors (Hardy? Whitman? Homer?), and distorts the troubling achievement of a poet like Douglas, whose work not only shuns pity but disparages it. ('The north-African [*sic*] poems

---

[26] Ibid. 15.   [27] Motion, 'Afterword', 136.
[28] Wilfred Owen, *The Complete Poems and Fragments*, ii: *The Manuscripts and Fragments*, ed. Jon Stallworthy (London: Chatto & Windus, Hogarth Press, and Oxford University Press, 1983), 535.

of Keith Douglas,' Motion blandly asserts, 'may take a seemingly insouciant attitude to battles, but they leave us in no doubt about war's misery and waste.'[29]) Nor does Motion realize that as anti-war poets have quietly ignored Owen's emphasis on experience, the relationship between pity and truth has become increasingly vexed. 'Owenite | Pity was excellent when burdened,'[30] writes Geoffrey Hill, suggesting that it is the burden of experience which earns Owen the excellence of his pity. Far from being truthful, unburdened pity risks lapsing into self-satisfaction as poets flaunt their finer feelings: as Patrick West argues, 'Our culture of ostentatious caring concerns . . . projecting one's ego, and informing others what a deeply caring individual you are. It is about feeling good, not doing good.'[31] When Tony Harrison, in 'Iraquatrains', describes 'a small child's shrapnelled scalp scooped of its brains',[32] his palpable design anaesthetizes the knowledge that children are butchered in war: expected to imagine a scene already presented as nothing more than caricature, readers will pity only if they allow themselves to be prompted into extra-textual images by the poet's ponderous cues. (Can a scalp be said to have 'brains'? Are they 'scooped' by an explosion?) But complacency may be the least of the dangers. 'Behind pity for another lies self-pity, and behind self-pity lies cruelty,'[33] wrote Auden; while Freud's account of pity as a reaction-formation to the sadistic drive finds unlikely support from a poem in Swift's anthology: 'are there children somewhere | waiting for wounds | eager for the hiss of napalm | in their flesh?'[34] Mistaking sadism for sympathy, this has less in common with Owen's pity than with Lewis Carroll's Walrus, weeping for the oysters even as he eats them.

[29] Motion, 'Afterword', 136.
[30] Geoffrey Hill, *The Orchards of Syon* (Washington: Counterpoint, 2002), 63.
[31] Patrick West, *Conspicuous Compassion: why sometimes it really is cruel to be kind* (London: Civitas, 2004), 1.
[32] Tony Harrison, *The Guardian*, 1 Apr. 2003, accessed at <http://books.guardian.co.uk/writersoniraq/story/0,12975,928753,00.html> on 16 Aug. 2005.
[33] Auden, quoted in Richard Davenport-Hines, *Auden* (London: Heinemann, 1995), 168.
[34] Robert Priest, 'Are There Children?', in Swift (ed.), *100 poets against the war*, 127.

In his draft preface for a book he would not survive to publish, Owen declares that 'All a poet can do today is warn'.[35] Motion quotes the maxim approvingly in his afterword to *101 Poems Against War*, and it is reproduced, contextless and in large font, on the back cover of the anthology. Motion remains in no doubt of the continued relevance of Owen's warning, arguing that his message has 'held firm through the years, even in wars (such as the war against Hitler) which are generally considered "just"'.[36] But this conflation of past and present falsely compares poets of 2003 with their counterparts of 1918 who risked their lives to send back dispatches from the front to an ignorant civilian population. Having no more experience of war than the majority of their contemporaries, it is unclear whom, and of what dangers, contemporary poets should be warning: what do poets know that others do not? Motion asserts that the anti-war poet's pity and truthfulness become especially important 'when the realities of war are blurred by euphemisms ("friendly fire", "collateral damage"), and by the strange separations of TV screens'.[37] This makes an extraordinary claim for the efficacy of such poetry—that television having caused the separation of its audience from the 'realities of war', poets should be able to reconnect that audience with realities which they themselves have not witnessed. The implication is that poets do not need to experience the truth of war because they know it instinctively. They can even smell it. Without saving irony, one of Swift's contributors condemns the pontifications of a 'distant observer' before falling into the same error of prattle without practice: 'Death is easy to pronounce. | It's the smell of burning children that's hard'.[38]

Explaining his preoccupation with the war survived by his father and uncle, Ted Hughes draws attention to the continued presence of the past. Having grown up in 'a kind of Mental Hospital of

---

[35] Owen, *Complete Poems and Fragments*, ii. 535.
[36] Motion, 'Afterword', 136.   [37] Ibid.
[38] Sampurna Chatterji, 'Easy', in Swift (ed.), *100 poets against the war*, 32.

the survivors'[39] of the Great War, he became witness to the after-
effects of their experiences, so that the war remained a shaping
influence on his childhood. Contemporary conflicts, by contrast,
seemed distant and less relevant: 'As we became aware of the
effects of the war in Eastern Europe, the holocaust, the Nuclear
Terror etc, they became just more news.' For every poet who
has risen to the challenge of turning news bulletins into poetry
(Shelley in 'The Mask of Anarchy', Tennyson in 'The Charge
of the Light Brigade'), many more have failed. Louis MacNeice's
McGonagallesque response to the dropping of atomic bombs on
Hiroshima and Nagasaki—'When I first read the news, to my
shame I was glad; | When I next read the news I thought man had
gone mad'[40]—is a potent warning to those who seek to versify the
latest atrocity. A contributor to Swift's anthology begins with the
observation that 'the war is on the kitchen table | waiting to be
read';[41] and the poem constitutes proof, if any were needed, that
war has been experienced only via the newspapers. Contemporary
poets are now as likely to watch as to read the news, and when
Motion attaches blame to television, he fails to acknowledge that
its rise to dominance has occurred alongside a growth in popular
anti-war sentiment which is partly indebted to it. Motion may
stress the 'strange separations' of the medium in order to praise
the supposed intimacies of anti-war poetry, but television effects
the instant closure of otherwise insurmountable distances. Most
beguilingly, it promises to bring about the transformation of viewers
into supposed witnesses (albeit witnesses who lack involvement and,
consequently, full understanding) from the safety of their armchairs.
Anti-war poetry, nevertheless, often considers itself superior to, and

[39] Ted Hughes, quoted in Antony Rowland, *Holocaust Poetry: Awkward Poetics in
the Work of Sylvia Plath, Geoffrey Hill, Tony Harrison and Ted Hughes* (Edinburgh:
Edinburgh University Press, 2005), 147.

[40] Louis MacNeice, 'Notes for a Biography', in *Collected Poems*, ed. E. R. Dodds
(London: Faber, 1979), 477. I am grateful to Peter McDonald for drawing this example
to my attention.

[41] Myrna Garanis, 'the war is on the kitchen table', in Swift (ed.), *100 poets against
the war*, 51.

suspicious of, visual representation of conflict: at best, television presents a displaced and mediated truth, and at worst it allows presidents to tell smiling lies to their nation.[42] Wilfred Owen was able to renounce the photographic art because his experience had taught him that it told only a partial truth, privileging one sense over the others: 'Can you photograph the crimson-hot iron as it cools from the smelting? That is what Jones's blood looked like, and felt like.'[43] That prejudice has continued among poets who have no experience to justify it. A poem in Swift's anthology, for example, criticizes a newspaper photograph of a woman who has hitched up her burqa and waded into a river. The woman's 'broad | ass',[44] in the original website version of the anthology, has been revised to her 'broad | backside'[45] in the printed version: attacking the camera's inadequacies and invasions, the poet quietly distracts attention from her own.

Writing in 1987, Tony Harrison insists that only poetry can offer redemption from the century's worst horrors:

In [drama] I find a reaffirmation of the power of the word, eroded by other media and by some of the speechless events of our worst century. Sometimes, despite the fact that the range of poetry has been diminished by the apparently effortless way that the mass media seem to depict reality, I believe that, maybe, poetry, the word at its most eloquent, is one medium which could concentrate our attention on our worst experiences, without leaving us with the feeling, as other media can, that life in this century has had its affirmative spirit burnt out.[46]

Harrison offers no evidence for this belief, nor any sense that by preserving the 'affirmative spirit' of life the poet is truer to the

---

[42] See Robin Lim, 'Good Morning Middle Age', ibid. 88.

[43] Wilfred Owen to Siegfried Sassoon, 10 Oct. 1918, in *Collected Letters*, 581.

[44] Susan Gubernat, 'Women washing clothes in the Kabul River', in Swift (ed.), *100 poets against the war*, 92, accessed at <http://www.nthposition.com/100poets0.pdf> on 17 Aug. 2005.

[45] In Swift (ed.), *100 poets against the war*, 57.

[46] Tony Harrison, untitled, in Neil Astley (ed.), *Tony Harrison* (Newcastle: Bloodaxe Books, 1991), 9.

events of 'our worst century' than the mass media. Affirmative spirits
haunt political rhetoric, with its feel-good promise of a better future,
without usually materializing into anything substantial; and a poetry
which 'concentrate[s] our attention' on such experiences as the death
camps while retaining that affirmative spirit commits a potentially
grievous offence. (Harrison's source is Auden, who hopes in the
midst of 'Negation and despair' to 'Show an affirming flame'.[47]) But
Harrison is an unlikely critic of the 'apparently effortless' depictions
of reality by the mass media, having complained of Geoffrey Hill's
poetry that it 'sort of gets quite difficult, and I think, if I can't
understand somebody's work then who can?'[48] Hill's difficulty
remains more responsible to the ethical complexities of the material
than the relative facility of Harrison's own art. Harrison also adopts
and adapts the techniques he affects to distrust. His Gulf War
poem, 'A Cold Coming', takes its inspiration directly from the mass
media—a photograph by Kenneth Jarecke in *The Observer* of '[t]he
charred head of an Iraqi soldier [which] leans through the windscreen
on his burned-out vehicle'.[49] Anyone can read the newspaper, but the
poet's special calling will not be subjugated into passive dependence.
Studying the photograph, Harrison starts, as even poets must, with
the merely visual: 'I saw the charred Iraqi lean | towards me from
bomb-blasted screen'[50] (an abbreviation for windscreen, but hinting
as well at the distance between the television viewer and atrocity).
But within a few lines he claims to be given a unique insight beyond
anything of which the photographer is capable, as the corpse singles
him out for its posthumous message:

> 'Don't be afraid I've picked on you
> for this exclusive interview.
>
> Isn't it your sort of poet's task
> to find words for this frightening mask?

---

[47] Auden, 'September 1, 1939', in *English Auden*, 247.
[48] Harrison, quoted in Rowland, *Holocaust Poetry*, 92.
[49] Anon., quoted in Tony Harrison, *The Gaze of the Gorgon* (Newcastle: Bloodaxe Books, 1992), 6.
[50] Ibid. 48.

If that gadget that you've got records
words from such scorched vocal chords,

press RECORD before some dog
devours me mid-monologue.'

Reporters with microphones might be expected to know that finding words is crucially different from recording words, but that is a distinction which Harrison, seemingly within touching distance of the 'crumbling bone', though in reality thousands of miles away, tries to obscure. Rhythmically leaden—'If that gadget that you've got records'—'A Cold Coming' also falls foul of the problem besetting its most obvious precursor, Hardy's Boer War poem 'A Christmas Ghost Story'. In each case, a poet exploits the dead as he gives his own preoccupations and politics a fraudulent authority by voicing them for a victim of war. Harrison's dead Iraqi seems most upset that he did not follow the example of three American soldiers 'who banked their sperm before the battle'; and the poem's title, 'A Cold Coming', is therefore as much a schoolboy joke as an allusion to Eliot's 'Journey of the Magi'. Harrison also uses the Iraqi to argue against a war poet who needed no convenient fictions to transport himself to scenes of death. The dead soldier states, sarcastically:

Pretend I've got the imagination
to see the world beyond one nation.

That's your job, poet, to pretend
I want my foe to be my friend.

It's easier to find such words
for this dumb mask like baked dogturds.

So lie and say the charred man smiled
to see the soldier hug his child.[51]

Recording this exchange (or rather, feigning that he records a feigned exchange), Harrison would have the reader believe that he does not 'pretend' or 'lie'. He therefore bears witness to a truth which

[51] Ibid. 53.

contradicts the dead German soldier in Owen's 'Strange Meeting': '"I am the enemy you killed, my friend."'[52] Owen, if Harrison's authority is to be trusted, may have been only pretending.

The most persuasive of Harrison's defenders, Antony Rowland, has argued that the poet 'confronts the bathos that no authentic voice exists anyway for the dead',[53] and praises 'A Cold Coming' for reminding the reader that 'the poem and the photograph refer to a real corpse'.[54] Yet the poem does not so much confront bathos as enact it. Too much of Harrison's war poetry is sentimental in the sense defined by Oscar Wilde: it desires to have the luxury of an emotion without paying for it. Harrison's travesty of the life and death of an Iraqi soldier is not a window on reality but a mirror returning his own gaze. Very few anti-war poets show concern that authentic voices from the war zone might struggle to be heard above the din of their own competing performances and ventriloquisms. No wonder Harrison should want to borrow the persona—and with it some of the authority—of the war correspondent; but the thinness of that charade is betrayed by comparison with the war poetry of James Fenton, who in his early twenties used money from a poetry prize to travel to Vietnam and Cambodia as a freelance reporter. The unexpected result of Fenton's journey, Dana Gioia notes, was a tactful poetic silence: 'It would have been different, he once commented, if it had been "one's own war." But to find a war just to write about it struck him as not only artificial but disgusting.'[55] Fenton spent three years from 1973 in Indochina; the poems inspired by his experiences did not begin to appear until several years after his return to England. They prove in relation to their own wars what Keith Douglas prophesied about his: that the important poetry would be written after the war was over. Fenton's prose account, *All*

[52] Owen, *The Complete Poems and Fragments*, i: *The Poems*, ed. Jon Stallworthy (London: Chatto & Windus, Hogarth Press, and Oxford University Press, 1983), 149.

[53] Antony Rowland, *Tony Harrison and the Holocaust* (Liverpool: Liverpool University Press, 2001), 77.

[54] Ibid. 78.

[55] Dana Gioia, 'The Rise of James Fenton', accessed at <http://www.danagioia.net/essays/efenton.htm> on 14 Sept. 2005.

the Wrong Places, describes the political views he held at the start of his adventure in terms which share broad affinities with those of most anti-war poets: 'I wanted to see a communist victory because, as did many people, I believed that the Americans had not the slightest justification for their interference in Indochina.'[56] Yet his artistic approach to war has far more in common with the soldier-poets. Fenton writes as a disciple of experience:

I wanted to see a war and the fall of a city because . . . because I wanted to see what such things were like. I had once seen a man dying, from natural causes, and my first reaction as I realized what was happening was to be glad that I was *there*. This is what happens, I thought, so watch it carefully, don't miss a detail. The first time I saw a surgical operation (it was in Cambodia) I experienced the same sensation, and no doubt when I see a child born it will be the more powerful. The point is simply being there and seeing it. The experience has no essential value beyond itself.[57]

If Fenton's accounts of war are more trustworthy than Harrison's, it is because he is seeing for himself, listening to others, relishing every detail, genuinely recording rather than pretending to record. Present at the fall of Saigon, Fenton hitches a ride on the first North Vietnamese tank to reach the palace and smash down the gates: 'I was very, very excited. The weight of the moment, the privilege of being a witness, impressed itself at once.'[58] Politics remains less important and less interesting than experience; and a politics (and poetry) which lacks experience holds itself vulnerable to the distortions and deceptions which proliferate in time of war.

'Poetry's function', Robert Duncan writes during the Vietnam War, 'is not to oppose evil, but to imagine it: what if Shakespeare had opposed Iago, or Dostoyevsky opposed Raskolnikov—the vital thing is that they *created* Iago and Raskolnikov [so that] we begin

---

[56] James Fenton, *All the Wrong Places: Adrift in the Politics of Asia* (London: Viking, 1998), 6.

[57] Ibid.

[58] Ibid. 86. Fenton later criticizes his own actions as an opportunistic attempt to associate himself with victory: ibid. 106.

to see betrayal and murder and theft in a new light.'[59] Himself
an outspoken peace campaigner, Duncan nevertheless criticizes the
oppositional poetry of his friend and correspondent Denise Levertov:
'It is a disease of our generation that we offer symptoms and diagnoses
of what we are in the place of imaginations and creations of what
we are.' Duncan's distinction between opposing and imagining war
is especially useful in evaluating the capacity of Fenton's best poems
not just to create but to re-create 'what we are.' They startle with the
amount of specific information contained in them. The opening of
'Dead Soldiers', for example, gives full official titles:

> When His Excellency Prince Norodom Chantaraingsey
> Invited me to lunch on the battlefield
> I was glad of my white suit for the first time that day.[60]

Fenton even remembers the exoticism of the menu—frogs' legs,
turtles with their eggs boiled in the carapace, marsh irisis in fish
sauce, the 'inflorescence of a banana salad'. But the details do serve
a larger purpose, as part of a ritual which, intimately involved in
violence, is at once impressive and hard to stomach. Discarded
brandy bottles are as close as the poem comes to battlefield corpses:
'They called the empties Dead Soldiers | And rejoiced to see them pile
up at our feet.' This is a re-created evil more persuasively insidious
than the cartoon effects of scooped scalps achieved in Harrison's
'Iraquatrains'. The poet-witness dwells less often on the dead and
mutilated than does the long-range commentator: Fenton works by
implication, conveying the eeriness of being at one remove from
the atrocities, sensing them all around but connecting to them only
through metaphor. The prince's aide—a 'club bore' who turns out
to be Pol Pot's brother—asks the poet a simple question: 'So, did
they show you the things they do | With the young refugee girls?'

---

[59] Robert Duncan, quoted in Marjorie Perloff, *Poetry On and Off the Page: Essays for Emergent Occasions* (Evanston, Ill.: Northwestern University Press, 1998), 210.

[60] James Fenton, *The Memory of War and Children in Exile: Poems 1968–1983* (Harmondsworth: Penguin, 1983), 26.

Fenton's restraint exacerbates the horror by leaving those matters to
the imagination of his readers.

Restraint is the conspicuous characteristic of Fenton's poetry of
Indochina. Caring so much about what he sees, sometimes he cannot
bring himself to write it: 'I had intended to include a full account
of my experiences in Cambodia. But I found it too painful, during
the years of the Khmer Rouge regime, to touch that subject, and
now it is too late.'[61] Anti-war poets, sharing little of that pain, rarely
share Fenton's restraint either. 'Poetry', Coleridge noted, 'excites us
to artificial feelings—makes us callous to real ones.'[62] As we listen
for poetic truths from those in the latest war zone—whether soldier
or civilian, medic or aid-worker—we might do well to consider
the humbug-shattering honesty of Jane Austen, writing to her sister
Cassandra during the Napoleonic campaigns: 'How horrible it is to
have so many people killed!—And what a blessing that one cares for
none of them!'[63]

[61] Fenton, *All the Wrong Places*, p. xii.

[62] Coleridge, quoted in Geoffrey Hill, 'Poetry as "Menace" and "Atonement"', in
The Lords of Limit: Essays on Literature and Ideas (London: André Deutsch, 1984), 3.

[63] Jane Austen to Cassandra Austen, 31 May 1811, in *Jane Austen's Letters to her
Sister Cassandra and Others*, ed. R. W. Chapman (Oxford: Oxford University Press,
1932), 286.

Bibliography

ASTLEY, NEIL (ed.), *Tony Harrison* (Newcastle: Bloodaxe Books, 1991).

AUDEN, W. H., *Collected Shorter Poems* (London: Faber, 1966).

——— *Collected Poems*, ed. Edward Mendelson (London: Faber, 1976).

——— *The English Auden: Poems, Essays and Dramatic Writings 1927–1939*, ed. Edward Mendelson (London: Faber, 1977).

———*Prose and Travel Books in Prose and Verse*, i: *1926–1938*, ed. Edward Mendelson (Princeton: Princeton University Press, 1996).

——— *The Complete Works: Prose*, ii: *1939–1948*, ed. Edward Mendelson (Princeton: Princeton University Press, 2002).

——— and MACNEICE, LOUIS, *Letters from Iceland* (London: Faber, 1937).

——— and ISHERWOOD, CHRISTOPHER, *Journey to a War* (London: Faber, 1939).

AUSTEN, JANE, *Jane Austen's Letters to her Sister Cassandra and Others*, ed. R. W. Chapman (Oxford: Oxford University Press, 1932).

BARTHES, ROLAND, *Camera Lucida*, trans. Richard Howard (London: Jonathan Cape, 1982).

BELL, VEREEN and LERNER, LAURENCE (eds.), *On Modern Poetry: Essays Presented to Donald Davie* (Nashville: Vanderbilt University Press, 1988).

BENTLEY, PAUL, *The Poetry of Ted Hughes: Language, Illusion & Beyond* (Harlow: Longman, 1998).

BLAKE, WILLIAM, *Complete Writings*, ed. Geoffrey Keynes (Oxford: Oxford University Press, 1966).

BLOCH, ERNST, *et al.*, *Aesthetics and Politics*, trans. Francis McDonagh (London: NLB, 1977).

BLUNDEN, EDMUND, *Undertones of War* (London: Penguin, 1937).

——— *Selected Poems*, ed. Robyn Marsack (Manchester: Carcanet, 1982).

BREARTON, FRAN, *The Great War in Irish Poetry: W. B. Yeats to Michael Longley* (Oxford: Oxford University Press, 2000).

BROMWICH, DAVID, *Skeptical Music: Essays on Modern Poetry* (Chicago: University of Chicago Press, 2001).

BROOKE, RUPERT, *The Poetical Works*, ed. Geoffrey Keynes (London: Faber, 1960).

BYRON, LORD, *Poetical Works*, ed. Frederick Page (London: Oxford University Press, 1970).

CAMPION, THOMAS, *The Works*, ed. Walter R. Davis (London: Faber, 1969).

CARPENTER, HUMPHREY, *W. H. Auden: A Biography* (London: Harper-Collins, 1981).

CHATTARJI, SUBARNO, *Memories of a Lost War: American Poetic Responses to the Vietnam War* (Oxford: Oxford University Press, 2001).

COLERIDGE, SAMUEL TAYLOR, *The Collected Works*, xvi: *Poetical Works, Part One: Poems* (Reading Text), ed. J. C. C. Mays (Princeton: Princeton University Press, 2001).

CRANE, STEPHEN, *War is Kind* (New York: Frederick A. Stokes, 1899).

DAVENPORT-HINES, RICHARD, *Auden* (London: Heinemann, 1995).

DAVIE, DONALD, *Under Briggflatts: A History of Poetry in Great Britain 1960–1988* (Manchester: Carcanet, 1989).

DICKINSON, EMILY, *The Manuscript Books*, i, ed. R. W. Franklin (Cambridge, Mass.: Harvard University Press, 1981).

DOUGLAS, KEITH, *Alamein to Zem Zem*, ed. John Waller, G. S. Fraser, and J. C. Hall (London: Faber, 1966).

——*A Prose Miscellany*, ed. Desmond Graham (Manchester: Carcanet, 1985).

—— *The Complete Poems*, ed. Desmond Graham (Oxford: Oxford University Press, 1987).

—— *The Letters*, ed. Desmond Graham (Manchester: Carcanet, 2000).

ELIOT, T. S., *The Complete Poems and Plays* (London: Faber, 1969).

EMPSON, WILLIAM, *The Complete Poems*, ed. John Haffenden (Harmondsworth: Penguin, 2000).

——*Seven Types of Ambiguity* (London: Pimlico, 2004).

FAAS, EKBERT, *Ted Hughes: The Unaccommodated Universe* (Santa Barbara, Calif.: Black Sparrow Press, 1980).

FENTON, JAMES, *The Memory of War and Children in Exile: Poems 1968–1983* (Harmondsworth: Penguin, 1983).

——*All the Wrong Places: Adrift in the Politics of Asia* (London: Viking, 1988).

FROST, ROBERT, *Collected Poems, Prose, & Plays*, ed. Richard Poirier and Mark Richardson (New York: Library of America, 1995).

FULLER, JOHN, *W. H. Auden: A Commentary* (London: Faber, 1998).

FUSSELL, PAUL, *The Great War and Modern Memory* (Oxford: Oxford University Press, 1975).

GARDNER, BRIAN (ed.), *The Terrible Rain: The War Poets 1939–1945* (London: Methuen, 1966).

GARDNER, HELEN, *The Composition of Four Quartets* (London: Faber, 1978).

GIFFORD, TERRY, and ROBERTS, NEIL, *Ted Hughes: A Critical Study* (London: Faber, 1981).

GOLDING, WILLIAM, *A Moving Target* (London: Faber, 1982).

—— *Darkness Visible* (London: Faber, 1979).

GRAHAM, DESMOND, *Keith Douglas 1920–1944: A Biography* (Oxford: Oxford University Press, 1974).

—— *The Truth of War: Owen, Blunden, Rosenberg* (Manchester: Carcanet, 1984).

—— ' "Out of the heart's sickness": Ivor Gurney as a Poet of War', *The Ivor Gurney Society Journal*, 7 (2001), 7–32.

GRAVES, ROBERT, *Complete Poems*, ii, ed. Beryl Graves and Dunstan Ward (Manchester: Carcanet, 1997).

GROSS, JOHN (ed.), *Rudyard Kipling: The Man, his Work and his World* (London: Weidenfeld & Nicolson, 1972).

GURNEY, IVOR, *Severn & Somme and War's Embers* (Ashington and Manchester: MidNag/Carcanet, 1987).

—— *Collected Letters*, ed. R. K. R. Thornton (Ashington and Manchester: MidNag/Carcanet, 1991).

—— *Best Poems and The Book of Five Makings*, ed. R. K. R. Thornton and George Walter (Ashington and Manchester: MidNag/Carcanet, 1995).

—— *80 Poems or So*, ed. George Walter and R. K. R. Thornton (Ashington and Manchester: MidNag/Carcanet, 1997).

—— *Rewards of Wonder: Poems of Cotswold, France, London*, ed. George Walter (Ashington and Manchester: MidNag/Carcanet, 2000).

—— *Collected Poems*, ed. P. J. Kavanagh (Manchester: Carcanet, 2004).

HAFFENDEN, JOHN (ed.), *Viewpoints: Poets in Conversation* (London: Faber, 1981).

—— *William Empson*, i: *Among the Mandarins* (Oxford: Oxford University Press, 2005).

HAMILTON, IAN, 'Tough Guy', *London Review of Books*, 8 February 2001, 17–18.

HARDY, FLORENCE EMILY, *The Life of Thomas Hardy* (London: Macmillan, 1962).

HARDY, THOMAS, *The Complete Poems*, ed. James Gibson (Basingstoke: Palgrave, 2001).

____ *The Dynasts* (London: Macmillan, 1978).

____ *The Collected Letters*, ii: *1893–1901*, ed. Richard Little Purdy and Michael Millgate (Oxford: Clarendon Press, 1980).

____ *The Collected Letters*, iii: *1902–1908*, ed. Richard Little Purdy and Michael Millgate (Oxford: Clarendon Press, 1982).

HARRISON, TONY, *The Gaze of the Gorgon* (Newcastle: Bloodaxe Books, 1992).

HEANEY, SEAMUS, *Preoccupations: Selected Prose 1968–1978* (London: Faber, 1980).

____ *The Government of the Tongue: The 1986 T. S. Eliot Memorial Lectures and Other Critical Writings* (London: Faber, 1988).

HECHT, ANTHONY, *Anthony Hecht in Conversation with Philip Hoy*, ed. Philip Hoy (London: Between the Lines, 2001).

HIBBERD, DOMINIC, *Owen the Poet* (London: Macmillan, 1986).

HILL, GEOFFREY, ' "I in Another Place": Homage to Keith Douglas', *Stand*, 6/4 (1964/5), 6–13.

____ 'Gurney's Hobby', F. W. Bateson Memorial Lecture, *Essays in Criticism*, 34/2 (April 1984), 97–128.

____ *The Lords of Limit: Essays on Literature and Ideas* (London: André Deutsch, 1984).

____ *Collected Poems* (Harmondsworth: Penguin, 1985).

____ *The Enemy's Country: Words, Contexture, and Other Circumstances of Language* (Oxford: Oxford University Press, 1991).

____ *Canaan* (Harmondsworth: Penguin, 1996).

____ 'Isaac Rosenberg, 1890–1918', Warton Lecture on English Poetry, *Proceedings of the British Academy*, 101 (1999), 209–28.

____ *The Triumph of Love* (Harmondsworth: Penguin, 1999).

____ *Speech! Speech!* (Washington: Counterpoint, 2000).

____ *The Orchards of Syon* (Washington: Counterpoint, 2002).

____ *Style and Faith* (New York: Counterpoint, 2003).

____ *Scenes from Comus* (Harmondsworth: Penguin, 2005).

____ *A Treatise of Civil Power* (Thame: Clutag Press, 2005).

HOLLANDER, JOHN, *Melodious Guile: Fictive Pattern in Poetic Language* (New Haven: Yale University Press, 1988).

HOLLIS, MATTHEW, and KEEGAN, PAUL (eds.), *101 Poems Against War* (London: Faber, 2003).

HOUSMAN, A. E., *The Poems*, ed. Archie Burnett (Oxford: Clarendon Press, 1997).

HUGHES, TED, *Poetry in the Making* (London: Faber, 1969).

_____ 'Ted Hughes and *Crow*', interviewed by Ekbert Faas, *London Magazine*, 10/10 (January 1971), 5–20.

_____ 'The Rock', in Geoffrey Summerfield (ed.), *Worlds: Seven Modern Poets* (Harmondsworth: Penguin, 1974), 122–6.

_____ 'Introduction', in Keith Douglas, *The Complete Poems*, ed. Desmond Graham (Oxford: Oxford University Press, 1987), pp. xv–xxvii.

_____ *Winter Pollen: Occasional Prose*, ed. William Scammell (London: Faber, 1994).

_____ *Collected Poems*, ed. Paul Keegan (London: Faber, 2003).

JARMAIN, JOHN, *Poems* (London: Collins, 1945).

JOHNSTONE, JOHN H., *English Poetry of the First World War: A Study in the Evolution of Lyric and Narrative Form* (Princeton: Princeton University Press, 1964).

KEATING, PETER, *Kipling the Poet* (London: Secker & Warburg, 1994).

KEATS, JOHN, *The Letters*, ed. Maurice Buxton Forman (Oxford: Oxford University Press, 1935).

_____ *The Complete Poems*, ed. Miriam Allott (London: Longman, 1970).

KERR, DOUGLAS, *Wilfred Owen's Voices: Language and Community* (Oxford: Oxford University Press, 1993).

KEYES, SIDNEY, *Minos of Crete: Plays and Stories*, ed. Michael Meyer (London: Routledge, 1948).

_____ *Collected Poems*, ed. Michael Meyer (Manchester: Carcanet, 2002).

KIPLING, RUDYARD, *The Five Nations* (London: Methuen, 1903).

_____ *Something of Myself*, ed. Robert Hampson (Harmondsworth: Penguin, 1987).

_____ *Wee Willie Winkie*, ed. Hugh Haughton (Harmondsworth: Penguin, 1988).

_____ *War Stories and Poems*, ed. Andrew Rutherford (Oxford: Oxford University Press, 1990).

_____ *The Letters*, iii: *1900–1910*, ed. Thomas Pinney (London: Macmillan, 1996).

_____ *The Complete Verse* (London: Kyle Cathie, 1996).

_____ *Traffics and Discoveries* (London: House of Stratus, 2001).

KIRKHAM, MICHAEL, *The Imagination of Edward Thomas* (Cambridge: Cambridge University Press, 1986).

KUROSAWA, AKIRA, *Something Like an Autobiography*, trans. Audie E. Bock (New York: Vintage, 1983).

LARKIN, PHILIP, *Required Writing: Miscellaneous Pieces 1955–1982* (London: Faber, 1983).

LAWRENCE, D. H., *Kangaroo* (London: Martin Secker, 1923).

LEIGHTON, ANGELA, and REYNOLDS, MARGARET (eds.), *Victorian Women Poets: An Anthology* (Oxford: Blackwell, 1995).

LEVI, PRIMO, *The Drowned and the Saved*, trans. R. Rosenthal (London: Abacus Books, 1986).

LONGLEY, EDNA, *Poetry in the Wars* (Newcastle: Bloodaxe, 1986).

LONGLEY, MICHAEL, *Poems 1963–1983* (Harmondsworth: Penguin, 1986).

LYCETT, ANDREW, *Rudyard Kipling* (London: Weidenfeld & Nicolson, 1999).

LYON, JOHN, ' "Pardon?": Our Problem with Difficulty (and Geoffrey Hill)', *Thumbscrew*, 13 (Spring/Summer 1999), 11–19.

MACNEICE, LOUIS, *Collected Poems*, ed. E. R. Dodds (London: Faber, 1979).

_____ *Selected Prose*, ed. Alan Heuser (Oxford: Oxford University Press, 1990).

MCDIARMID, LUCY, *Saving Civilization: Yeats, Eliot, and Auden between the Wars* (Cambridge: Cambridge University Press, 1984).

MCDONALD, PETER, *Serious Poetry: Form and Authority from Yeats to Hill* (Oxford: Oxford University Press, 2002).

MAHON, DEREK, *The Hunt by Night* (Oxford: Oxford University Press, 1982).

MASON, PHILIP, *Kipling: The Glass, the Shadow and the Fire* (London: Cape, 1975).

MENDELSON, EDWARD, *Early Auden* (London: Faber, 1981).

_____ *Later Auden* (London: Faber, 1999).

MEW, CHARLOTTE, *Complete Poems*, ed. John Newton (Harmondsworth: Penguin, 2000).

MILTON, JOHN, *Paradise Lost*, ed. Alistair Fowler (London: Longman, 1971).

MONTAIGNE, MICHEL DE, *The Essays of Montaigne*, i, trans. John Florio (London: Dent, 1910).

MONTEFIORE, JAN, *Feminism and Poetry: Language, Experience, Identity in Women's Writing* (London: Pandora Press, 1987).

MOORE, MARIANNE, *Complete Poems* (London: Faber, 1984).

MOTION, ANDREW (ed.), *First World War Poems* (London: Faber, 2003).

NEWBOLT, HENRY, *The Sailing of the Long-Ships and Other Poems* (London: John Murray, 1902).

——— *My World as in My Time* (London: Faber, 1932).

ORWELL, GEORGE, *Inside the Whale* (London: Victor Gollancz, 1940).

OWEN, WILFRED, *Collected Letters*, ed. Harold Owen and John Bell (Oxford: Oxford University Press, 1967).

——— *The Complete Poems and Fragments*, i: *The Poems*, ed. Jon Stallworthy (London: Chatto & Windus, Hogarth Press, and Oxford University Press, 1983).

——— *The Complete Poems and Fragments*, ii: *The Manuscripts and Fragments*, ed. Jon Stallworthy (London: Chatto & Windus, Hogarth Press, and Oxford University Press, 1983).

PEARSALL, CORNELIA, 'Complicate Me When I'm Dead: The War Remains of Douglas and Hughes', a paper given at the MLA conference, San Diego, 27 December 2003.

PERLOFF, MARJORIE, *Poetry On and Off the Page: Essays for Emergent Occasions* (Evanston, Ill.: Northwestern University Press, 1998).

PIETTE, ADAM, *Imagination at War: British Fiction and Poetry 1939–1945* (London: Papermac, 1995).

PITTER, RUTH, *Collected Poems* (London: Enitharmon, 1996).

RAINE, CRAIG, *Haydn and the Valve Trumpet* (London: Faber, 1990).

——— *History: The Home Movie* (Harmondsworth: Penguin, 1994).

RAMAZANI, JAHAN, *Poetry of Mourning: The Modern Elegy from Hardy to Heaney* (Chicago: University of Chicago Press, 1994).

RAWLINSON, MARK, *British Writing of the Second World War* (Oxford: Clarendon Press, 2000).

REILLY, CATHERINE (ed.), *Chaos of the Night: Women's Poetry and Verse of the Second World War* (London: Virago, 1984).

RICKS, CHRISTOPHER, *The Force of Poetry* (Oxford: Clarendon Press, 1984).

_____ *Essays in Appreciation* (Oxford: Oxford University Press, 1996).

RIDLER, ANNE, *Collected Poems* (Manchester: Carcanet, 1994).

ROBERTS, ANDREW MICHAEL, *Geoffrey Hill* (Tavistock: Northcote House, 2004).

ROBINSON, PETER (ed.), *Geoffrey Hill: Essays on his Work* (Milton Keynes: Open University Press, 1985).

ROSENBERG, ISAAC, *The Collected Works*, ed. Ian Parsons (London: Chatto & Windus, 1979).

_____ *The Poems and Plays*, ed. Vivien Noakes (Oxford: Oxford University Press, 2004).

ROSSETTI, CHRISTINA, *The Complete Poems*, ed. R. W. Crump and Betty S. Flowers (Harmondsworth: Penguin, 2001).

ROWLAND, ANTONY, *Tony Harrison and the Holocaust* (Liverpool: Liverpool University Press, 2001).

_____ *Holocaust Poetry: Awkward Poetics in the Work of Sylvia Plath, Geoffrey Hill, Tony Harrison and Ted Hughes* (Edinburgh: Edinburgh University Press, 2005).

SAGAR, KEITH (ed.), *The Challenge of Ted Hughes* (Basingstoke: Macmillan, 1994).

SASSOON, SIEGFRIED, *The War Poems* (London: Faber, 1983).

_____ *Collected Poems 1908–1956* (London: Faber, 1984).

SCAMMELL, WILLIAM, *Keith Douglas: A Study* (London: Faber, 1988).

SCANNELL, VERNON, *Not Without Glory: Poets of the Second World War* (London: Woburn Press, 1976).

SCOVELL, E. J., *Collected Poems* (Manchester: Carcanet, 1988).

SERGEANT, ELIZABETH, *Robert Frost: The Trial by Existence* (New York: Holt, Rinehart & Winston, 1960).

SEYMOUR-SMITH, MARTIN, *Hardy* (London: Bloomsbury, 1994).

SHELLEY, PERCY, *Poetical Works*, ed. Thomas Hutchinson (Oxford: Oxford University Press, 1967).

SIDNEY, PHILIP, *The Prose Works*, iii, ed. Albert Feuillerat (Cambridge: Cambridge University Press, 1968).

SILKIN, JON, *Out of Battle: The Poetry of the Great War* (Oxford: Oxford University Press, 1972).

_____ (ed.), *The Penguin Book of First World War Poetry* (Harmondsworth: Penguin, 1981).

SKELTON, ROBIN (ed.), *Poetry of the Thirties* (Harmondsworth: Penguin, 1964).

SMITH, ANGELA K. (ed.), *Women's Writing of the First World War: An Anthology* (Manchester: Manchester University Press, 2000).

SMITH, STAN (ed.), *The Cambridge Companion to W. H. Auden* (Cambridge: Cambridge University Press, 2004).

SORLEY, CHARLES HAMILTON, *The Poems and Selected Letters*, ed. Hilda D. Spear (Dundee: Blackness Press, 1978).

SPENCER, MATTHEW (ed.), *Elected Friends: Robert Frost and Edward Thomas to One Another* (New York: Handsel Books, 2003).

SPENDER, STEPHEN, *Collected Poems 1928–1953* (London: Faber, 1955).

—— *The Thirties and After: Poetry, Politics, People (1933–75)* (London: Macmillan, 1978).

STALLWORTHY, JON, *Wilfred Owen* (Oxford and London: Oxford University Press and Chatto, 1974).

—— *The Anzac Sonata: New and Selected Poems* (London: Chatto & Windus, 1986).

—— *Anthem for Doomed Youth: Twelve Soldier Poets of the First World War* (London: Constable, 2002).

STEWART, J. I. M., *Rudyard Kipling* (London: Gollancz, 1966).

STEWART, SUSAN, *Poetry and the Fate of the Senses* (Chicago: University of Chicago Press, 2002).

STUBBS, JOHN, 'A Soldier's Story: Keith Douglas at El Ballah', *P.N. Review*, 47, 12/3 (1985), 26–9.

SWIFT, TODD (ed.), *100 poets against the war* (Cambridge: Salt, 2003).

SWINBURNE, ALGERNON CHARLES, *The Poems*, vi (London: Chatto & Windus, 1904).

SWINGLER, RANDALL, *Selected Poems*, ed. Andy Croft (Nottingham: Trent Editions, 2000).

SYNGE, J. M., *Collected Works*, i, ed. Robin Skelton (Oxford: Oxford University Press, 1962).

THOMAS, EDWARD, *In Pursuit of Spring* (London: Thomas Nelson and Sons, 1914).

—— *Collected Poems*, ed. R. George Thomas (Oxford: Oxford University Press, 1981).

—— *A Language not to be Betrayed: Selected Prose*, ed. Edna Longley (Ashington and Manchester: MidNag/Carcanet, 1981).

THOMAS, HELEN, *Under Storm's Wing* (Manchester: Carcanet, 1988).

VAN WYK SMITH, M., *Drummer Hodge: The Poetry of the Anglo–Boer War 1899–1902* (Oxford: Clarendon Press, 1978).

WALDER, DENNIS, *Ted Hughes* (Milton Keynes: Open University Press, 1987).

WEST, PATRICK, *Conspicuous Compassion: why sometimes it really is cruel to be kind* (London: Civitas, 2004).

WHARTON, EDITH (ed.), *The Book of the Homeless* (New York: Scribner's, 1916).

WHEATLEY, DAVID, 'Posturing for Peace', *The Guardian (Review)*, 24 May 2003, 25.

WHITMAN, WALT, *Complete Poetry and Collected Prose*, ed. Justin Kaplan (New York: Library of America, 1982).

WILSON, ANGUS, *The Strange Ride of Rudyard Kipling* (London: Secker & Warburg, 1977).

WITTGENSTEIN, LUDWIG, *Tractatus Logico-Philosophicus*, trans. D. F. Pears and B. F. McGuinness (London: Routledge & Kegan Paul, 1971).

WORDSWORTH, WILLIAM, *The Fourteen-Book Prelude*, ed. W. J. B. Owen (Ithaca, NY: Cornell University Press, 1985).

_____ *Lyrical Ballads and Other Poems, 1797–1800*, ed. James Butler and Karen Green (Ithaca, NY: Cornell University Press, 1992).

YEATS, W. B. (ed.), *The Oxford Book of Modern Verse* (Oxford: Clarendon Press, 1936).

_____ *The Letters*, ed. Allan Wade (London: Rupert Hart-Davis, 1954).

_____ *Essays and Introductions* (London: Macmillan, 1961).

_____ *Yeats's Poems*, ed. A. Norman Jeffares (Basingstoke: Macmillan, 1989).

Index